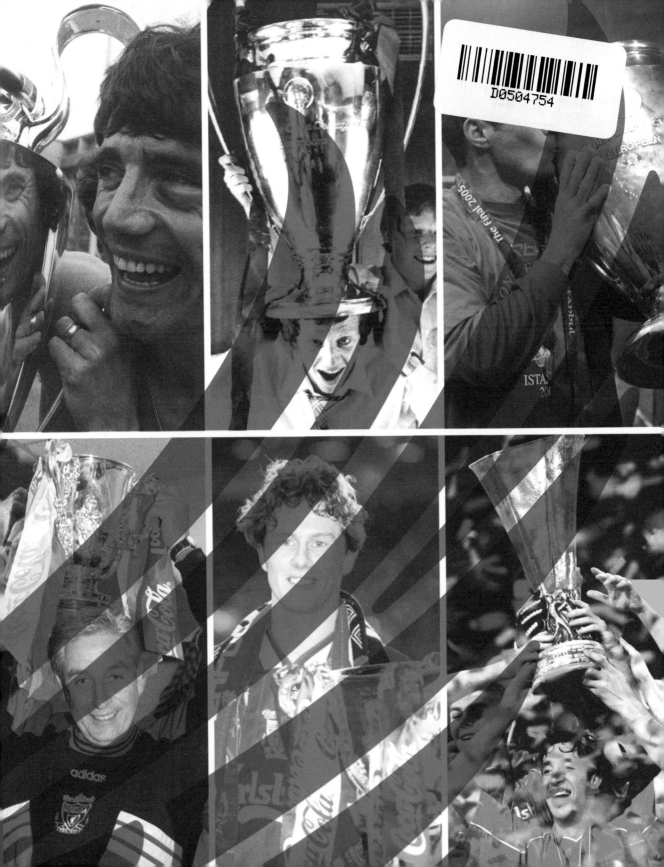

LIVERPOOL FC
HEROES

Ragnhild Lund Ansnes

Contents

Foreword

When I was sat at a desk signing a contract for Liverpool Football Club with Bob Paisley standing beside me on October 9th, 1974, I didn't realise that my life would change forever.

What happened over the course of the next 11 years was beyond my wildest dreams. I went on to play 650 games and the Reds went on to win countless trophies, including four unforgettable European Cup triumphs. It was a magical spell that made Liverpool the most successful team in the history of British football and along the way made me the most decorated player in the English game.

It is special to recall the many great days in our club's illustrious history, but this book is about more than that. Liverpool FC Heroes gives some Anfield legends the opportunity to tell their personal stories. I'm sure that you won't have heard many of them before.

I had the pleasure of meeting the author, Ragnhild Lund Ansnes, when she was writing and promoting her first Liverpool book. She reminded me of the standards we set as players in order to succeed every season. Her initial 30-minute interview lasted for hours!

I know that she left no stone unturned when it came to speaking to the legends and understanding them as people, as well as heroes.

There are players interviewed in this book who span the Anfield generations and, as well as homegrown players, there are a few adopted Liverpudlians.

I'm sure that all are now right behind Kenny Dalglish as he restores the spirit and belief to the club after some difficult times. I know that the atmosphere he creates every day in training, as well as picking the right team for the game ahead, is giving everyone associated with Liverpool FC confidence and optimism for the future.

Whatever happens over the coming seasons, some things will always remain the same. The game has not changed that much; it is still about commitment, passion and togetherness – for the players as well as the fans.

Enjoy the book.

What is it really like being a person in the world of football?

"The pleasure of meeting this lady for the first time reminded me of the standards Liverpool FC players set themselves in order to succeed every year."

Phil Neal

It was March, 2011. King Kenny's return to the Anfield managerial hot seat had reinvigorated the club. The Reds had lost just once in the previous 10 games, a spell which included an impressive 1-0 win over Chelsea at Stamford Bridge and a 3-1 victory over Manchester United courtesy of a Dirk Kuyt hat-trick. The team that had looked so fragile and downbeat in the gloom of November and December under the reign of Roy Hodgson, had transformed itself by the early spring. There was the new hope that comes with the beginning of a new era.

If the Reds had been reborn, then Liverpool the city remained the same. It hadn't changed since my last visit. It was still the same colourful, friendly and opinionated place I had come to know as my second home. Many trips had been made from my home in Norway for a game and a chance to renew acquaintances. Now I was back, and not just for a match visit. I was to stay for three months, over the course of a spring and early summer during which I would meet some of the club's greatest legends face to face.

I had become fascinated by the club. First as an outsider looking in, trying to understand the passions that drove my husband to so fervently worship these men with the Liver bird on their chest. And, then, with the enthusiasm of a believer, hooked on the thrill of Anfield on a matchday, hungry to play the role of the twelfth man, as a fully-fledged Kopite.

Now I would stay in an apartment with my husband and two kids, in the heart of the city centre, on Back Colquitt Street. During the day, it would prove a perfect hideaway, tucked away from the shops and traffic. By night, it would come alive, especially on the weekend, as I watched the crowds pour into neon-lit bars and restaurants, many of them perhaps out on the town after a Liverpool win.

From the start, I didn't want Liverpool Heroes to be just another book about the Anfield legends and stars. I wanted it to be different, to get underneath the surface and discover what makes these great men what and who they are. I thought I had a chance of doing that because

7

of who I was. I wasn't one of the familiar faces from the press the former players see on a regular basis, nor was I a young reporter looking for a news angle for the website or that day's paper. They all have their job – and they do it superbly – but I was looking for something different. Perhaps it also helped that I was not from the city, or, indeed, the country. Maybe it also made a difference that I looked at some things from a woman's and a mother's perspective.

***

There are many people who have served the club and deserve their part of the glory, from the groundsmen to the stock clerks. Among them are the cleaning ladies; the tea ladies; the talent scouts; the ticket office staff; physiotherapists; doctors; executive directors; coaches, and, of course, the managers. But, most of all, it is the players who provide the key to a club's fortunes. The destination of a glittering trophy can swing on a misplaced pass or a moment of inspiration on the pitch. A season will stand or fall on the performances of the men who cross the white line. They carry your hopes and fears.

It is hard for us to fully understand the players' experiences. From following their own set routines in the dressing room before a match, they are suddenly thrust into the spotlight. It is a spotlight that is more dazzling than ever. The crowd's emotional outbursts echo all around, nerves pound in your ears and cameras focus on your every move. With the heart hammering, you are to perform your best, knowing that many fans have given up a lot to be able to afford seeing you play live – and win. Because a winning instinct drives most players on an international top level – or does it?

I wonder what it is like to be a human in this circus. What was it like before and how is it today? How are you shaped as a person by the pressure of market forces, media coverage, and mobile phones with cameras flashing wherever you move when away from the pitch. How is it possible to be a family man in all this? Today's top-flight football world is cut-throat and uncompromising. What kind of person makes it in this arena?

Also, what was this all like 10, 20, 30, 40 or 50 years ago? How is it possible to play 857 matches for Liverpool the way Ian Callaghan did? What stuff is he made of? Is that kind of stamina in your head or your body?

And what does it take to deal with the pressure and score as many goals as Ian Rush? What goes through the mind of such a goalscoring machine during matches?

Before arriving at Anfield in 1981, Bruce Grobbelaar had served as a soldier in Rhodesia, with the abominations and terror of warfare. How did that affect his football career and how did it help him when he landed in a battle in court to clear himself after allegations of match-fixing?

What about John Barnes? What does he think of the young Africans coming into the game today? He had bananas thrown at him and was peppered with racist harassment as one of the first profile black people in the English national team and as a high-profile player at Liverpool.

Kevin Keegan was another legend who fascinated me. I wanted to find out why he felt he had to leave Liverpool at the height of his career after the 1977 European Cup triumph in Rome. Was it still the right decision, all these years later? Then, there was Phil Thompson, the Scouse captain who lifted the European Cup and whose post-playing career at Anfield was cut short by Graeme Souness – the man who had inherited his captain's armband – only to later return during Gérard Houllier's reign. And Jamie Carragher, the modern day legend. How is his experience different to those heroes from the 1970s and '80s?

No other English club has a history like that of Liverpool. I had read about the amazing Bill Shankly, who put the Reds on the European map with his remarkable energy and vision; I had studied his successor, the ever shrewd Bob Paisley, who plotted success after success; I knew about Joe Fagan and Kenny Dalglish, too, the latter now fittingly back at a club that is so in touch with the value of learning from its past.

I also knew about Roy Evans. Himself a former manager but, perhaps even more importantly, the last of the famous Boot Room boys – or so he was called when, with tears running down his cheeks, he said his farewell to Anfield as he made way for Gérard Houllier. Not only did I know of the legend Roy, I had also come to know him as a person and friend as well.

***

I cast my mind back to August, 2010. It was 3.55pm. Panic. It was exactly five minutes before the new season kicked-off and Liverpool were facing Arsenal at Anfield. I was wandering aimlessly between the buildings in the sleepy city centre with Roy Evans. We met one locked door after another. We were in a great hurry.

We were at 70 degrees North – more precisely in Alta, Norway – hunting for a pub that was showing the match. Dressed for hiking, we were slightly frozen after encountering two seasons in one day – warm summer and icy, rain-filled autumn – on a riverboat trip to Northern Europe's largest and most spectacular canyon, at the very top of the Alta-Kautokeino waterway. Evans was one of several legends who had travelled to Norway to help me promote

my first Liverpool FC book and to celebrate the 30th anniversary of the supporters' club.

We had made a stop to see former Liverpool player Vegard Heggem, who sacrificed the opening game for 24-hour fishing in the legendary river. Heggem is like my father was; a passionate fly fisherman. I have many good memories from my years growing up, spending the night along the Alta river. One of my favourite photos of my dad is where he is smiling proudly, bearded, holding a whopper of a salmon of as much as 16kg. My dad is about to pour a small cork of whisky down its throat, as tradition goes.

Many years had gone since I last sat in a riverboat, but the scenery, the smell of waders, bonfire and woodwork – as well as the beautiful eagles circling above us – brought out many good memories. And a flash of grief. But our trip had lasted longer than planned, so we were not back at the hotel until 15 minutes before the start of the match. They had promised us Premier League coverage.

Now, the game was about to start and the channels still did not work. We almost could not believe our eyes. Here I was, having lured the Boot Room legend – the man with an incredible 34 years of service to Liverpool Football Club – as player, coach, physiotherapist, reserves coach, assistant manager and manager – all the way up to Alta on the big opening weekend of the season and we could not find a single pub with TV rights open on a Sunday in my hometown! The centre, that used to be nothing but a big moor, was sleepy and deserted. Sunday afternoon is not the time for urban mingling for the Alta population.

I called my friend Magne Ek, journalist in the newspaper Altaposten and a massive Liverpool supporter. He was poised for the match at a friend's house, about 10 minutes' drive away, towards the old centre of Alta: Bossekop. We scurried to our car, threw ourselves inside and made our way through the many roundabouts. Magne ran out to point us down the right byway.

The scene that followed was priceless. It was six minutes into the match between Liverpool and Arsenal when Bjørn Christian Eriksen opened the door to his unusually tidy bachelor's den. He had the typical stressed look of someone not keen to miss even a few seconds of the action – and then discovered Evans at his front door wanting to get in!

Bjørn Christian was speechless. Dressed in his red home kit, he pattered

inside and took out his best Cognac for the guests, who then sat down by his unpainted living room table and began sipping brandy, strong coffee and eating crisps while analysing and commenting on this year's team. No sooner had we sat down than the mayor of Norway's biggest Sami municipality showed up, Klemet Erland Hætta. He has also been a Liverpool supporter since childhood and is a man who has learned a lot from football which he now applies in politics. He, too, was wide-eyed with surprise to see the white-haired expert commentator lounging on the sofa. When we said our thank yous after the match, our host said he would never forget this day. Just imagine, sitting in your own home to watch a match, and then a proper Liverpool hero turns up out of the blue!

Fast forward to December, 2010 and the secretary of the official LFC Supporters' Club Scandinavian Branch (LFCSCSB) Tore Hansen, Roy Evans and I are driving along the south coast of Norway. A little later, we would be drinking gluhwein and signing books in the Christmas town Egersund. However, right now, we are discussing a possible greatest-ever Liverpool team.

The idea of writing an honest and powerful book about the Liverpool legends would not leave me and I was accompanied by the perfect men to offer me advice. I had travelled with greats such as Bruce Grobbelaar, Phil Neal, Gary Gillespie, Alan Kennedy and David Fairclough during the autumn. It had been pure joy getting to know all these representatives of the club and to hear countless stories of their time at the club.

Now, I was consulting the man who knew Liverpool FC inside and out, from Bill Shankly's reign and beyond, on who would have to be included.

The former Liverpool boss, Tore and I put together names to form a Greatest Team supposed to represent the last 50 years, with all positions on the field covered. We had problems right from the start with strikers – we could not possibly land on just two. There were obviously more than a pair of strikers in Liverpool's incredible history that needed inclusion and Evans concluded that choosing only 11 was mission impossible.

Choosing a Greatest Team is an incredibly subjective task. There are so many different arguments for one or the other all-time favourite. Also, it was a bit of a limitation that I did not grow up watching the heroes. My relationship with at least some of Liverpool's history and former players had been formed through other people's memories and experiences, not least through meeting and travelling with a lot of Liverpool heroes during recent years following publication of Liverpoolhjerter, my first – and successful beyond my wildest dreams – book about the club which was published solely in my home country.

I realised that I had to choose my personal list based on the stories people have shared with me and which have left the biggest impression, choosing what they represent of the human side of professional football. I would have to choose names that had been repeated and that had been important figures and idols for thousands of people. Besides, I wanted to choose representatives from Liverpool's past 50 years of history that I had the pleasure of meeting in my inquisitive journey to the core of the club's culture and history.

Now, I was back in my new 'home' city, desperate to catch up again with my old friends and find out more about what makes them tick, as legends of our great club and as people. Where better to start, I thought, than with the man who had taught my daughter to walk?

As I headed by train to Phil Neal's house in the suburbs of north Merseyside, I sensed that my spring and summer would be an amazing journey.

And one that I would never forget.

Phil Neal
The Sacrifice

"What a great player he was. To play as long as he did and never miss a match through injury. He was one of those who never complained. He just got on with his job. True style, my mate Nealy.'

Phil Thompson

 I am in the home of Liverpool's most decorated player, Philip George Neal. The midday sun has warmed the glass house that was built as an extension to the brick house. I look out on his beautiful garden, and the elegant statues. There has been a lot of work put into the land, I consider – my mum is also passionate about gardens. I notice that there is a bench like no other, standing alone, offering good support for your back. The former Liverpool captain had custom-built it and dedicated it to his mother and mother-in-law, and it now sits at the bottom of a huge old tree.

Phil was my first interview for this Heroes project. In one respect, he should always come first because he is the full-back whose boots all Liverpool FC players must aim to fill. Nobody has won more medals than him while wearing the Liver bird on their chest.

This wasn't the only reason why I started here, however. It was also a natural choice to speak first to the man who I have come to know so well. In many ways, the chats we enjoyed during the course of the past 12 months or so had reminded me of the conversations I had shared with my own dad. Little chats I had missed for more than six years.

Phil had just come from a meeting at the club, agreeing to take over a lot of the ambassadorial work that Kenny Dalglish and Ian Rush have been doing up to now, travelling all over the world. With Dalglish back as manager, Rush would need someone else on board to help spread the word. Neal will be the man for occasions such as major sponsor events and trips to The Far East and elsewhere.

Now that he will be travelling a lot for Liverpool FC, he must take care to book good holidays for himself and his wife Sue as well. Long work trips must be evened out, I am told. It seems like there is an imbalance here. In Phil Neal's past, there are paths he has chosen that have left a black mark on his conscience. He has to carry that weight. That is a heavy load, decade after decade.

He played 417 matches in a row, never missing a game. In addition, Neal never missed a single day's training, not even to heavy colds. It did not occur to him to call his boss, Bob Paisley, and say he could not make it because of a headache or a cold. He did not call in sick to training even when he had stomach problems either. Instead, he went to the session with the team but, when he got home and felt ill, his wife put him to bed and dosed him up. That way, he got some rest before the next day's training, instead of going to get the kids from school, as he would normally have done.

His conscientious commitment did not start at Liverpool. He did not miss a single day of school either. But why on earth did he train even when he was sick? Everybody knows that is not the way to preserve good health.

"I didn't want Steve Nicol to nick my No2 shirt! So I was doubly determined. The club and the staff made us feel like gladiators. If I was to fail the fierce competition to be in the starting XI, I'd have had to go out with a bang. They'd have to tell me to my face that I wasn't wanted on the team. Not because I was at home feeling sick!"

This attitude even saw him playing matches with a broken toe. Ronnie Moran made him a plaster cast, but then his shoe did not fit. Pain shot through the entire foot when he tried. Moran knew a way around it – he got hold of a much bigger shoe for the injured left foot. It also made it easy to spot Neal's match boots for the next six weeks as on the floor was a pair of shoes, right foot size seven, left foot size eight-and-a-half. The "little and large" boots side by side brought a lot of laughs from the team, but the solution also helped Neal avoid breaking his impressive run of league matches.

During a Saturday match against Derby County, his attitude would truly be put to the test. Suddenly, a loud crack. It followed a clash with a Rams player. Neal recalls that he felt his opponent caught him in the face on purpose. Neal's cheekbone snapped. He was in a large amount of pain; his cheekbone was indented and had to be lifted. The defender was taken to hospital and had an operation immediately. The surgeon told him not to play football for six weeks – his face and bones needed time to heal. On Monday, he was discharged from hospital and, by Tuesday, he was back at Melwood, watching the lads train. Paisley asked him how he felt and he said: "Pretty good, considering the circumstances."

Neal remembers that, luckily, there was no midweek match that week and, come Wednesday, the manager asked: "Do you fancy a little kick-around? If I tell the lads to stay away while you're in possession, you can play a little. While we're doing the warm-up,

you go and kick the ball against the wall and see how you feel, then we train together the last half hour and see how it goes?"

And so they did. Two days after his discharge from the hospital, he was back in training. Same thing Thursday. In training on Friday, Paisley asked him if he wanted to go with them to London for the match against West Ham United. Of course he did. It was great to be able to go with the team and see how they fared. When they arrived at the hotel, Paisley asked: "Fancy a little fitness test tomorrow morning around the hotel grounds?"

Just one week after his cheekbone was put back in place, Liverpool's No2 agreed to the test, and Paisley said: "If you play today, you'll only be up against a small chap called Alan Devonshire. He's not exactly a Wimbledon type. West Ham only play a little football."

The boss asked him, a full-back, if he could play, despite the injury. You can imagine how important he felt.

"Okay, boss, I want to give it a try!"

John Toshack eventually scored the first goal in the 63rd minute and within 12 minutes he had scored again. The prospect was looking good to last through the match, and keep

the continuous run of played matches unbroken. Toshack had scored a hat-trick by the 82nd minute and Kevin Keegan sealed the game by scoring Liverpool's fourth goal just before the end. Neal had got away with playing with a broken cheekbone. The next week, no one even gave a thought to how Neal was. Strictly speaking, he was still on four weeks' sick leave. He was back in full training while the bones in his face were slowly but surely healing underneath his skin.

Paisley had a cunning plan that took him a week to accomplish – to get Neal back on the pitch. There were no flaws in the psychology of his plan. Seeing how accommodating they were when he was injured, and how eager they were to have him back on the team, Neal's self-confidence got a boost: "By doing everything they could to get me to play matches, it was like they told me, *'You've given away nothing in defence. It's been rock solid and that's the way we want it!'* They made me feel wanted. And I was just a common player from Northampton. By including me in every team he picked, Paisley gave me a feel-good factor. It was an incredible feeling."

This way, Phil went on to win 23 trophies in his 11 years at the club from 1974 to 1986. He won the league eight times and lifted the Uefa Cup in 1976. He also played in five European Cup finals, winning four of them. Not many people have a career like that. What is it like, being the player with most winners' medals in the history of Liverpool Football Club?

"It's a nice title to have, especially when you think of all the stars who were there with me. But they didn't stay quite as long as me, more than 10 years. It's a great feeling, carrying that title. I managed not least because, already halfway through my Liverpool days, I was put under pressure because Bob Paisley – who kept breaking teams up, building new ones – had bought the much younger Stevie Nicol as my replacement. I told the boss I wasn't finished at the club. *'I want more!'* I think that was obvious from my mentality, my game and my principles – that you had to be ambitious and 100 per cent committed to make it 365 days a year."

However, although the club and the fans appreciate his dedication, there is another side to the story. Such a commitment came at a price.

"If you speak to my wife Sue about family life at the time, I missed certain things going on here (at home), just through being idolised by the Liverpool people. We were bringing in trophy after trophy while I ignored family issues. I'm sorry to say that now, looking back."

It's a point reiterated by Sue, who hears Phil's comments and calls from the kitchen: "I still hate football!"

When Phil was 15, he was offered a contract with Tottenham Hotspur. At the time, though, his father was dying. He warned Phil that "football is a fickle game," and said that he wanted his son to stay home another year and finish school first. He listened to his dad, rejected the offer from Tottenham and finished school while he counted on other big clubs to come for him. But no other offers appeared, so he joined the local side Northampton Town FC, who were plummeting through the divisions.

"It was a disappointing place for a young footballer with high ambitions. But the boss there gave me a chance: he made me a striker and I had no complaints. In the first nine matches I scored eight goals. Even though we were on a lower level, the papers wrote that Northampton's goal-getter Phil Neal was followed by the big clubs. I was certain this would bring me a step forward, eventually."

Six months later, he was called in to his manager's office at Northampton. His hopes were high. "I wonder who wants me?" he wondered. He was rubbing his hands. Is it Manchester United? Liverpool FC? Newcastle?

The manager asked him to sit down and told him straight: "We have accepted an offer for you from another club."

"Fantastic," Neal thought.

"Where am I going?"

"Aldershot," came back the reply.

"What? Okay…"

Aldershot were in the old Fourth Division back then.

"I don't want to speak badly of Aldershot, it just wasn't what I had been impatiently hoping for. The whole offer made me giggle, but I decided not to be arrogant, so I went down to meet them, before I politely turned them down," Neal laughs.

It was to be almost another three years before he received a far better offer. Phil was 23 and Sue had just had their second baby, their son Ashley, but was still in hospital because of high blood pressure. On the weekend, Phil played his last match for Northampton. In training on Monday, his manager asked: "Do you want to go join Liverpool FC?"

Seven long years of waiting for something bigger could finally be over. All he could think was: "Where is the car?" He could hardly wait to get to Liverpool as soon as possible.

There were, of course, no mobile phones back then. He left a message for his wife with his mother-in-law to let her know he had gone to Liverpool and that he had no idea what was going to happen.

"I didn't consult my wife at all before I leapt into the car and drove to Liverpool. I think she's still mad at me for that. I couldn't have done things differently. This was my only opportunity to sign for Liverpool FC. I had done it the long way. For seven years I'd felt like I was moving further and further away from the dream of a football career. I was thinking I'd have to take up teaching soon. I wanted so much to give my family a better income than teaching would bring. I wanted to give them a better life than I'd been able to at Northampton. Then, suddenly, this Monday morning I was asked, 'Would you like to come work for Liverpool FC?'"

On his way to Merseyside, Phil worried about the medical test. How tough would it be? Would he pass it? The doctor at Liverpool tapped his knees, took a few X-rays and asked him a few questions. He knew that Neal had played more than 260 matches for Northampton and was generally fit. The player passed his medical in less than an hour. Then he was able to go upstairs and sign his contract with Bob Paisley, who had just – very warily – taken over after the great Bill Shankly. Phil Neal was his very first signing. The newly-fledged Liverpool player no longer remembers how long his first contract was, only that he made £10 more a week than at Northampton.

At seven o'clock that evening, Neal was back in Northampton and went straight to the hospital to tell the new mother-of-two the good news – they were moving to Liverpool.

While Neal is telling me about his career, it starts pouring down on the roof of the conservatory, so we go into the living room, next door to the dining room – where Sue is laying the table. She pops her head in to say she cannot stand listening to all these football stories. She is getting worked up. I feel I have to defend her husband.

"I've travelled all over my country with your husband. I wish you'd seen how happy he makes people, simply by being there. I've received numerous emails after our travels, from people who say meeting him was the biggest moment of their lives. He makes a lot of people happy, because of his football career," I say.

Sue's anger takes me by surprise, but I realise there are many sides to a story. Sue Neal's experience of Liverpool FC is very different to that of most Reds. She has had good reasons to be angry. But it must be hard when the anger will not let go.

Phil's amazing career was an intoxicating trip – a feeling of overwhelming happiness. But even though he was successful with Liverpool all over Europe, the atmosphere was totally different on his own home ground. He sighs and starts to tell me how his wife suffered from depression after their second child was born.

They had left behind their network and support of family and friends in Northampton. Phil was away a lot. In addition to never missing a single training session, he was often away for midweek matches, and always from Friday to Saturday. The team was always at a

hotel the night before a match, so that fathers with young children, like Phil, could have the most relaxed build-up possible.

"I just wish I'd realised how poorly Sue was. The pressure on her was immense, with two small children at home and no help from our parents, who were too far away. This made her quite depressed for 18 months, and I didn't recognise that fact. I should have done. My head was in the clouds and I just wanted to win more with that red shirt. After seven years at Northampton I was finally living the fairy tale. Within 18 months I'd become an England player as well. But I didn't acknowledge that she was quite ill. It is my biggest regret in life, that I didn't understand."

He quickly played his way into the starting XI and worked vigorously to keep his place. The competition was cut-throat and it was his sole focus. Sue doubts she will ever be able to fully forgive him.

"I hate football," she tells me again, while setting the white-clad table with porcelain plates and pouring rosé wine into crystal glasses. Just hearing about football makes her angry. It must be hard when football, and the glorious career of her husband, still finances their lives.

Sue talks about cruises with other football couples, where media tagged along. They were often interviewing the wags. Beautiful ladies talked about their amazing lives.

"They've never been interested in *my* story. The one that's not so great. I think it's important that this comes out, too. That people know what life *can* be like in a family where you give your all for football," Sue says.

It is an unpleasant question to ask, but I have to, because I wonder if he – despite the anger and pain later in life – really had a choice?

"Phil, do you think you'd have won all those medals and trophies with Liverpool FC if you'd stayed home more, and been less devoted to football?"

"No."

This was the price the Neal family paid. The glass cupboards in the dining room hold a lot of crystal, a hint of something gained for her sacrifice – they were often given crystal when they won. Fortunately, Sue's life improved when she got to know other football wives, like Barbara Hughes and Vivian Clemence, who also lived nearby. Slowly, but surely, Sue worked her way out of her worst depression.

There were even upsides to combining professional footballing with having small children. Phil would always pick his kids up from school. It was perfect timing – he finished training at 1.00pm and was home by 1.30pm. He had the chance to see many of the things that mean so much: he was there to teach Natasha and Ashley to walk, talk, read, and play the tin flute. He was there when their son, who turned out to be a big football talent too, kicked a ball for the first time. They also had the opportunity to go abroad on holidays and see a lot of the world.

That was quite uncommon for England in the 1970s and '80s. In the latter decade, with unemployment high and the city of Liverpool set at odds with the Thatcher era, it could be a time of hopelessness for the working class in Britain. It's something we see returning among the young again today. The wheel has turned full circle and the world seems neither to learn nor remember very well. However, the Neal family was able to travel and broaden their horizons. It was like further education for Phil, Sue and their kids, Ashley and Natasha. The money was coming in steadily and the family was happy on these trips. The children loved travelling.

I'm in the elegant dining room with Sue, looking through the open veranda door, leading out to the garden. We're sipping champagne while Phil is coaching my son. He's giving orders about which foot Elias should kick the ball with – they're passing to one

another. Even playing with my son, who had just turned five here in Liverpool and celebrated with an LFC cake, I can see Phil's winning instinct waken. Even in suit shoes and grey, ironed trousers, he is a stubborn opponent for Elias – and the boy is beaming with happiness.

Phil's kids were raised on the kind of winning instincts my son is now getting a taste of. Sue has had to intervene, as mediator, a number of times – in games of snooker or tennis between father and son.

"Dad's cheating!" Phil chuckles.

"I think I've taught my kids the sharpness of a winning attitude. I hope you give certain genes away, because I think competitiveness is a good thing to share. Then, if you've got that '*go*', if you have ambition and determination, you can make your dreams come true."

Despite having played in five European Cup finals, a league match from his second season as a Liverpool player stands out as his strongest Liverpool memory.

Bob Paisley and his crew had exited the FA Cup in the fourth round after losing 1-0 to Derby County at the Baseball Ground. The pressure was building up on Paisley after his first trophyless season and the press was speculating about how long he would last as Shankly's successor.

The perfect response to any doubters would be delivering the league title back to Anfield. The Reds were just one game away. That match took place on May 4, 1976, at Wolverhampton Wanderers. The only problem was, the home team also *had* to win to avoid losing their place in the division. There was massive interest in the game. A crowd of Liverpool fans had gathered outside Molineux.

In the crowd, Phil Thompson spotted his brother, and a couple of his mates from Kirkby. They had no tickets. Thompson asked Paisley if there was any chance they could let the boys in through the back, through the changing room. Nobody would notice... Bob was under severe pressure and would not risk causing his players to be upset just before the match. He said it was okay for Thommo to let his family and friends through.

In the meantime, rumour spread among the rest of the crowd that you could get into the stadium through Liverpool's changing room. When Paisley opened up to let Thompson's people in, Scousers poured in. He had no chance to close the double door. People fell in between the 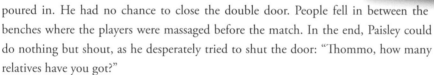 benches where the players were massaged before the match. In the end, Paisley could do nothing but shout, as he desperately tried to shut the door: "Thommo, how many relatives have you got?"

"I love this story," adds Phil, "and tell it fondly when I talk about my days at Liverpool as this was the turning point for Bob Paisley. In his first season, we won nothing. Now Bob achieved his first goal – we won the league that day, and I won my first medal.

"Fifteen days later, Kevin Keegan scored from a free-kick in the return match against FC Brugge and we won the Uefa Cup. The next year, we also won the Double, winning the league and the European Cup, and Paisley was named Manager of the Year.

"This gave him the self-confidence to build the team in the way he did during the rest of his time in charge. It was absolutely fantastic. I got to be in this along with Paisley. He had so many huge bottles of whisky, being named manager of the month so many times. God only knows if he ever managed to drink any of it."

So, what is Neal's secret? Why did he end up in the history books of Liverpool FC as their most decorated player? A dominant winning instinct, a focus so narrow he sacrificed his family and good health through fierce determination and hard work.

And, he says, that he was extremely lucky to be there at that period, with the great Boot Room staff, good managers and fantastic team-mates.

"Ian Callaghan was still there when I started, so was Tommy Smith. They were the stalwarts of our city and our team. It's vital to have a local base in a team, just like the modern team has Steven Gerrard and Jamie Carragher."

"Why is that?"

"They gave us a feeling of what it was like for our supporters to lose a derby game. They gave us the passion to beat Manchester United. Those inner city boys who were brought up on Scotland Road, Huyton – Terry McDermott, Jimmy Case and David Fairclough, and Thommo, from Kirkby. They were all from hard parts of the city and they were all working so hard for the team. They showed me what winning for Liverpool really meant to them, on every occasion.

"Ian Callaghan was probably the prime example. He was a gentleman and a diplomat, whereas Tommy Smith was in your face. A very different type, he'd tell you plainly if you were doing things the Liverpool way or not. Just what you need when things weren't going quite right.

"Despite my 23 trophies in 11 years, there were moments of trouble – and then it was great to have seniors in the team who could help straighten things out. I hope and believe I grew to be a figurehead like them, influencing players like Jimmy Case and Ian Rush, who were attempting to make it in the first-team. Not quite so in your face like Smith; maybe more diplomatic, like Cally."

Neal has no doubt the local lads he played with had great influence on the loyalty of new arrivals at the club. Thanks to the commitment of Phil Thompson, Ian Callaghan and Tommy Smith, Neal stayed at Merseyside instead of moving back to Northampton at the end of his career.

"Those Liverpool people were fantastic. They gave me confidence and taught me everything about the city. You could see how they gave everything for the team and I tried to imitate them."

It is the same way with Steven Gerrard and Jamie Carragher today. They are both as dedicated and fight just as hard as they were brought up to. Neal says Carragher has an amazing personality and can play in a number of positions on the pitch. He is the modern

Tommy Smith, with strong, plain messages to his team-mates to keep them on their toes and motivate them to work even harder.

Gerrard, not as verbal as Carragher, has the ability to settle matches on his own. Neal, and many with him, will never forget the glorious goal Liverpool's captain scored in the FA Cup Final against West Ham in 2006.

"Gerrard is a model player – he never gives up, will never submit to a loss and will fight until the very end. Besides, there are many times when he has pulled the team by the scruff of the neck through a match and salvaged points all by himself. He could have played in every team from 1974 to 1986. The only problem is, who would you drop to replace with Gerrard?"

The old Liverpool captain hopes the fantastic abilities of the current local stars will be continued through other local players in the future. As long as Kenny Dalglish is boss, he is not worried about local recruitment.

"I would hate my club if sometime in the future they totally discarded the local lads and left the Academy to itself. That would be hurtful for me. There are a few local talents in the making and I hope they'll be able to take over after Gerrard and Carragher, because even they can't be there for ever.

"I have a feeling that, now Kenny's back at the helm, the heritage from Shankly and Paisley will show."

He has no doubt that Liverpool supporters are even prouder to win with local talent on the team.

"See how the seats fill up for matches now that the club's own Kenny Dalglish has made a comeback as manager and given several local talents the chance to show off. Now the stalls are filled again, just like when David Fairclough knocked in the winner against St Etienne en route to our first European Cup. Dalglish is quite similar to Paisley. He knows when to break up a team and build a new one. Kenny has showed his quality already by getting rid of Fernando Torres."

As I took the train back to Liverpool city centre, I was moved by Sue and Phil Neal's strong story. I felt for both parties. I know first hand what it is like to be suffering from a long-term sickness, with a newborn baby, while your husband is travelling more than one third of every week. I also understand that Neal could not have just dropped his amazing Liverpool career, that he pushed his limits as far as he could, earning a place in the history books forever, with his unsurpassed list of achievements. But, after all these years, you would think there was room for reconciliation. It is not easy.

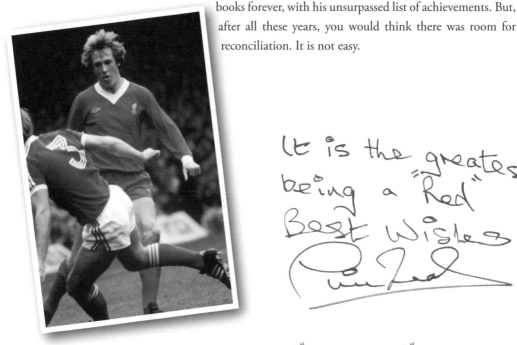

It is the greatest being a "Red"

Best Wishes

28

Liverpool FC Career: 1974-1985 🦅 *Appearances: 650* 🦅 *Goals: 59*

Ian Rush
One Big Family

"The best goalscorer in Britain"

John Barnes

In the 1980s and 90s, whether you liked football or not, you could not avoid noticing Ian Rush: the tall, thin striker with his trademark black moustache.

My childhood was spent in a two-storey house built just before I started primary school. It had plenty of space, a dashing oriel and a spacious garden on the verge of a big forest with blueberries and exciting tree huts. We were among the first to establish in the new housing estate. Dad was a commuter and usually he would only be home every other weekend. So, most of the time, I shared the house and garden with my older sister, our mother and the cat, while Ian James Rush had a lot less space to himself growing up.

He grew up in Wales – less than an hour away from Liverpool – with his mum, dad and nine brothers and sisters. Doris May Rush must have been quite a woman. She had 10 children in just 15 years. Her husband was mostly away; either at work or at the pub. I find raising two children busy, while this woman dedicated her life to her family and children. She must have been a strong and courageous woman.

"She was, yes, God bless her, she's not with us any more. All she did all her life was look after us. She put family in front of everything. My dad was always working and my mum was waking my brothers up to go to work, and then the rest of us to go to school. It was a very, very tough life for her," says the man who is now one of Liverpool FC's foremost ambassadors.

The family of 12 shared a council home with three bedrooms. His parents had one bedroom, four sisters the other, and the third held six brothers in bunk beds.

"As you may understand, it was easy for me to find space inside the penalty box, easier than finding space in a small room with five brothers," Rush chuckles.

He looks out over the centre of Liverpool, bathing in sunlight beneath us. We are in the Panoramic restaurant in the West Tower, the tallest building in the city, with a spectacular view. Our talk goes straight on tape, as a Norwegian TV channel has tagged along to make a story about my new book project. The filming makes us more honed during the interview. Rush thinks back on his childhood and the densely populated bunk bedroom.

31

Second youngest, he would be in one bed and was constantly woken up by brothers rising with the lark to get ready for their shifts, or coming home from shifts or after a night out. His childhood was a series of broken sleep. Quite a few times, Rush was in bed listening to his older brothers turning in while dreaming that he scored in an FA Cup final.

If growing up with so many brothers and sisters deprived him of sleep, it had other benefits; with so many brothers, there were always someone he could play football with. His brothers were decent, local players. The fact that Rush played daily with boys a lot older than him made him push his limits from early on.

"To reach the very top I think you need more than just skills. You need to be very determined and mentally strong to succeed. Nobody helped me more with this than my brothers, who loved to play local football alongside their jobs. They helped me an awful lot."

Having so many people so close every day, how does this affect your ability to function in a team where people are close for long periods of time?

"In my family, we're very close to one another and that probably made it easier for me than for a lot of others to become part of, and adapt to, a team. I was used to socialising with different types of people. We were brought up to respect others and get behind those who struggled. I've found that, in life, when you're successful, everybody wants to know you, but when you struggle, that's when you need your family.

"When you're successful and winning, people may well criticise you, but I don't feel it's right to criticise someone who is down.

"That's what I found happened at Liverpool FC, the culture was to support players who were out of form or didn't play so well, rather than criticise them. This way, you would see other players working extra hard for you at times when you couldn't hold your own on the pitch."

Rush found a lot of similarities between the values he grew up with in his family and the extended family of Liverpool Football Club. He sees the club as his real, extended family. The father figure of the LFC family when he joined the team was Bob Paisley. He did what a lot of fathers would: he gave each child no more space or a higher status than the other children, despite the number of superstars on the team. No one was bigger than the club. Every single one – from Kenny Dalglish

to the tea lady and the supporters – were important factors, all contributing in different ways to the enormous success of the club.

Paisley used to make sure everybody went in to greet the cleaning lady and the tea lady every Monday morning.

"That made them feel six feet tall as well."

Nobody in Liverpool FC's history has scored more goals than Ian Rush. He hit 346 goals for the Reds during an incredible career over two spells from 1980 to 1996 – interrupted only by a stay at Juventus from 1987-1988.

When Rush and the boys scored for the Reds, their first task was to run back to the man who made the goal, usually the second last man on the ball. If you thanked him, he would work for you to score more goals. If you did not, he might try himself the next time.

Ian Rush has thanked no man more often in his career than Kenny Dalglish. The two of them formed one of the most special and successful partnerships in the history of English football. However, the magic between them was not there right away. In training they did not quite hit it off – and off the pitch they hardly talked. They did not mix unless the whole team did something together. They were very different. Dalglish liked golf

while Rush loved horse racing. They did not have a lot to talk about. But playing together was a different story.

Even though they did not hit it off socially or in training, something happened in the games. Dalglish helped the youngster from Wales to gain self-confidence by saying that his only job was to score goals, not make goals. Others would take care of the rest.

"I basically couldn't understand how a person could put the ball in the space where he said he was going to. I was quite quick in those days, so I just made the run and Kenny would put it straight to my feet. I realised Kenny could put the ball wherever he wanted to."

Dalglish didn't even look, he would just put the ball in the perfect spot where he knew Rush would be. This way, the moustached chap often gained a metre on the defenders before he hammered the ball into the back of the net.

How was such a precise interaction possible when they hardly spoke? Firstly, Rush used to study Dalglish, and Dalglish used to study Rush. They both had well-developed football brains. Besides, they instinctively knew what the other was thinking.

"It was telepathic, really. It was no good talking. People say you need to talk when you play football – and you do sometimes – but we didn't have to talk because we were on the same wavelength and had a special understanding for each other's game. That's why I scored so many goals."

In addition, it was about trust. After Dalglish had done a lot of running for Rush early in his career, now Rush worked extra hard for Dalglish, so he would still have the possibility to pass him the ball.

It was exactly the same when the local young talent Robbie Fowler won a place in the first-team. Now it was Rush's time to say: "Robbie, your job is to score goals. Nothing else!" The next generation was under way. That was Liverpool FC: they helped each other and made each other play well.

"That is why Liverpool Football Club is such a great club. When I played badly, Kenny would help me more than usual and vice versa."

Only lately has Rush and his former team-mate Dalglish hit it off on a personal level. Now, they are big mates and talk almost every day.

They have a lot to thank each other for. The most important lesson Dalglish taught

Rush was that you never stand still on the pitch, you had to always be on the move. Pass and move! But Dalglish's most important task, both before and during his time as player-manager, was his ability to inspire everybody on the team.

"He kept us all going. If I scored a hat-trick, he would come over and congratulate me, but he would never go over the top. However, if one of us had a bad day, he would help us even more, to keep your confidence going.

"Self-confidence is vital for a striker. If you lose that, you don't get in the right position and you are too scared to have a shot. When I went through a bad patch and he was player-manager, he would take me aside in training and we'd go back to basics, and practise shooting. When my confidence came back and I started scoring again, he left me alone."

A partnership like that of Rush and Dalglish does not form just anywhere and definitely not between anyone. Rush has no problems realising how lucky they were with the timing.

"Without a doubt. We were the number one pair. But, when you play, you don't realise how special that is. After I stopped playing, I've watched videos and realised I was very, very lucky to play for Liverpool Football Club and with Kenny Dalglish. I can say, 'Yes, job well done!' Now that I'm not playing, I can't be pig-headed, but...

"Of course you can! I'll allow it!" We laugh. Rush has a peculiar laugh. It's almost boyish, even though it hits the deep notes. "No one can take that time away from me, or the goals I scored – and that is something to be proud of."

As an 18-year-old, Rush had never thought he would be the record goalscorer for Liverpool FC because he was struggling to find his place. He really only wanted to quit.

"I hated my first year at the club. I was very shy and I was changing next to these superstars: Ray Clemence on one side, Alan Hansen on the other. It was very, very difficult.

"The environment was brand new. People were joking in the dressing room and I didn't know how to take it. Good or bad? And I wasn't playing well for the reserves, so everything seemed to be bad and I really needed some help to get into the team spirit.

"There were no bouncers there to protect you. Even the supporters – they are all known as comedians and jokers, and you need to get into that – but I hated it. In the dressing room, they took the mickey out of every newcomer and it really was sink or swim. I took it all in and said nothing because I was so shy. It was eating away at me and affected my football.

"Deep down I knew I was good enough. That's what made me so determined – even though for two or three months I did feel that I wasn't good enough for the team. That didn't help. I thought loads about leaving. If I wasn't good enough, I could go back to Chester City, I'd been happy there."

After three months of training with the first-team, he knew his worth. He kept that feeling and his strength to himself. His mental strength showed itself. The first six months at the club were probably the most important in his entire career. It seemed impossible to play your way into the team; they were always winning and you did not change a winning team – unless someone got injured or sick.

Rush played for the reserves but trained with the first-team on Thursdays and Fridays, even though the first-team and reserves trained separately then. He would still play for the reserves on Saturdays.

In training, Paisley had noticed that the Welsh youngster performed better against better opponents and with better team-mates. So, even though he did not play too well for the reserves, Rush got his chance in the first-team. When he had seven games under his belt for them, he felt like part of the first-team and asked the manager for a pay rise. They had won most of the games he had played and, even though he had not scored, he thought: "This is a team sport and my team, that I'm part of now, have done well." Paisley wouldn't give it to him.

"What do you want?" Rush had said.

"You're not part of this team," the manager huffed. "You're not good enough. You haven't scored any goals! You have to become more selfish on the pitch!"

It turned into an argument that ended with Rush, hurt over the refusal and being told he wasn't part of the first-team, asking for a transfer. Paisley accepted. Rush left his office agitated and with only one thought in his mind: "From now on I'm only playing for myself!" In two games for the reserves, he scored five goals.

In a cup match at home at Anfield, Rush started on the bench when they met the Finnish club Oulu Palloseura. In his mind, he was leaving the club, as they would never let him play. Then, he got a chance after all: "I'll show them selfish!"

In front of the Kop, Rush then wrote history. The striker got the ball four or five yards from the goal line and punted it home. Rush had scored his very first goal for the first-team. He cannot remember who made the assist. He was not that bothered, since he was training to be selfish. With the goal, a magic process went through his head: "Once you score, it's amazing how much better you feel. And you feel confident and want to try out new things on the pitch. That's when I took off, I think. Liverpool won the match 7-0.

"Two months later, Bob Paisley called me to his office and said he wanted to give me a new contract. He'd never actually put me on the transfer list. He'd said that to annoy me and it worked! Because I listened to him and showed him I'm a quick learner, he offered me a new contract. At this level, you have to learn quickly – and I learned a lot in a short time from Bob Paisley."

Slowly but surely, Rush became part of the team and his self-confidence grew.

"In the end, I just entered the field knowing I would score. I wasn't conceited, but I had a lot of confidence and I was given many chances to score in every match because we had such a great team."

The ability to be selfish is vital, but you also need to be a good team player and make each other good, just as Rush and Dalglish did. But it is confusing and contradictory, if you ask me, having to be selfish and a team player, to juggle and balance inside that duality. It cannot be easy. What more do you need to be a striker like Rush?

"It's a mental thing. Mental toughness and strength are needed. I coach a lot of kids these days, and I can see they're often scared of failure. Once they make a mistake, they're scared of trying it again. Watching kids over the last five years, I've seen that a lot of them are scared of not doing everything 100 per cent right.

"I wasn't like that, neither was Michael Owen. We weren't afraid to miss. If you miss five and hit the sixth, people forget your misses and remember the one you scored. But, today, if the kids miss, they're scared of doing it again because they think they're a failure. It takes mental strength to say, 'Listen, I don't care if I missed that one.'

"I used to get stick from the supporters when I missed the goal, but I shut it off because I was concentrating so much on my football. However, when I scored, I heard what they were saying, because the feeling is so overwhelming you open up again."

Rush concentrated in the same way whether he played at home against a bottom team or at Wembley in front of a crowd of 100,000. He shut off the surroundings completely. He neither heard nor saw the supporters, focusing solely on the game and on trying to hold the opponents. If their full-back had the ball, Rush was thinking three or four steps ahead to where the ball would end up. That creates goals. Lots of goals.

"Many times I didn't even see the ball hitting the net as I was already on my way to the centre line, knowing it was a goal, because the supporters would be singing my name when I was back at the centre line. But I was focused on scoring again. I wanted more goals!

"Right away?"

"Yes! I want to score one, I want to score two, I want to score three!"

"That sounds like a song about you."

He laughs his typical laugh, breathes in, and smiles widely: "Yeah!"

"You must feel proud when you hear The Kop sing about you – and it is a song that is still popular years after you finished playing. What do you think about that?"

"I think it's great. It's good they still think of me and sing my name. My two sons often say, 'They still sing your name!' It just goes to show what fantastic supporters they are. But when I was playing, I didn't really hear it. They still sing Kenny's name and mine, and it makes me feel really proud."

I grew up in a time and culture where sporting heroes were in regular contact with their fans. So, it has been odd seeing some of these young footballers in hip suits and clean shirts, newly ironed by professional launderers, quickly hopping in and out of buses, preferably with earphones to keep out the noise of the cheering crowd of young and older fans with a pen or camera at the ready, pursuing memories from one of their big heroes. Often, the players disappear into tunnels that are stretched out as close to the bus door as possible. They enter the stadium, with styled hair, and are practically unapproachable. How does this compare to the 1980s and a good part of the '90s, when Rush was one of the biggest stars on Merseyside?

"We used to talk to the supporters and have a laugh and a joke. As you probably know, Liverpool people are very funny, great characters. You'll never see a shy Scouser. They are fantastic people and very friendly. It's funny to think about how different people are – even only a 40-minute drive away, in Wales, where I am from.

"I met the fans going to and from training. They were good to me and I respected them. But, today, things are very different for the fans; the game has become too big. That's why you'll rarely be able to chat to the players."

"I'm relatively new to football writing and grew up somewhere without 'superstars', far north of the Arctic Circle. Am I naive to think, 'Boys playing football – they should act normal and mingle with people?'"

"You can be annoyed that it's like this, but you have to look after players today. You always get one silly idiot who wants to fight or cause trouble, which is why they're overprotecting the players. I'd rather have it that way than not."

"It sounds a bit lonely in there?"

"It is! At times it's very lonely because most of them can't just go to the pub or play a game of golf. It can be very hard on them – remember that many of them are normal working class people who ended up like this because they have fantastic skills."

Normal working class boys or not, there is one thing I am certain of – they would not have been allowed to moon or bare their backside, if you like, to the Kop in a testimonial. When Alan Hansen played his testimonial, Rush had gone to Italy to play for Juventus. However, he came home to play the match for his old team-mate. Rush scored two and The Kop were shouting for Dalglish to sign him back. They were also yelling at their star striker: *"Why don't you show us your arse?"*

Rush laughs heartily: *"So I did!* There are too many cameras today. But the fans used to make us laugh!"

I am thinking about how playing for one of the world's greatest football clubs shapes you as a person, and how this has changed during the last 50 years. For Liverpool FC's record scorer, all his years at the club taught him a lot about respect for other people and what it is like to be part of a club family. About how you help those who struggle and hold back your criticism, but dare to criticise in better times.

The characteristic moustache is gone, the dark hair is now silvery, almost white, but the intense, light blue husky eyes are the same and they glitter. It is a silly digression for anyone but me, but they remind me of my father's eyes. There are few people in the world with such ice blue, bright and kind eyes. The kind you notice. It is like they can see right through everything, even what you desperately try to hide. These days, Rush travels as one of the club's foremost ambassadors. He represents the club in all corners of the world and often goes to arrangements with the largest sponsors.

"With all the travelling I do now, I realise just how big Liverpool FC are – especially when we go to the Far East and meet lots of people who have watched my years in the red jersey from there. Back then, I had no idea how big we were outside Europe. We had pre-season matches in Scandinavia and elsewhere in Europe. The world is a small place now. Liverpool FC are a global club and many people we meet on our travels will never have the chance to go to Anfield, even though they are fanatical supporters.

"It just goes to show how big our club has become. Our family is getting bigger and bigger!"

When I was young, I spent altogether a year and a half in Australia, where I experienced my greatest adrenaline kick so far in life. It wasn't the time that I almost stepped on a giant poisonous snake that was worming itself across our street, fat and greyish-brown, in the dark. No, the biggest shot of adrenaline I have had pumped into my blood was when I parachuted. I threw myself out of a plane, 12,000ft up in the air. My fingertips tingle just thinking about the feeling I had in the doorway, watching the landscape, and my friends sink like stones in the air below me, before their chutes opened above the ochre landscape. Then I had to make the choice to jump off myself. After all, that was what I had paid for.

I will never forget the feeling of so much adrenaline pumping in my body. The feeling of flying, even after we had landed, almost like gravity had ceased to exist. I laughed all the time, constantly looking up in the sky and longing to experience the same free fall again, when seconds raged and stood still at the same time. I was perfectly happy. Happiness filled my entire body, lived in every single cell.

I have also heard the urban myth about the mother who – in an adrenaline rush of fear after her child had been run over by a car – managed to lift a car to save the child. Which is why I wonder what it does to someone, having so much adrenaline pumped into your body regularly, as footballers do? Can you really accomplish anything with enough adrenaline?

"Yes. The adrenaline floats around the body of a player. It's what makes football so special. Sometimes I've been asked how on earth I managed this or that, but I can't give them an answer because it's the adrenaline and the energy that drive you and make you accomplish incredible feats without even thinking. Sometimes I had to ask myself the next day, 'Did I really do *that*?'"

He played for one of the world's top football clubs for many years and had large doses of adrenaline coarse through his body. It must have been a happy life, playing for the Reds?

"Sometimes you don't know how lucky you are. When I played, people told me to enjoy it because nothing would ever be the same afterwards. I thought, 'Yeah, right...' But it's only when you stop playing you realise you can't beat it. I've had the best life ever.

"When people say, 'I bet you wish you were playing today, with all that money?' No! I wouldn't swap my life with anything. Now, I'm working for the club, and our players today make lots of money – good luck to them! Jealousy is the worst thing. It's not right. Let these lads enjoy themselves, but I wouldn't swap my career for anything in the world."

"With all the money they make today, does it affect motivation somewhat?"

"Absolutely. We played and, if we weren't in the side, we moved on because we wanted to play as much as possible. Now, the money is so big I think that some players are happy sitting on the bench. And, if they get enjoyment out of that, I... I think they're lying. The only enjoyment they have then is money-wise – and all players should enjoy playing, not being on the bench.

"If we couldn't get regular game-time for our team, we left the club, because all we wanted was play football."

Rush played an incredible 660 games for Liverpool and has many vivid, great memories from his years at the club. But, if you rewind to his childhood wishes, one wish topped the list, one that turned out to come true.

Let us go back to 1986. All the players and the people around them pretended that everything was normal. They followed their routines and tried to think this match was just another game. They made the same preparations as they used to – the menu was the same, they talked about the same things. But there *was* one difference: they were in a London hotel and in and around the hotel there were huge crowds of Liverpool fans.

Rush could not help but feel his body tense up a little extra. His stomach felt it. The view from the bus going to the stadium did not help either. A sea of Everton and Liverpool supporters wandering together like pilgrims towards Wembley.

"That's when it kicked in, that this was something special. It was going to be a Merseyside derby in the FA Cup final. For me, we were the two best teams in Europe then, not just in England."

It was a boiling hot day. When they arrived at Wembley, they had another reminder that this was the real thing – the changing rooms were a lot bigger than elsewhere.

Rush tried to think it was just another day at work. He did what he always had: he immersed his boots in hot water. He had done so ever since they played Luton Town in

1983 and his boots were way too stiff. He wet them in water to soften them and ended up scoring five goals. Therefore, ever since, regardless of the weather, he has played in wet boots. His mother cannot possibly have been impressed with her son voluntarily running out in the icy cold winter with soaked footwear.

On the Wembley grass he was met by a sea of waving red and blue fans from Liverpool, his head and heart throbbing. The seriousness of it all really hit him when the national anthem was played. He was marked by the gravity of the moment and suddenly had no choice, he had to take note of his surroundings. He could not shut them out like he used to during the warm-up and match. He had goose bumps and again he realised that this was something really, really special.

He could hardly wait to show everyone what he could do. The world was watching. His head pounded. The last warm-up session made him focus again.

The first half was blue, and Everton were 1-0 up before half-time. But the second half was a different story altogether.

Liverpool was the dominant team. Jan Molby played a little like Dalglish. The Dane knew where to put the balls for Rush. He put them in the space in front of the striker and suddenly Rush was on target and reached the ball just before Everton keeper Bobby

Mimms. The forward touched it with his right foot and knocked it in with his left – being two-footed was one of his great assets. Craig Johnston had tried to reach it but, if he had, it would have been offside. After 56 minutes it was 1-1.

"When the equaliser came, we knew we would win. You see, for the previous six years, if I scored, we never lost. I think the supporters and the opponents knew about this."

The Reds' self-confidence grew, while a fear of losing hit the Blues. Johnston scored Liverpool's second goal, just six minutes after Rush. When there was less than 10 minutes left, Rush was back, helping to defend the lead. Then, he saw an opportunity to attack and used his pace while Ronnie Whelan was on the ball. He had two possibilities: either pass to Dalglish on the left side or Rush on the right.

"Luckily for me, he chose me. I controlled the ball and hit it hard and low at the bottom corner, where it hit a camera. It was 3-1 in the 83rd minute and then we knew we weren't going to let this slip."

The man who had accomplished his childhood dream of scoring in an FA Cup final had done it not only once, but twice, that day – and secured the Double in the process.

Happiness filled his body. He forgot all about running over to thank Whelan. He ran over to the supporters to celebrate his goal. It didn't matter, all the other players joined him there.

"Everything came together in this match. It was an incredible feeling. A little later, I had a chance to score a hat-trick, but I wasn't bothered, it wasn't like me. I regret that now – there aren't many who have scored hat-tricks at Wembley. But I was simply too cocky at this stage. It was just too much to grasp. We had won the Double, and my dream from when I was a wee lad wasn't winning the league, but to score in the FA Cup final. Now I'd scored the winning goal, against our city rivals, even.

"I never went to bed that night. There was too much going on in my head. It wasn't the goals, but the whole match and the whole atmosphere that made this a perfect day for me."

The goal machine from Wales; the man who entered the pitch knowing he was going to score and, sometimes after he hit the net, found lying underneath his delighted team-mates who had dived on him like a heap of penguins. Rush cannot describe what it is like lying there squeezed under several hundred kilos. When you lie there filled with adrenaline, endorphins and happiness, you do not feel pain – and you do not think of the consequences of jumping on your team-mate at such a time that you may actually hurt him. Celebrating a goal, even in a pile like that, it's just an incredible feeling, he says.

"You must have been hugged a thousand times by men?" Ian Rush bursts out laughing as I ask.

"Yes! And, honestly, I did enjoy it!"

Ian Rush – perhaps the most hugged football player in the history of English football. Embraced by his big Red family.

Thank you very much
for everything
Ian Rush

45

Liverpool FC Career: 1980-1987 & 1988-1996 *Appearances: 660* *Goals: 346*

Phil Thompson
Burying The Hatchet

"Thommo, great mate; great Liverpool fan; great player; good reader of the game. He was very quick at identifying danger. He calls me Whip, I call him Skip. He will always be one of my number one captains."

David Fairclough

 When you achieve something you have worked hard for, or wanted for a long time, it is only natural to celebrate it with people you have known all your life. It is as if recognition counts more if it is from the people around you.

My mother Synnøve has told me that ever since my first years in primary school, I have dreamed of becoming a writer. I filled notebook after notebook with stories and pretended they were books. When my first book was published, I was 34, I wanted to celebrate the publication in Alta, the place at 70 degrees North where I grew up, but had not lived for 16 years.

Why did I want that? I had not given it a second thought until now. It just seemed natural to share my dream come true with 'my people'. My time in Liverpool has made me think more about these mechanisms.

The majority of Liverpool legends choose to stay on Merseyside. Does recognition last longer if they stay? A lot of them have jobs related to the football club, but not all. Some are commentators for national television, like Alan Hansen. But Liverpool is still his home, he prefers commuting – as does John Barnes. He is a football expert on two other continents but, in between battles, he returns to his base on Merseyside.

Another frequent topic among supporters and the whole culture is the significance of local players. The more players who have grown up in working class areas of Liverpool in the team, the happier supporters are for a win. Is that not part of it, that local lads who make it with the club, make the whole city shine? We are on a spot of Earth made of people who generate success and high esteem for all of us. We have breathed the same air, have been shaped by the same culture, and grown up with the same heroes, and just look:"That's what winners are made of!"

Phil Neal told it to me straight: the local lads were the most important factor as to why his team won so much back then. Ian Callaghan, Tommy Smith, Sammy Lee, Chris

Lawler – and not least Phil Thompson – they all gave that little extra, and showed the rest of the team how important it was to win every single match. They knew what it meant to the fans that the team won – and to many who had little, Liverpool FC's achievements were something that would keep them warm all week.

Spring 2011. Phil Neal had asked his friend Phil Thompson if he would consider helping my book project and, only a few days later, he had found time for me. Last time I met him, I was interviewing him for Liverpool Hearts (Liverpoolhjerter), and we tested the theory that football improves your memory. 'Thommo' confirmed it through numerous examples of how he still remembers detailed information of matches and incidents from a long time ago.

This time, we were going to meet at a gym, The David Lloyd Centre, right next to Liverpool FC's Academy. I almost missed it. I had called a taxi for Back Colquitt Street, but it turned out to be waiting on the wrong road. I called the head office several times. My pulse quickened. Luckily, I had allowed for extra time, but I was getting rushed. I started legging it, looking for the taxi, as the woman at the office stubbornly claimed the car was waiting for me right where I wanted it. I was quite grumpy by the time I found it – in Colquitt Street. The taxi driver was also crabby, and worse so when I told him to hit it so I could be in time for my meeting with Thompson in Kirkby. I should not have said that because, afterwards, when I had calmed down, I noticed the Everton pennant in his windscreen.

"Phil Thompson!" The driver snorted. "I don't care about him at all! He has mocked us Everton supporters too much. He has it coming to him!" (Well, that's the version without the swear words anyway!)

The cafe area at the gym is large and light. I am thinking how well Thompson bears his years. His commitment to the club is massive and he is a very trustworthy personality. He gesticulates and talks in a deep, sonorous voice. He has a Bond cleft in his chin and a nose he makes fun of himself. It seems most football players during his time had nicknames, often shortened version of their names, such as 'Thommo' in his case. However, it was unavoidable that the lads also named him Pinocchio.

In Norway, journalists usually wait on the people they interview. But cast among well-brought-up Liverpool lads, I have no chance. Thompson is up and has already got our drinks from the bar – black coffee and mineral water – before I have even got my coat off. We start the recording.

"My name is Philip Bernard Thompson. Now you know that, I'm going to have to kill you," he laughs.

He was born in 1954 and grew up in Kirkby, a tough area of Merseyside. His dad Owen was an Evertonian and his mum June an avid Red. They had seven children. His dad was away a lot, which left mum with all the room she needed to recruit her young to the right team.

"My mum was an absolutely passionate Liverpool fan with her twin sister, auntie May. They went to matches to support Liverpool from when they were kids and she did all she could to get us over on the right side. When my dad came home from sea, he tried to tempt us with sweets, toys and gifts. But he couldn't do it – we were already too long in the tooth as Liverpool fans."

"And your parents remained married?"

He laughs: "They did stay married, yes. And, once I became a Liverpool player, my dad, like a lot of people – Jamie Carragher, Michael Owen, Robbie Fowler – turned from Evertonian to Liverpudlian. He gave me great support."

When Thompson grew up, Everton were kings and they had all the money. But Liverpool had started their wonderful journey with Bill Shankly. Still, it was never a good thing, going into school after a derby game. If Liverpool had won, Monday mornings were great and Thommo would wear his red and white scarf to school. Had they lost, he braced himself. He would be humiliated and mocked by Evertonian pupils. They grew up to resent each other. Ever since childhood, they learned that they were bitter enemies. That is why some acts still hurt.

"When my autobiography came out a few years ago, I actually apologised to the Evertonians for something I did as an 18-year-old at Goodison Park: Alan Waddle scored the only goal of his Liverpool career, in the Gwladys Street end. A young Phil Thompson ran towards the Gwladys Street stand, waving two fingers on each hand aggressively at the Everton supporters. Not a clever thing to do. Luckily, not that many people picked it up at the time. With the media involvement today, it would have been scrutinised and I would have been in big trouble. It took many years before I had a chance to apologise for what I had done, through my book."

These things make sure you are remembered and hated by your enemies. The taxi driver who took me to Kirkby to see Phil Thompson was one of these Blues. If you cross

die-hard fans like that, it sticks, and a few decades cannot wipe these acts out of people's minds.

The derby matches against Everton are among Liverpool's biggest games every year – and *the* biggest match for Thompson.

"Some people think the Manchester United games are the biggest, but not for me. I think it's because I was brought up in this city and the passion to beat Everton FC as often as I could drove me. I was lucky enough to take part in seven years when we never lost to Everton! That's a long time, and that's how important it was to me."

Liverpool has experienced a dramatic rise in fans, more than Everton. When Thompson was growing up, the teams were more even. Sometimes he would get into fights at school after derby matches. He hated being ridiculed if the Reds had lost. That made him really mad. There were cliques of Evertonians and Liverpudlians, and Thompson went to matches with the Liverpool lads.

He never forgets 1965. His mum could not get tickets to the famous Cup final against Leeds United, but she had got tickets for the first leg of the European Cup semi-final against Inter Milan at Anfield. He was 11 years old and this was one of his very first matches at Anfield. They were on what was then the Kemlyn Road – now Centenary Stand – where you look over to the Kop on your left. He was wearing his red and white scarf, his pride and joy. It was always ready in his bedroom.

"I'm not sure if I watched The Kop and the fans there more than I watched the match, the swaying of the crowd, that was absolutely packed. There must have been 28,000 on The Kop alone. I was in awe. If it's possible to have a love affair with a place, that's what happened to me.

"I'd been to a few matches before. But this was a night game against the great Inter Milan, so it was the first match of its kind for me. I was sold, completely hooked after that night. For people who've supported the club since the '60s, this is the game. We beat Inter Milan 3-1."

He had pictures of Liverpool players all over his bedroom, and was already an avid supporter. Roger Hunt was on his headboard, next to Ian St John. Team photos and cut-outs of the Red heroes covered his walls.

"It must have cost my mum a fortune to take us to that match. We couldn't go to Wembley, so she got us these front row tickets. It's great that, in time, I was able to pay my parents and my brother back for all they helped me with."

Thompson played for Kirkby boys when he was 14. He was good, but, according to himself, not exceptional. People develop differently. He was very tall and skinny, but he could run. He would run all day and was North of England cross-country champion at 13. He was a midfielder at that time and played five-a-side, Sunday league, for his school team and the Kirkby boys. Every week.

His Sunday league team was managed by Billy Gamble. He was also a steward at Anfield and he brought down a talent scout to come watch the boys. The scout picked skinny Thompson and a lad called John Roberts. Thompson was developing as a 15-year-old and was just hoping someone would pick him. He was training with Everton on Tuesdays and Thursdays. As soon as the scout invited him to Liverpool, Thompson started training Tuesdays and Thursdays at Melwood instead.

However, he did not sign straight away. There were four other apprentices there on a six-week trial period. This was in 1969.

"It was awful and demoralising. I was playing with these guys, and lads a year older than me, and I felt out of it. When the season started and we played our first match against Bury's B team at Melwood, I invited my mum to come and watch. Then I told her to please ask Tom Bush, the youth coach, whether I had any chance at all."

June asked him after the match. Then she and Phil walked along Melwood Drive to get the bus and his mum was very quiet, saying nothing. But eventually she cracked: "I can't keep this to myself any longer. They're going to sign you tomorrow!"

"What!"

"He told me not to tell you, but I just had to. They'll have the contract ready for signing tomorrow when you come in for training."

Thompson was absolutely delighted. None of the other four got contracts, even though they all played for England's schoolboys.

A couple of months before his 17th birthday, Thompson had been injured. He recalls: "Shanks was infamous for not talking to injured players."

"So that's true?"

"Oh, yes. If you were injured, he didn't want to know you. He'd look in the treatment room in the morning, and say, '*Good morning, Bob. Good morning, Joe*', and walk away. If there were players on the treatment bench he didn't acknowledge them.

"It really was not much of a treatment, anyway. If you managed to stand on your foot, you got down to Melwood and started walking. When you could jog, you'd jog, when you could run, you'd run and, when you could sprint, you'd sprint – and then you were ready to play. You told them when you were ready."

This November day in 1970, Shankly came in and asked Thompson about his injury. Then, he said: "Your birthday is in January, isn't it? 21st January?" Thompson nodded and gasped a little. He thought: "That's nice, he's going to send me a birthday card."

"Listen, son, I know you're injured, but I just want to put your mind at ease. You've done very, very well. All the coaches and myself are pleased with you. You don't have to rush yourself back too soon. We'll give you a professional contract on your birthday."

Phil was dumbstruck.

"But don't tell the other lads about this," Shankly added.

It was very difficult to keep it a secret for two months. The boss kept his word and gave him a contract for his birthday, while the other lads privately expected contracts on their birthdays and were disappointed.

In 1971, as a very young lad, he travelled with the team to Wembley and saw his first FA Cup final. He watched Liverpool play Arsenal, in his professional Liverpool FC blazer. At 1-1, he could not watch anymore. He wandered aimlessly around the halls.

"I was so frightened. Then I heard a roar from inside, and I thought, 'That wasn't from our lot.' I ran in; Charlie George had scored his famous goal."

Thompson was devastated. He was outside the stadium crying his heart out. But, in 1972/73, he won the league and the Uefa Cup. It was an amazing journey in such a short time.

The first time I saw Thompson was in Florø, Norway, in 2008. The small, idyllic west

coast town was full of Liverpool legends. They were playing an exhibition match against former national players of Norway, and they were having a Reds party with thousands of visiting Liverpool supporters from all over the country. Friday night out. I was at a small table with my husband.

The atmosphere was relaxed. The Liverpool lads were left in peace at their long table. Florø has hosted several Liverpool legends matches in a row now. The boys enjoy coming back to the place because they get to relax; reminisce about old times; go boating in the spectacular archipelago; play a match; eat and drink to their hearts' delight; go to concerts in the tent at night; have a dance and talk to the locals.

All of a sudden, a skinny, well-groomed man with a freshly ironed shirt came in. Immediately, people gathered around him. The laid-back atmosphere was washed away, because supporters could not stop themselves – they had to go talk to the newcomer. I understood that here was a man with higher status than most of the other lads from the Liverpool FC Legends team. He had a natural authority, politely greeting people, shaking their hands and talking to them.

"We played for the club during its best period and have some kind of a legend status today. I'm not sure many of the younger ex-players who finish their Liverpool careers now have the same mystique as lads from my time: Alan Kennedy, David Fairclough, Phil Neal, Jimmy Case. All these guys are real heroes. Real Liverpool heroes.

"All players who play for Liverpool are legends, but I think there are some bigger legends than others – and I make no apologies for that. They were great times. I see my old colleagues and how warm they were with the fans, the humility they showed them – you don't see a lot of that now," Thompson said, pausing for a sip of water before continuing: "That's why I worry a little about the new generations. Today, we have many foreign players who come here, play their part and go back to their countries. They'll never feel the warmth of that iconic status you get when you go to countries like Norway, other parts of Scandinavia and to South-East Asia and experience what the fans feel about you.

"Stevie Gerrard and Jamie Carragher will probably feel some of that warmth, but I wonder if any of the foreign players worry about how they will be received after their career is over? I hope they think about it long and hard, how they behave and meet the fans now, because they will be bumping into Liverpool fans all over the world later. Will they feel the passion that we do?"

"Is this about the loyalty you get from playing on the same team for a long time, or is it about being a local player?" I ask.

"Let's get it straight: it's a great pride and privilege to be a local lad and play for Liverpool, or Everton, even. A lot of guys have come in from other parts of Great Britain – players like Dalglish, Souness, Hansen and Nicol. The team becomes part of their life because they stay in our city and become Liverpudlians. Now, things have changed a lot. It's not the same loyalty anymore. I can say that; it doesn't mean I'm bitter, that's life these days, – players come, players go.

"Just look at Fernando Torres: a player we'd taken to our hearts more than most other players and he leaves us for Chelsea! Quite easily, he broke our hearts – and, yes, he said he couldn't win the Champions League or the league with us. And? So? You come to Liverpool and here you play with passion and commitment. You move on to other clubs if you're not good enough or you can't stay fit. You leave the club when it wants to sell you, and not when you want to go. I just can't get my head around that, how people feel they can enhance their career by moving away from Liverpool FC. I just can't understand that! And I don't care who you are or how big you think you are!"

During Thompson's playing days, the regulars on the team played match after match under intense pressure from the fans. You had to play and perform every single week.

"It becomes part of your life. Phil Neal always says that I helped him loads and that's very kind of him. We had a lot of unwritten rules that were passed down to me from Ian Callaghan and Tommy Smith when I came into the team in 1972. Thanks to the likes of Emlyn Hughes, we enjoyed ourselves, but we knew when that enjoyment had to stop. There were plenty of rumours in the '70s and '80s, too. We had to live with that.

"But, the pressure, did it help the players? I'd like to think so. In turn, Ronnie Whelan, Ian Rush and Steve Nicol learned these unwritten rules about club values from us: the good habits; training hard; enjoy yourself; what you need to do when you cross that white line on Saturdays at three o'clock – that was when we always kicked off. That was when we went to battle – and we went into battle with one another and fought one another until we'd won. It's like Manchester United now; we never knew the feeling of defeat."

When new players came in, they learned the rules as well. They had the mickey taken, had to serve the older players, get their drinks and fix everything for them.

"Nobody put these rules down in writing, but they were good learning habits. I ran all the errands for Smith, Ian Callaghan and Chris Lawler.

"People who came in and played for Liverpool in the early '70s, like Ray Kennedy, said it took him a good 12 to 18 months before he understood what they were. You had to listen, work hard and learn. It was intense. You had to embrace that intensity and say, 'I am going to play and I am going to win'."

"During that period, the team seldom lost big games. Would you say football is also about the will of the mind?"

"Absolutely! We shouldn't be so up and down. You should always be able to perform at the top of your ability, play an eight out of 10 every week. Some of the current players vary between four and eight. Yes, it's about attitude and mind power, motivation, focus and the will to win. Phil Neal used to say to me: 'We needed you most when we played Bristol City or Southampton.' Maybe this sounds arrogant, but, because I was a Liverpool fan, I just couldn't believe I could get beaten by these teams.

"Tommy Smith was the same. He drove us insane with his passion and commitment. He could have the worst day on the pitch, but he'd make sure the rest of us were doing our jobs. I was also obsessed with Shankly's teachings, that it was a crime to give away the ball. People talk about Barcelona now and their concept that it's a sin to lose the ball. Well, we were taught the same in the early '70s – and Shankly had been just as mad when someone lost the ball to an opponent in the '60s.

"When new players came into the team, I was right at them in the dressing room, making sure everybody went on the pitch to win, whether we were playing Southampton or Coventry. That attitude was part of us. Not everyone played eight out of 10 every week – some would drop to a six – but, then, somebody else would go up to a nine.

"You never had a long down period. If you started playing poorly, you were out of the team. Paisley or Shankly would always give you some time to right your bad form. They wouldn't dismiss you after one bad match because you were an integral part of the team."

When Emlyn Hughes was at the end of his career, Paisley gave the captain's armband to Kenny Dalglish. The Scotsman seemed uncomfortable with it, according to Thompson. Phil Neal had a few matches as captain as well. When Thompson got the armband in 1979, Neal had said: "Rightly so. You were destined to be Liverpool captain."

In 1981 he saw his big dream come true: as captain, he got to lift the trophy with the big ears first after Liverpool's European Cup triumph in Paris.

However, the next season was not so good for Thompson. He struggled to find his form for a while, and, just after New Year, Paisley gave the captaincy to Graeme Souness. A man the defender admired greatly on the pitch: "He was not only Liverpool's greatest midfield player, he was one of the league's best midfield players. One of the world's best players.

"He was superb. He could dominate the game. People say you could grab it by the scruff of the neck – that was Souness. That expression must have been invented for Souness, because he could turn a game single-handedly, he was that good."

However, the change of captain made Thompson furious at the time.

"I wasn't very happy about that decision and I stopped talking to Souness. Before I was captain, I always went out last. When I was captain, I always went out first. Now that I wasn't captain anymore, I was going out last again.

"Just when I was about to go out to my first match without the armband, Moran and Fagan said: "Phil, look, you've got to forget what's going on.' I said: 'Hey! You don't need to tell *me* how to behave or how I do this. When I cross that line out there, we're a team, and we're going to fight together, so don't tell me how and when I have to talk to Graeme Souness. You've got no right!'

"They looked at me like they understood what was going on. We won 4 - 0 and I had one of my best games since the start of the season. It had been a masterstroke by Bob Paisley. He realised I had taken on way too much responsibility as a captain. I was angry and annoyed about what happened, but my performance level rose from a six to an eight or nine in every match. *That* was psychology!"

It was an amazing turnaround. The team were 12th in the league, 18 points off top spot, and went on to win the title that year.

"That way, Paisley got the best out of me. I used the same psychology with Sami Hyypia,

when Houllier and I took the captaincy away from him and gave it to Steven Gerrard. It was a tough decision, because Sami was such a fantastic guy, but he didn't perform at the level he should. Sami's performance also improved when he didn't have the captaincy anymore."

"How long did it take you to get over this loss of status?"

"I'd like to say I was a professional and got over it right away, but I didn't. Souness and I didn't talk for months. After a while I realised this had made a positive change to my performance."

"How was it for your role as team inspirer?"

"I backed off a little. It wasn't my job any longer. Still, captain or not, I was one of the most experienced senior players, so I did still have a motivational role. I read the game, talked to the others, moved players around – almost like a chess player. It was hard for me to stop doing that, after Souness became captain. It affected me for a while. On the pitch I was the same, shouting and encouraging people. However, in the dressing room and in training I changed. It took a little bit of the edge off me for a while. My relationship with Souness was strained, but then things normalised and we became friends again."

This was not the only time Thompson found himself in conflict with Souness. If the battle of the captaincy had anything to do with the later and much bigger conflict,

57

Thompson does not know. When Dalglish stepped down as manager, Thompson – who was reserve team coach at the time – thought it a masterstroke to hire Souness as new boss. However, soon there would be dramatic changes within the club.

It was a Thursday towards the end of the 1991/92 season. The staff had come in to do the training kit for next season. Ronnie Moran, Roy Evans and Thompson were numbering the clothes. Usually, there would be an envelope with a bonus from last season there, but Thompson could not find his. Evans and Moran looked at each other and said: "Ooh, that's what happened to Chris Lawler! You'd better go talk to Peter Robinson."

"I went up to Peter, who looked sheepish and a little embarrassed. I asked: 'Peter, what happened? How come there's no bonus for me? Roy and Ronnie had theirs.' Peter said, 'You've got to see the manager.'

"Then I get it – 'Oh-oh, I'm a goner!' – and I went down to tell Roy and Ronnie. I felt awful and nervous. I rang Souness all day to get in touch with him. It was early evening before I got hold of him after trying everywhere. I said, "What's happening? I haven't got my bonus."

"Come talk with me on Monday."

"I can't wait from Thursday to Monday. I need to know what's going on. If I'm out, tell me I'm out!"

"Well, okay. Then, you're out."

"Why are you doing this?"

"Come talk with me on Monday, then I'll let you know."

"I can't believe what you're doing!"

"Come to my office on Monday."

On Friday, Thompson tried to find out what had happened. He talked to the chief executive, Robinson, again, and did what he could to try and keep his job. But the decision had already been made. Someone had leaked it to the press. The Sunday paper read:"Phil Thompson sacked, Sammy Lee comes in as assistant manager."

"That was incredible, because the previous Friday I'd seen Sammy Lee, who was stepping down as player and wanted to work as a coach. I knew Souness was at Melwood, so I told Sammy to go and talk to him. I thought maybe one of our coaches, John Bennison, was planning to retire. Sammy went up straight away, and then I didn't hear any of it until this Sunday. He ended up getting my job!" he laughs.

"It wasn't Sammy Lee's fault, the job was there. But it was incredible that I'd sent him in to get my job. It was a very difficult time for me. One of the low points of my career."

His letter of dismissal stated that he shouted too much at the lads on the reserve team and was "denting their progression".

"It was the heritage from Joe Fagan, Ronnie Moran and Roy Evans. The way I worked was the normal communication. It was a legacy from the Boot Room boys."

"Liverpool FC was your life, how long did it take you to reconcile with this?"

"I never really got over it. Liverpool was a part of me. I was down, depressed. I stopped going to games at Anfield. It was hard in itself. I had a business in Liverpool that I fell into and after a while I started working for Sky Television, who'd started doing Premier League. I saw a lot of football with them."

It took a few years before he returned to Anfield. It was a hard time for the whole family.

"I decided to tell my kids of just seven and 10 what had happened at the weekend, before they went to school on Monday. It really hurt when Souness sacked me and it was painful for my family and my boys. It was hard to bear and to hear what they went through in school because I'd been sacked. I vowed then I would never speak to Graeme Souness again."

"What haunted you afterwards?"

"Doubt was the worst. '*Why?*' Especially a few years later, when I found out he thought I was disloyal to the club. I thought, 'Where and how could you ever question my loyalty?' I was astonished. I just had to try and get on with it. Feeling that someone didn't trust *me*, Phil Thompson, hurt a lot – and not least because it hurt my family who'd enjoyed me being at Liverpool. I love Liverpool and I thought I'd be there for many years to come as a coach. I was passionate and loyal, and for someone to doubt that was just awful."

Thompson says he has no idea whether Souness saw him as a threat.

"If so, I don't see why, because I wasn't ready for management, certainly not for Liverpool Football Club. I was too wet behind the ears. There were a lot of people out there more competent than me. I was full of loyalty, but that's the thing he questioned. I think that's why I was sacked. Not for professional reasons, but personal. He said he didn't trust me."

When Souness was sacked as manager in January 1994 and Roy Evans took over, going back to Anfield became much easier. Thompson finally felt he was part of the community again.

At the end of the 1993/94 season, there was to be the final match in which there would be standing room on The Kop before seating was to be introduced. All the legends, the

ex-players, were supposed to be paraded on the pitch before the match. The former footballers had to wait in the tunnel with the players and staff before Liverpool against Norwich.

"Then I thought, 'I'm really going to milk it.' I took my two sons onto the pitch with me and wore my red jacket for the day. It ended up as a good day: Philip and his little brother Daniel didn't realise at the time. They hadn't been to Anfield for a long time. So, I held their hands going into the tunnel and they were thinking, 'What's going on here?' It was very, very emotional when we walked out on the pitch."

Later, he got the chance to be assistant manager for Gerard Houllier.

"I think nobody was more loyal than me. When I was manager while Gerard was recovering from major heart surgery, I pleaded with the media that I was only minding it for Gerard until he came back. A very good and loyal companionship with Houllier evolved. That's what we really were – good friends and loyal coaches."

It took 15 years to break the silence with Souness. It was at the funeral of Sheila Walsh, who had been the secretary to Paisley, Fagan, Dalglish, Souness, Evans, Houllier and Benitez. Everyone was there. Previous managers were on the front row, including Thompson. Before the ceremony, he and Souness met. They shook hands out of respect for Sheila.

"When we left the church we actually shook hands again, when he came over to me and said: 'We have to start talking again. We've acted like schoolchildren all our lives'."

"You might have done, I haven't!" Phil laughs at the memory of what he should have said, but did not. Instead, he shook Souness's neck slightly and said: "Yes, we have."

Thompson's wife had been saying for years that a lot of water had gone under the bridge since the two football heroes had fallen out and that they should start talking.

"Souness was supposed to leave right after the funeral but actually came with us to Anfield for a bite to eat and a bit of a chat afterwards. We haven't got together since."

Taxi driver Bob Millan, who took me back home after my meeting with Thompson, had just been having dinner at his home in Kirkby when he got the call. He grew up almost next door to Anfield Road, in 77 Hartnup Street. As a kid, he used to take over his big brother's parking space on matchdays, and look after whatever was parked there during the match for a bob or two. He'd see the last 25 minutes of the matches for free, when the gates opened.

Bob, born in 1948, followed all of Liverpool's games both home and away every year growing up. He has seen thousands of matches live up until seven years ago. The solution then was paying for Sky Sports. Match tickets got too expensive.

"They're taking the man's game away from the man," Bob sighed behind the wheel.

These days, he takes comfort in things like Thompson as a football expert on Sky Sports every Saturday. Bob knows the former defender and was in their local in Kirkby – The Falcon – when Thompson came in, happy to have lifted the most coveted trophy of them all as captain for Liverpool after the triumph in Paris in 1981.

Thompson had been all smiles and told them that 'Big Ears' itself was in the boot of his car outside! He went out and got it, and all the lads got to lift the giant cup one by one. Bob Millan, too. He looks at me in the rear-view mirror and grins: *"It was heaven!"*

Millan has been chairman of Children's League for many years – children's football of Liverpool. A lot of talents and future stars have started there, and Thompson will come in to give the kids their prizes.

"Thommo does anything to help kids play football," he says.

This time, my taxi driver is all Red and cannot find enough words to describe his admiration for my interviewee.

Thompson belongs to the generation of local players who grew up living and breathing LFC – and they still do. I like to think he represents the good old days when money meant little or nothing, where the joy of playing for your team was the top motivation. It was that way for many of them.

Bob Millan took out a rolled-up A3-size paper – it turned out to be a copy of the payslip for all the first-team players and staff in 1959, more specifically November 1.

The big stars – Billy Liddell and Roger Hunt – made £20 a week, and Joe Fagan, reserve team coach, made £15. Bob Paisley was first-team coach and made all of £17. Phil Taylor, the manager, received a "staggering" £29.

In total, the whole stable of coaches, secretaries and everyone at Liverpool FC cost £618 a week. *Those were the days...*

I studied the payroll while thinking about what Phil Thompson had told me when I asked him what Liverpool Football Club had meant to him: "Everything! Every single thing I've done from the age of 15 – or, really, ever since I was boy, a singing member of The Kop. Even when I was 17 and played for the reserves I'd go to the Kop for midweek matches. Besides, the club has also made my family proud and happy: my dad was very proud, although discreetly. My brothers and sisters were also very proud. They travelled to see my games."

When Thompson was a lad, his big brother Owen used to give him 50p out of his salary as pocket money – and he only earned £3.50 a week. His money was spent on tickets to The Kop so the brothers could go to matches together. When Liverpool played away, Thompson the younger saved his money.

"I think I got to pay him back, because I paid for him to travel to see us in Europe from my second season in 1972-73. We went to play the return match against Borussia Mönchengladbach and Owen got to come out on the pitch with us. So, he was there to share these fantastic days with me. When I became captain in 1981, my entire family was there, as was my wife's family.

"My mum worked at the Fazakerley Hospital. She could get on people's nerves because as soon as the talk was about Liverpool FC, she would tell them soon enough, 'Hi, I'm Phil Thompson's mother.' When she went to the bingo, she'd have a glass of bitter and people would come over to her and ask her about me, then she was like a queen bee. She loved it.

"I touched a lot of hearts being a local lad from Kirkby playing for Liverpool. You affect a lot of people's lives, more than just your own. Now we're here at David Lloyd in Kirkby, in the area where I was brought up, a place I'm very proud of and that I haven't moved away from. You have to work for it. Both as a player and former player, people here want to know what went wrong if Liverpool don't win. As a player, you knew all the answers, but I don't anymore. However, it's been a wonderful journey, from standing on The Kop to where I am today."

To all our fans in the "WORLD" "BELIEVE" Y.N.W.A.

Phil Thompson

Liverpool FC Career: 1972-1983 🦅 *Appearances: 477* 🦅 *Goals: 13*

Kevin Keegan
Never Look Back

"We were in search of a hero and out of nowhere came Kevin Keegan."
Phil Thompson

This is it. From the Fourth Division to the First Division in the course of a summer. Kevin Keegan is a little tense, driving up alone in his little old Ford Cortina. He had never been to Anfield on a matchday and is overwhelmed. At his previous club, Scunthorpe United, they did not even have stewards at the stadium. The team he just left used to have a crowd of about 3,000 people and when the players arrived, there would only be one or two supporters there with their scarves on. But, here, within half a mile of the ground, you cannot really get any nearer to the stadium because of the crowd. The dimension of it all is dawning on him. The big debut match.

He had moved to Liverpool in the summer and lived in digs about two miles from Anfield. This was before the team started going away to a hotel before home games.

Anfield stadium was blocked and a steward stopped him with a curt: "Yeah?"

"Hi, I'm playing today."

"Yeah, and I'm on the fringe of the team as well!"

None of the players had admission cards. Everybody knew who Ron Yeats, Ian Callaghan, Ian St John and Emlyn Hughes were, but nobody knew this short chap or his maroon car. The steward would not let him through. Keegan had never played for the club before. With 51,000 people heading for the stadium, this Anfield steward did not believe Keegan. He could have been anybody.

Easter 2011: Time flies when you are in Liverpool for only a short trip and have ambitions to meet a lot of stars. I had a few good helpers out there trying to fix interviews for me. But now my diary was empty, time was ticking and I desperately needed to secure one of my top three: I decided to go for it, and ring the one and only Kevin Keegan. I knew Phil Neal had sent him a text, saying he could trust me, but I had not heard of a reply.

I admit it freely – I was nervous. What if he hung up on me, an unknown Norwegian lady, disturbing his Easter? Then my chance to interview Liverpool FC's superstar would vanish. To settle my nerves and to convince myself, I said to my husband Jostein: "I'll go call him now. He's only an old man in a pair of shorts!"

I took shelter in the bedroom and looked out the window down Fleet Street, packed with nightclubs and bars. I took three deep breaths, found comfort in Neal's text message about my project, and then I dialled his number.

"Kevin."

"Hello. My name is Ragnhild Lund Ansnes. I'm a Norwegian author who writes books about Liverpool FC. Tell me, is the weather as great where you are?"

"Hi! Yes, it's wonderful here. I'm out in the park with the dog, my wife and our daughter."

He sounded like he was smiling. I breathed a sigh of relief.

"This is my first Easter here in Liverpool. I'm from the top of Norway and I'm used to going skiing in the mountains this time of year, but I have to admit I could get used to this, what lovely weather."

"You know, it could be our summer, you'd better enjoy it!" Keegan laughs.

The ice was broken on satellite signals between the outskirts of Manchester and Liverpool by using the oldest trick in the book, talking about the weather. I asked him if he had five minutes, and told him briefly about my project, and if he would consider joining?

"Yes, I'd love to, why don't you come over here one day?"

Liverpool's first modern superstar asked me to email him some dates of when I was available. Later that same night, I got his reply, accepting one of my proposed dates:

Hi Ragnhild,
Good to talk to you earlier. The best day for me is April 28th.
Cheers,
KK

And, so, the world spins. I now had a date with Joseph Kevin Keegan. He has not been a hero to me personally, but I know how important he has been for a huge number of people. His hero status, along with the stories from the other Liverpool legends, has done something to me.

April 28 came and I took the train to Manchester. Travelling through bright green landscape of new-leaved trees and fresh grass. Everything was light green and beautiful, between the endless rows of brick houses and fields surrounded by trees that are accustomed to the whipping of the North West wind. The sun was shining and I was full

of anticipation. I had packed a Liverpool bag full of retro shirts and pennants. I was nervous about asking him to sign them and reminded myself how 'Mighty Mouse' is described: both fans and other legends have emphasised his incredible patience and friendliness about signatures.

In general, I am no collector of autographs, but on this occasion I wanted to get my very first signed shirt. I was not quite sure why. Whether I was coloured by everybody else's starlit eyes when the name Keegan came up, or if it had started to dawn on me that I was meeting someone who will just continue to rise in status in my own life as I grow as a Liverpool supporter.

Besides, I have two small children who will grow up as Liverpool supporters, and they might wonder why mum, who got to meet so many of the greatest living legends, did not take the opportunity to transfer the personal meetings into something more tangible.

Also I had good helpers that I wanted to thank. Without them, I would never have had access to the big stars. And I had decided to help the fantastic organisation OGSY (Old Is Gold Slum Youth), that helps single mothers in the slums of Nairobi. I also wanted a way to thank the bravest man in my first book, Mr Jan Holten, who hid his secret for many years, but who told me the story of his miserable childhood that included bullying and violence at school. Jan became a Liverpool supporter the first time he saw Keegan on TV. He fell head over heels, but the other boys in school told him he was not cool enough to be a Liverpool fan. So, he had to support his team in secret to avoid worse beatings than he had already suffered. I had brought along a big, beautiful LFC pennant with "YNWA" across it and I was hoping to get a personal greeting on it.

I had agreed to meet Kevin in Hale Village, where he lives. They bought the house when he was manager of Manchester City. His wife Jean liked it so much they decided to stay, at least for a while. Keegan is a restless soul who just might end up in America to enjoy the sun and play golf. You never know. He is a man who likes to think ahead and never looks back.

Hale Village is a charming place with trees in bloom and as many as 17 restaurants on the short strip of brick houses with shops and places to eat. Football players from a lot of teams live here – from Manchester United and Manchester City, of course, but also quite a few from the likes of Everton and Bolton. A lot of clubs are within tolerable commuting distance of this place.

At Keegan's request, we met at the Piccolino restaurant. Inside, the couches are intensely green, quite an eye-catcher. Photographer Tony and I were looking at photo opportunities on the first floor as Liverpool's former star came up the stairs, smiling at me. I knew he had been nicknamed 'Mighty Mouse', but I was still surprised to see he is shorter than I am.

Keegan's watch has a black dial. At the bottom of the dial, small diamonds form the number '7'. There are no other numbers on the watch. He is surprisingly wrinkle-free, considering he turned 60 in 2011, the year of this interview, and it is 40 years since his fantastic debut at Anfield.

His childhood was nothing like the life of a superstar. He grew up in a big, old council house in Doncaster, Yorkshire, with his parents, sister and little brother. His father Joseph was a miner and the house was from the mining company. The toilet was at the bottom of the garden, there was no hot water or electricity and the house was run on gas. Even the lighting was gas-operated. Electricity was never installed, and the place was never refurbished at all, because it was supposed to be knocked down. So, as a newborn, Keegan stayed at his aunt's house, that had electricity. His mother Doris was a full-time housewife and his father was a rare sight.

"I almost never saw my dad. He worked in the mine, came home, went to the pub and then to bed. Except for the one week's holiday every year, I can't remember spending much time with him, he was working all the time."

"Didn't he watch you play at all?"

"Yes, he'd come to watch me play for the school team. He was very proud when I started playing for Scunthorpe and used to come to my games with my brother, sister and mum. When I started playing for Liverpool, he got a guy called Harry to drive him. Mum and dad didn't drive. They never had a car."

"Because they didn't need one, or because they couldn't afford it?"

"Probably both. It makes you a little different being brought up like that. Now if I meet people who've got money and they say, 'I'm not going to give my kids anything, they'll have to fend for themselves like I did', I think it's a terrible thought, because they'll never be like you, who built everything from scratch. They've grown up in a fancy house.

"When I hear people say they won't leave anything for the kids, I go, 'Wow, get a life!' It's the most stupid thing. We've pulled them up here and now you'll push them back down and say, 'Make your own way.' I think it's a bit cruel."

Keegan was discovered by Bill Shankly's talent scout Geoff Twentyman and signed for the Merseyside club at 20. Just before the start of the 1971 season, he came to his first training session with the first-team. Up to then, he had been training with the reserve team.

After training, Shankly asked him: "Where do you want to play on Saturday? First-team or reserves?"

Keegan's reply was calm and confident:"I haven't come here to play in your reserve team."

And Shankly said: "Okay."

On the Friday, Shankly's team selection was up and Keegan was in the first-team. His only problem turned out to be getting into the stadium! After he was stopped in his old car, he had to think quickly.

"So, I drove around to the other side, the Stanley Park side, and the steward there believed me, luckily. So, I got in that way. The guy on the opposite side was only doing his job. I really could have been just anyone."

Keegan had a flying start to his Liverpool career. Only 12 minutes into the game against Nottingham Forest, he scored his first of many goals for the club. According to himself, it was a lucky goal because he scuffed the ball. However, it brushed the floor, rolled past the keeper and in.

Shankly had been clever. By surprising Keegan with such short notice before his debut, he relieved him of a lot of pressure. It paid off. Liverpool's new No7 scored three times in his first five matches and secured his place in the first-team. Not only did he go straight from Fourth Division – without stopping by the reserve team – he also played his way into the hearts of both fans and sponsors. Kevin Keegan became Liverpool's first modern superstar.

"I didn't feel like one. Everything happened so quickly the first two or three years at the club. We won the league the second year I was there, and I made the England squad. So much happened. People wanted to pay me for using their boots instead of me buying my own. George Best was the first to land personal deals like that. I was the second.

"George Best also had a newspaper column that I took over eventually. Best wasn't really interested in the conditions of these contracts, he did what he wanted to do, and I admire him for that. However, because of his reluctance to turn up on sponsorship arrangements, I fell into a lot of his contracts, despite not being half the player Best was. I had long hair like he did and I played for a big club."

"And you looked like a pop star! I've seen pictures!"

Keegan laughs.

"Everybody looked like pop stars back then. People take the mickey out of our hair, but if you look back to 1971 to 1974, everybody had that – in Denmark, Sweden and Norway, too. It was ABBA fever. The Beatles were huge just before I arrived in Liverpool as well. All pop musicians had hair like that, not just footballers. We all had that image. In addition, shorts were smaller and shirts a little tighter!"

"Please, bring that time back," I laugh, and Kevin gives me a big smile before he continues: "People started growing 'taches – Souness after me, McDermott and Smith."

"You know, forget about bringing back the old times; drop the moustache. Anyway, did you mingle with the pop stars, like they do today?"

"No, that started in the '80s. Football and showbiz started to mix. Remember, in the '70s, when I came to Liverpool I earned £35 a week. Where would you go and who would you mingle with, with so little money? However, you could live off that money, and the biggest money I made at Liverpool was £160 a week. I didn't make that much. I think Tommy Smith was the best paid player back then. Still, there was only £35 between us. No one begrudged Tommy Smith being the best earner. Even though he wasn't the star player, he'd been there longest and was the captain. That's how it worked in those days."

When Keegan arrived, there were no superstars in the team – and that was probably one of the reasons why Liverpool were so successful. Now, the clubs have their megastars who are worshipped as icons. They are well protected, but visible in club advertisements. Keegan did not go through all that, yet he ended up as the club's superstar – worshipped by fans and sponsors alike. What does *he* think was his X factor, the little extra that made him the chosen one? Among all these great players, why him?

"I don't know," he answers quickly. "If you'd asked a hundred different people, all would have given different answers, like '*Because he worked hard, we know he really cared about the club.*' I don't know, there could be a million reasons. You can't say yourself what it is. I just went out and played and people liked what I was doing.

"When fans started to queue up for my autograph I thought, 'Wow! That's unbelievable!' But, you're quite right, Liverpool weren't about superstars at that time. We were all team players and we did well. Also, the lot of us made a decent enough living for the time and maybe I did a few more things outside of football."

He avoids mentioning probably the most important reason for his status – he was Liverpool's best player, with a voracious game and great offensive qualities.

At this stage of his career, Tommy Smith was an incredible support, Keegan tells me. He was manager for the players, while Shankly managed the club.

"Tommy educated us. I remember throwing my big, black jumper on the floor once, and he went, 'Ay, we don't throw jumpers on the floor around here. Come on, pick it up, or else Betty who cleans here will have to do it, and it's not her job.' Every club had someone like Tommy."

"Tommy Smith has told me he was like a father figure to you."

"Yes, he was. I always went to Tommy for advice, to sound him out. I had tremendous respect for him and he supported me all the way. He was so direct, but he got into a little bit of trouble with the club as a youth coach. His language was pretty rough, so it didn't work out. Tommy is Tommy, and that's why I like him so much. What you see is what you get.

"Sometimes when he says something, I think, 'Perhaps you should have bitten your tongue rather than speak. Yes, you believe what you're saying, and you're probably right, but should you be saying it? Maybe not.' Because, you know what football clubs are like – even though Liverpool are among the best in looking after their players, you can't look after all of them, and some really mess up for themselves."

Keegan still meets with his old team-mates from time to time, but when he played for Liverpool, he did not spend a lot of time with them outside football. When he moved to Liverpool he had already met the 17-year-old beauty Jean. She lived a seven-hour drive away, but after some time moved into digs in Liverpool 6, near where Emlyn Hughes lived. Keegan had a room in Liverpool 7. Jean got a job in Liverpool and on Sundays the lovebirds went for drives, using the Mersey Tunnel and on to the Wirral. They would drive into North Wales, the part you can see from Liverpool across the Mersey on a clear day. Eventually, they moved there.

"We really liked North Wales. It doesn't look that far, as the crow flies, but it took me about an hour to drive to Liverpool. But, then again, Formby, where most other players lived, was half-an-hour away from Liverpool.

"We looked around and found this place near the foot of Moel Famau, the big hill you can see with a little tip on it when you look towards Wales from Liverpool. The place cost us £19,000 and was in 2.5 acres of land, so we could have horses and go riding, go out the gate and up Moel Famau. We enjoyed ourselves a lot, especially as I became more well-known. In North Wales you could just relax and be yourself.

"We got to know the farmers and people around us, and some of them had probably seen me on TV. However, there was no stress and no fuss about my person, as it would have been in Formby. That was a good thing."

Kevin was no party animal. He liked to spend time on the farm.

"My wife is my best friend. I have known her ever since I used to pick her up from school. We've done everything together, that's why I haven't got that many good friends. I don't need them. I consider all my old team-mates from Liverpool FC my friends, but I don't really see them that much."

Just after he retired from football, Kevin and his wife made an important decision. They moved to Spain to enjoy life, watch the kids grow up and play a bit of golf. Later, they went travelling with the girls. He says there is only so much you can learn in a classroom or from a book, you have to get some experience as well.

They travelled to Australia, New Zealand and Malaysia when the youngest daughter, Sarah Marie, was about two, and the oldest, Laura Jane, was five. He played a few exhibition matches, held some after-dinner speeches and guest-trained a few young teams. The rest of the time they were out exploring. Laura Jane still remembers the smell of hot springs in New Zealand and the holes in the ground that served as toilets in Malaysia.

His daughters are now around 30. Jean is probably happy not having to wait for her husband as much as she used to when he was one of the biggest stars in European football.

Over the years, Jean learned that if Kevin went somewhere and she came along, she wouldn't be noticed. She also says that when she is with him, everybody knows her, but when she is alone, nobody knows who she is.

"She used to say, 'It's like I'm invisible.' It annoys me a little, because she's a person in her own right. But that's the way it is – and a lot of my old team-mates' wives I wouldn't have recognised either without their husbands there."

Sometimes, when they were leaving Anfield, Jean would have to wait for her husband for more than an hour, but she understood that was the right thing to do.

"All the other legends who are in this book give you the same credit, that you were absolutely incredible with the fans and nobody took more time than you. Did you do this out of obligation, or was it natural? I know Shankly urged you all to spend time with supporters – but there's a difference between writing a few autographs and working your way through the whole queue. Why did you do it?"

"It's simple, really. Meeting the fans, you have a chance to show them you really care. When we played matches, we'd park the bus, then walk past the fans, talk with them or just say hello. And the people at the back of the queue deserve it most, they have waited the longest. Nowadays, you don't usually see the players until the warm-up; there are underground car parks for team buses, big fences and other constructions to separate the players from the supporters. This sends a message to the fans, '*I don't want to talk to you. I don't even want to hear you.*' The truth is, these modern footballers often lack communication skills. These chaps turn 35 or 36, their career is over, and they might say, '*Okay, now I want to go on TV.*' But you can't learn communication in one week at school. You have all your life to communicate with people."

Keegan and the rest of the Liverpool team often went to visit people at the hospitals, many of them dying, to try and lift their spirits in some way. They made such visits regularly.

"It made a deep impression on us when the doctors said, 'We can't do more for him, but you can.' For us to go in and do something like that, give them a day of pleasure, was an extreme strain, but you just stay strong and do it, even if it's tough. If you don't do things like that, what are you going to learn? Nothing."

I ask Kevin to choose his strongest Liverpool memory. He finds it tough because there are so many to choose from. But, eventually, he settles for the time Shankly went on the Kop, to the delight and surprise of Kopites! He had retired as manager and the fans were chanting his name, so he went in to join them!

Keegan admits that none of the players could understand why he quit.

"He used to threaten to quit every year. The board would then, according to rumours, give him an extra fiver or tenner, and he'd sign a new contract. But this time he meant it.

"I went to take a corner and the fans were chanting, '*Shankly, Shankly, Shankly.*' There he was, the already legendary manager, in the Kop with his hands over his head. He was immaculately dressed in a suit and, as always, with a tie that matched his shirt rather poorly. It was incredible. He stood on the right-hand side, a few rows into the crowd."

Keegan did not want to be at Liverpool without Shankly. There is a time for everything. It was 1976 and Kevin announced he would quit at the end of the season. Why? Some people never got over him leaving Liverpool to play for German side Hamburg SV. Liverpool were champions of England, Uefa Cup holders and in the European Cup when he made his announcement. Did he not have all he desired at Anfield?

"I loved Bob Paisley, Joe Fagan and Ronnie Moran, too. I loved them all. However, when Shankly went, the club wasn't the same for me. Maybe I'm not a 10-year person, more of a five-year person, who needs to change pastures every five years."

Keegan is eager to talk about his departure from the Reds.

"I needed to move on. When everything in the garden is rosy, I'm looking for new

challenges. It's the way I am. Ian Callaghan couldn't understand that, but I said to him, '*For you, Cally, it's fantastic. You're a local boy, born in Liverpool. You grew up watching the team, you achieved your dream and you want it to go on for ever. I get it, but it's not for me'.*"

Back then, it was highly unusual for high-profile players to leave England and the country's long and proud football traditions. Fernando Torres was my little son's first big hero, and he broke Elias' heart when he gave us only a couple of days' notice between saying he wanted out and joining Chelsea. Almost a year later, he was still not over the grief and the loss of Torres.

Kevin, on the other hand, gave almost a year's warning that he was going to change clubs. It changed some Liverpool supporters' opinion of him. Was he being too honest? Should he have kept his plans to himself? What did this openness do to his last year at the club?

"I don't think it affected my performance, and we nearly won the Treble, so I don't think it took anything away from the team, either. We lost the FA Cup final, admittedly, but we won the European Cup final, and the league."

"I was thinking about you personally. Did your decision to leave change your relationship with the fans or your team-mates?"

"I think some fans understood me. Others definitely didn't. I know it sounds terrible, but it was something I just had to do. I think some fans were thinking, '*He came to*

Liverpool and nobody knew him. Now he's a big star and off he goes.' Others said things like, *'If that's the way he feels, he should go.'* The thought of staying another three to four years, which would be the case with a new contract, just wasn't right for me. Fans need to understand that sometimes.

"Telling them a year in advance was a lot better than if we had left them in the dark while I and the club knew for one year that I was leaving. That would have been misleading the supporters. It was all out in the open. I was going for that amount of money, and I wasn't leaving until the club got £500,000 for me, that they were using to get my replacement. That sum was set when I signed an extension to my contract. It was very important; it gave the club a whole year and a lot of money to find my successor – and they found Kenny Dalglish.

"So, even though many felt this was an unusual way to go about things, it was a fantastic solution for everybody. I wasn't deceiving anybody. The club knew I was going, they knew how much money they were getting for me. So, in many ways, it gave them the chance to forward plan."

When I listen to Keegan's story, I think of what my father would say when I was annoyed at having to come home from a party before it was over.

"Ragnhild, remember to leave while the party's at its best."

I feel his advice works for Kevin Keegan, as well. I wonder if one of the reasons why so many Liverpool supporters around the world still love him so much is because he left the club at his best?

"I think I left before I was at my peak. I achieved a lot afterwards, too. But, yes, it's sound to leave a party at its best.

"There's another saying, 'Never outstay your welcome.' I could have stayed longer at Hamburg, too. I had three great years there – why spoil it? I moved on while people still respected what I'd achieved, and I respected them. It was the same way with Newcastle. But always leave a club when they've found a good replacement, as I had in Kenny when I left Liverpool. The team went on to become even more successful after I left. It's a good way to finish something.

"Look at a company. If you leave your position and everything topples, have you really done a good job there? If everything revolves around one person and is depending on this one person, everything collapses if this person leaves. That's not the way a football club should be. When Shankly left, there was Paisley, Fagan, Moran – a good team. When Paisley left, it was the same way. That's what I mean by leaving a legacy, instead of bringing in a manager to change it all in two years. I don't believe in that. It might have done other clubs favours, but it hasn't worked for Liverpool Football Club – they need someone with an emotional attachment to the club, and they've got that now in Kenny.

"It takes years to learn what Liverpool Football Club are like – you can't learn it from Wikipedia."

Kevin also admits that he never goes back to visit his old clubs. Why not?

"I don't like to go back to anything in life."

"Do you mean to say you don't return to anything in life?"

"Yes. I don't like to go back. I went back to Wembley for the very first time last week, since I walked off as England manager."

"You're joking?"

"No, it was the first time I was back, because I don't like going back. I think far too many people live in the past."

"And forget about the present?"

"That, and they forget about the future. It would be really easy for players like myself and Tommy Smith to think of what we did for Liverpool, but we need to remember what the club did for us, too. Without Liverpool, I have no idea where I would have been now. What I'm getting at is, I don't understand why players want to go back to their old club, but I don't knock them for it"

"Some people need the money they make that way?"

"Yes, but that's my point exactly – it's right for those who go back every matchday and make £100 to £300. But, to be honest, a few of us shouldn't be doing that, it's not in our nature. As I said, I'm not criticising those who do, but it isn't, and can't be, for everybody.

"Should I have returned to visit one of my former clubs? I'm not a nostalgic person. I thought maybe I would change as I got older, but I haven't."

"Just wait, I'll ask you again in 10 years, when you've started to look back!"

We both break out laughing. But, while we laugh, I both envy and feel sorry for Keegan and his lack of nostalgia. Envious because he does not have to suffer the way I do: I have an aversion about throwing things away, anything from birthday cards and letters from my childhood to scribblings by my own kids – their first efforts with a pen. My nostalgic disposition makes me catch moments on camera almost daily. I bring my camera everywhere, because I want to preserve every moment, the good ones, and never forget them.

Still, I would not say I live in the past, like Keegan suspects a lot of nostalgic people do. However, I do like to think back on what has been, at the same time as I am living in new dreams and ambitions and try the best I can to savour each moment of everyday happiness and take delight in my kids' little gems of wisdom and steps of development.

Which is why I am also a little sad on Keegan's behalf; he does not know this beautiful, blue nostalgic feeling of happiness that good memories bring. He never takes time to return to the past of who he used to be.

Meeting people and places of the past gives you a lot of answers to who you are today and how you have chosen to lead your life. I am also a little sad on behalf of all the fans out there who will never forget Keegan's achievements in the red shirt. When the team fails and the supporters are despondent, they take comfort in what Keegan achieved in his time and that way remind themselves why they chose this team.

"Are you a restless person?" I enquire.

"Oh, yes. The day I stop being restless, I might just move to America and get out in the sun and laze my life away. But I'm not ready for that, I still want to do a lot of things. The day I start looking back is probably the end of me."

"How far ahead in life do you think?"

"Not too far. But I think that, even though I'm 60, I'm still young. Sometimes, I walk down the street here and see people who are younger than me and they're old. Maybe they've been unlucky and got an injury or other health problems. I still go running and do anything I like. So, if you look at it like that, I'm a very lucky man."

Thanks for your Support

78

Liverpool FC Career: 1971-1977 🦅 *Appearances: 323* 🦅 *Goals: 100*

Tommy Smith
Tougher Than The Rest

"He gave his whole body to Liverpool Football Club."

John Barnes

We get out of the car in the spring sun. Sea air tickles my nose. Tommy Smith greets us with parking gesticulations, a smile and a firm handshake. My first impression is that this is a man who has been to war – both on and off the pitch. His wife Susan waits behind him; a nimble little lady, with half-length hair, a warm smile and quick with a witty comment. She treats us to tea while photographer Tony and his assistant turn the dining room into a photo studio, hanging up a black backdrop that almost cuts the room in half.

Their lovely detached home is in Crosby, only a short walk from fellow Scouse defender Jamie Carragher's impressive house and about 200 yards from the beach.

While we are all settling in, the Smiths exchange humorous and loving remarks. I get to see the warm, caring side of the iron man chatting with his wife. They have both had a lot of health problems, but still this wonderful mood. On the shelf in the living room there is a small framed photo of the couple when they were young. She is in a lovely dress, he in a stately coat with slicked-down hair. On other shelves sit photos of their grandchildren and a wedding photo of one of the kids. On the wall of the TV room, next to the couch, the grand proof of services to football – an MBE.

Like a true serviceman, Smith sacrificed his entire body for Liverpool FC to earn every one of his medals of honour. Sometimes he cannot get out of bed. His body has been through a lot over the years. Numerous injections have kept his injured legs going in matches with no substitutes. Year after year, they ran out on to the pitch and played through the biting winter cold, with the only warm-up being a small swig of whisky.

I was wondering what it had been like to play in such tough surroundings, and not least what he was really like off the pitch. Rumour has it he wound up in quite a few fights. What kind of person is he, the much talked-about man who quickly earned the nickname 'The Anfield Iron'?

I had been a little apprehensive about meeting him, I admit.

During the day, Liverpool's former captain is keen to tell me tales of one fight after another, and not least how the rumours of his fighting abilities started to spread from an early age. Tommy was an only child and a very shy kid. He had never been involved in fights. He used to go with his friends to the local baths that was just around the corner from his Catholic school, St John's. They had to queue up to get in. One day, a guy jumped the queue in front of him and Tommy wasn't impressed.

"Sod off!" the guy said. He butted Tommy. Tommy got back up and battered him. Afterwards, all the classes of 10 to 11-year-olds said: "Don't go near that lad!"

"So, I found out early on that it was smart to scare people I didn't like!" he smiles.

From that day forward, he does not know if it was his reputation, his attitude or his looks that put him in constant trouble. However, when somebody else wanted to pick a fight with the boy who was big and tall for his age, he drily replied: "Don't mess with me. If you do, you'll end up having to call an ambulance."

It became his favourite saying.

At St John's, he won a scholarship to Cardinal Godfrey. When he was playing for the Under-15s, at the age of 12, he found himself in trouble again: 'Fatty Mac' was as tall as him, but chubby. Smith was at his desk, working between classes. Next to him, Fatty Mac was having an argument with another boy and tried spitting at him, but it landed on Tommy's shirt and blazer.

"Hey! Are you going to take this off?!"

"No!"

"You should have done!"

Tommy jumped over his desk and butted him. On the floor, he kept hitting him.

Their football fanatic teacher came in.

"What's up, Smithy?"

"He spat at me!"

"Listen, I know you come from a place in Liverpool where you need to make sure that people don't get on top of you. But you're in school now. It's different."

On the floor, Fatty Mac was whimpering: "He butted me, he knocked me down!"

The teacher turned to the wailing boy on the floor: "If I find out you're spitting any more, *I'll* butt you!"

If there is one thing Smith hates on the pitch more than anything, it's spitting. One day, Liverpool were playing Nottingham Forest. They had a big centre forward, a Scottish lad. Smith tackled him through the whole match, making sure the Scot hardly had a kick all day. He had been teasing him, too, saying this was a man's game, not a girl's game, and told him to go down the road where he could find some girls to play with. In the end, with 10 minutes to go, the Scot was so fed up he spat at him.

"You just signed your own death warrant!" barked Smithy.

"Did I, now?"

"Yes, the first thing I'll do, besides killing you, is call an ambulance!"

The referee blew the final whistle and the Scottish player set off running. Tommy ran after him like a furious bull into the away dressing room, but he could not find him.

"If you hit somebody, you hit them, but you don't spit at people. It's just not good."

Tommy washed, got changed and went to the lounge where the players had a drink after the match asking about the guy. Had he been there? Tommy was still mad and did not stop looking. Even Nottingham Forest's players' coach was examined. The spitting striker was nowhere to be found.

"During an after-dinner talk a few years ago somebody asked me, funnily enough, what happened to the spitter. I told them, truthfully, that I had no idea. I was asked whether I'd looked inside the skip with all the sweaty Nottingham Forest kits? That's where he'd been hiding!"

Tommy had learned to handle himself from an early age, but that became even more of a harsh reality when he was 15.

He was on the bus on his way home from training with Liverpool Schoolboys. They were preparing to play Manchester Schoolboys the following week. As he got off at the bottom of Everton Valley, his cousin Rosie was waiting for him at the bus stop.

"Tommy. Your dad has died…"

He could not believe it. His father was a big and popular lad. He had contracted double pneumonia and died after only a few weeks in hospital.

After the funeral, they went back to their terraced house in Lambeth Road where Tommy grew up. The priest from St John's got drunk. Tommy watched in utter disbelief as the priest bounced into the fronts of all the houses on his way home from the funeral gathering. He struggled getting up the hill and he hit every bay window on the way up.

"I just couldn't believe it. It was so embarrassing. I've never been to church since that day, only to funerals and weddings. I can't get enough energy to go into a church and say, 'This shouldn't have happened. It was my father's funeral.'

"The man could have got drunk, but in his own time, not at my dad's funeral. It was so unfair. The guy was an idiot."

Like Tommy, I cannot help think about when my own father died back home in Norway, and I think aloud: "I can't imagine what it must have been like." You see, I also lost my dad way too early and it was an incredibly vulnerable time. It's the last farewell with your dad and you want it to be beautiful and respectful. I would have been so mad!

Tommy picked up on his experience: "Yes! During the funeral supper, I could see the priest tumble over the threshold. I was just 15. If there's one person you should be able to trust at such a time, it's the priest. I decided there and then to stop going to church. Six months later, my mother and I moved to my grandmother's. My mother used to work for St Alphonsus doing the washing and cooking.

"If St John's was told of the incident, I don't know. But, now and again, a priest would come knocking at our door. They must have known."

It was a difficult time and it would have been natural for Tommy to feel the need to fill his father's shoes and look after his mother, but she obviously didn't see it that way – and that was clearly the case when she received a letter that was going to change everything. It was from Liverpool FC asking them to please come and have a talk with Mr Bill Shankly.

Tommy was over the moon, but also a little concerned, because his mother knew nothing about football.

They dressed up for the big meeting. Tommy wore jeans, which was considered very flash, and his dark college blazer with the school badge on. His mother, as small as his wife Sue, had a dress and coat. Her blonde, short hair was well presented. There were three barbers near the road where they lived and in the past Tommy had visited all three to find the one he liked best. The one he had chosen used to cut his hair for nothing, so it was a good choice. That barber was naturally the one he visited before the meeting with Shankly. Everything had to be in order. Well-groomed.

Arriving at Anfield for something other than finding the best spot on the Kop for a match was new to Tommy. He had never previously seen the place as having a sort of engine inside, with the manager's room, the Boot Room and the dressing room with the kits hanging up.

Now they were inside this new universe, and Shankly said to his mother: "We've heard he's a decent player. We're thinking of signing him on to play for the A, B or C team."

Then he looked straight at Tommy and said: "Would you consider playing for our junior sides? Would you also like to come to work for the club? It means working through Christmas. No holidays, just the two weeks in summer."

At the end of the meeting, his mother stood up and said: "Mr Shankly, you've never won the cup, have you?"

"Mum, what are you doing?!"

"No, we haven't," Shankly replied.

"I'll give you a bit of advice: when Tommy plays for the team, you'll win the cup," Smith's mother added.

"I'll take that," Shankly responded.

On their way out, Tommy cheeks blazing, said: "Mum! You don't say things like that to managers! You just do what they say!"

"You just wait and see. It'll be all right," said his mother as she smiled under her carefully laid hair.

Liverpool started paying Smith £7 a week. In 1960, £364 a year was a lot of money. So, Smith came to Liverpool only six months after Shankly had arrived. He was a pawn in the Scottish manager's plan to build a new team and better the facilities. The charismatic, but authoritarian, new boss at Anfield promised Tommy's mother he would take good care of the boy.

Tommy Smith is prettier than Sophia Loren

"I think he felt a little sorry for mum and me."

That was how he came to work at the club. He played for the junior team and, among other things, he helped paint the stadium.

"I think I painted the Kop three times. We dug up the Kop end of the pitch and threw sandstone in to drain it. We painted the dressing rooms, all the stands, it was an ordinary job. There were no Christmas holidays or Easter holidays. Liverpool played Saturdays and we came in to clear up and fix everything on Sundays and Mondays; pick up rubbish, fix equipment.

"The other day, I was talking to the old gardener who knows one or two of the boys at the Academy and he told me what a youngster of 18 can earn these days!" Smith gives a big laugh: "It's unbelievable!"

When Tommy signed a professional contract his weekly pay was £15. If they won a game in the reserve team or first-team they got a £2 bonus.

In the early 1960s, some of the players were complaining and saying they should be better paid. When Smith and his team-mates took Liverpool all the way to Wembley and won the FA Cup, he made £30 a week. With a sold-out Wembley – 100,000 people – he wonders where all that money really went.

Smith was a born leader. At 15, he captained both the college team and Liverpool Schoolboys. Both Everton and Liverpool had wanted him, but he was a Liverpool supporter like his father and grandfather.

He ended up as captain for all the teams he played for. At Liverpool, he got the captaincy in 1970.

"I became like a father to many – Jimmy Case even called me dad! I took care of Joey Jones, too, a couple of lads who looked a little out of place in the team."

I try to get Smith to talk football. After all, behind the 'Anfield Iron' exterior is an extremely talented player. This often gets overlooked because of his reputation. However, it was that fighting spirit that set him apart and helped ensure he won any battles to keep his place in the side.

He had a wonderful ability to stay in the team, even if that meant he had to change position on the pitch. Smith played 638 games for Liverpool.

He was already playing for the reserves at 17. When he turned 18, in 1963, he got a taste of how Shankly ran the club. The manager told him he would make his debut for the first-team against Sheffield Wednesday. Tommy was gobsmacked.

"*Thanks, boss!*"

At that time, you had to see what boots were under the shirt in the changing room to know if you were playing or not. Shirt No1 was the goalkeeper, two was the right-back, three was the left-back, four was the right-half, and so on. If your boots were under the bench, you were in.

Smith's heart was pounding when he entered the changing room.

"Where are my bloody boots?"

Shankly had not put Smith's boots out after all.

"Boss, why aren't I playing?"

"It's okay, it'll be all right. Just leave it now."

But he was tired of waiting. During the next week, he went and knocked on the manager's door three or four times and said: "Excuse me, boss."

"Oh no, not you again!"

"If I can't get a game when the team isn't playing well, how am I going to get a game if they are?"

"Don't worry, it'll be all right, Tommy..."

But Smith did not give up, he'd turn up the next day as well.

"I was really down his throat in my desire to debut for the first-team," Smith recalls.

Then came a game against Birmingham. The night before a match, Shankly would

bring 14 or 15 players to a hotel. Smith was in the group this time. He did not think he would be playing, but there they were – his boots under the No4 shirt.

"The reason Shankly did it like that was not to put too much pressure on the youngsters. That is why we never knew quite when we were playing, as in the FA Cup semi-final a few years later.

"I'd played a couple of games, so I thought I'd be playing. We came to Sheffield, I don't remember who we were playing. Chris Lawler, from my school team, was my roommate. He's a year older than me; a nice lad, but very quiet. On the bus, I said to him, 'I've got to go to the toilet. It's the FA Cup semi-final and I'm nervous.'

"I ran to the toilet when we got there. However, when I came out and said, 'Thank God for that, Chris', he said, 'Get out of the way! You're not playing today, but I am!' Then, he went to the toilet. All these experiences helped us mature."

He laughs at the memory.

"It was a tremendous gang, the team I was brought up in. The loyalty was fantastic – I'd still do anything for them. Most of us still meet up."

It was Tommy Lawrence, Chris Lawler, Gerry Byrne, Big Yeatsie (Ronnie Yeats), Ian Callaghan, Gordon Milne, Willie Stevenson, Peter Thompson, Ian St John and 'Sir' Roger (Roger Hunt) – and Tommy Smith.

"The '60s team was the best team I played for. If those boys had been playing today, they could have played in any team. I think only a couple of the current players could have played their way into our team. Jamie Carragher could, and Stevie Gerrard."

"What is your strongest Liverpool memory?" I ask.

While he is pondering this, his wife cheerfully adds: "Going out and getting drunk!" We all laugh.

"Really, there are two memories running equal. The first is from the 1977 European Cup final. We'd beaten FC Brugge in the Uefa Cup the previous year and everybody had been going crazy. Now, assistant manager Joe Fagan told me to go up for a corner. 'We scored two headers last year!' Fagan shouted, while I ran in position.

"Stevie Heighway took the corner and I headed it into the back of the net.

"Afterwards, we got a penalty that Phil Neal sorted. 3-1 was a fantastic result; we won the European Cup for the first time."

"And that was your last goal for Liverpool, too?"

"Yes."

"What a way to finish!"

However, it was not the end of his career. Swansea offered him twice as much money as Liverpool, so he went there to play for a year.

Not only was Tommy with Liverpool FC when they won their first European Cup final in 1977, he was with the Reds when they won their very first FA Cup final twelve years earlier in 1965. That is the second memory he holds highest. He did not score any goals, but it was a big moment because it was the club's first FA Cup – and not least because his mother's prediction came true.

Let us rewind to the start of the season that ended with lifting the sought-after trophy at Wembley. In 1964, Liverpool had won the league and the team went to America, leaving the internationals out of the squad because England, Wales and Scotland were playing. Smith, who was 19, had met his Susan and was getting married in the summer. However, because so many international players had to stay home, he got the chance to go to the USA.

"But I'm getting married," the newly-engaged footballer told his manager.

"Get married after you come back!" came Shankly's reply.

Susan agreed to postpone the wedding, and so he got the chance to show what he could do in the first-team.

"At the end of the following season we won the FA Cup. If we'd played a little more attacking football, we wouldn't have had to go into extra-time in the match against Leeds

United. But we won! And I'll always remember it. Afterwards, Shanks put his arm around me and said, 'Smithy, your mother must be one of the greatest foreseers of the world!'

"He remembered something my mother had said five years before! Can you imagine?"

"It must have made an impression on him that a mother came in to do the talking. That was probably rare?" I suggest.

"Absolutely, but she had to, as dad had died. I think it was the only time she was up at Shankly's office."

Our time was running out. Soon, grandad Tommy would have to do his pleasant duty and pick his grandchild up from school, as he does every Wednesday. I was thinking about what Kevin Keegan told me of the medical support team when he and Tommy were playing. I had heard horror stories about Smith's many injuries – but I had not heard the worst.

He has given his two knees and an elbow for Liverpool FC. They are replaced with metal. He has been through numerous operations and is suffering from rheumatism. The way I see it, Tommy Smith is a man who has sacrificed his entire body for his team.

"I don't really see it as a sacrifice," said Smithy. "I was lucky enough to play for

Liverpool FC and I didn't want to let them down. Once, against a Swiss team, a little winger came down on my knee. I don't know why I didn't stop. I just played on. At half-time I asked for a massage on my knee. We won 2-0.

"After the match, Bob Paisley said: 'I think we must have a look at you tomorrow.'

"What for?"

"Your knee doesn't look too good."

When Smith went to bed that night, his knee ballooned. He was at the door for his physio at 8.30am the next day, because he knew Bob used to be there at that time. Bob told him to call his wife and have her come and get the car, because they had to go to the hospital. He was examined and they discovered that the Swiss winger had taken the side off his kneecap.

Tommy laughs: "When I tell this story, a lot of people don't believe me. I played a full 80 minutes with a broken kneecap."

Those who have given birth with no pain relief, like me, know what real pain is. As a woman, I am often annoyed by men who whimper with a slight headache. I am deeply convinced that women are born with a higher tolerance for pain than men because we are made to bear children through a narrow birth canal. I am not joking. But it strikes me that Smith may be the first man I have met who could probably have taken the pain of giving birth. Has he got a higher pain threshold than normal?

"Probably. My two knees are -metal now. I don't have much trouble with them, just a little. Last week, I was at the hospital and they tapped the knees for fluids, and said they'd be okay. However, they think one metal kneecap might have started to erode. The other one is also worse for wear.

"The Iron Man's gone rusty," Susan says.

Tommy continued: "I can't straighten this arm. This elbow is also metal. Sometimes I have problems getting out of bed in the morning."

"Do you blame the arthritis or your injuries?" I ask.

"I think it's both. My mother had arthritis, too. It's hereditary, I think."

"When you think about all the pain you've been through, and that you can't go anywhere without being stopped for an autograph, was it worth it?" I ask.

"Erh, the pain I've been getting used to over the last 30 years. I don't blame football and I don't blame my mum. I used to do my own garden, but I've got a gardener now. A few years ago, when I came in from the garden, I shouted at Sue to call an ambulance because I'd had a heart attack.

"I grew up as a Liverpool fan. When I made my debut against Birmingham and we won 5–1, I walked around the stadium twice afterwards. I've no idea why – nobody knew me. It was my first game. Now I can't go anywhere without being recognised. I don't want to sound big-headed, but I only go a few yards before I'm stopped. Then a few more yards, and I'm stopped again."

"Actually, he seems to be getting more attention from fans lately," his wife adds.

Tommy replied: "Just look at the Olympic games; you can win even if you're not the best one.

"You get used to the attention. It's like getting married. I'm married to Sue and I'm married to Liverpool FC. We have got the best fans in the world, they never give up."

"Just like yourself?" I ask.

"Yes, I'm a Liverpool lad, which means I don't quit. I can't describe it. I really can't go anywhere. Crosby, Liverpool centre, Southport, Manchester...

"It's not a problem to start with, but after a while it can get too much. Especially if we go to a restaurant and someone comes over to our table and I have to tell them we're eating. That's when I don't like it. But the fans have followed me for so many years. After a defeat, they like saying things like, '*Where's your boots?!*'

"I don't feel any different to anybody else. I'm a Liverpool lad, I've lived here all my life and have no intention to go anywhere or to emigrate. It's a good place to live. I can't imagine anything else."

Liverpool FC Career: 1963-1978 🦅 *Appearances: 638* 🦅 *Goals: 48*

David Fairclough
The Window Smasher

"He will always be remembered as the super sub. I know he used to hate it, but God, he was terrific. He scored the most fantastic goal under pressure."

Ian Callaghan

SMASH! The jangling of glass is followed by a thud as a ball lands inside on the carpeted floor. Down the driveway, there are four boys in shorts looking up with concern at the broken window and the pieces of shattered glass outside the house. They had been playing two against two when one of the lads, a redhead, hit a "perfect" shot which accelerated, gained height and flew in an elegant curve... until a window got in the way.

The narrow Carmel Street in Everton, only 800 yards away from Anfield, served as a football arena for kids. They played all the time. The grown ups who lived at the house had not yet noticed the accident. The mother had left for her afternoon shift, the father was not home until six. The boys played on, but moved to the open area between the houses a little further away, an area that had been destroyed by a bomb during the war and had just been left as an open piece of ground. It was now a makeshift football pitch.

At 5.45pm, the little window smasher saw his dad come walking up the street. He went over to confess. His dad looked up at the window and smiled wearily. Another window to change. They did not have much, it was a cost he could do without, but the little boy never got told off. Not this time, either. His dad simply went in for the meal his wife had prepared for him before she left.

David Fairclough smashed his first window at eight – and continued for years after. They regularly replaced windows at his small, brick two-up, two-down, when David and his playmates had been busy again. At other times it was the neighbouring houses that needed windows changed. More often than not, David was to blame. David. *The window-smasher.* But the kids had a rule – whoever was playing all clubbed together to pay for broken windows.

I had met Fairclough several times before. He was always smartly dressed, a little reserved, but polite and friendly. While a lot of other Liverpool legends will fool around when they are out travelling, David is always the most serious of them. But appearances deceive. He was entertaining at the book launch party for Liverpool Hearts (Liverpoolhjerter) in the Shankly

95

Suite at Anfield. From the stage, he told stories. They were lively and adventurous, but not all were rose-coloured. And, while all the other ex-Liverpool players I have heard talking always speak very highly of the great managerial legends that are Bob Paisley and Bill Shankly, or mimic their peculiar manner of communication, Fairclough will tell you that Paisley could also be quite ruthless. He has personal reasons to say this.

In the summer of 2010, I also got to see the lighter side of David, when I went fishing for king crabs (horseshoe crabs) with him, Alan Kennedy, David Johnson, John Durnin and coaches from the Liverpool FC Academy. In addition to the Anfield legends, a few local chaps from Nordkapp Fotballfestival (North Cape Football Festival) and some other Norwegians had been invited. We were all dressed in orange survival suits as we set off at high speeds in the roofless boat.

We chased the waves, sea rafting. We were constantly sprayed and there was a lot of laughter on the boat heading towards the crab pots. We were heading between the high mountains diving into the sea on the roof of Europe, at 71 degrees North, where mainland Europe ends. It was a beautiful, warm summer's day and the adrenaline that was building up during the high speed journey did not lessen as we started pulling up the crabs.

Neither my English visitors nor I had ever seen live king crabs before. It was quite a sight, the rust-coloured monster crabs crawling on the bottom of the boat. To me, they looked like a mix of dinosaurs and monsters from an horror movie from the sea. The boys lifted the crabs by the claws and posed for photos. The biggest crabs, when you lifted them, were as long as one third of an adult body and their claws can snap a finger off. I did not dare hold one. However, when we got ashore, I held one together with Fairclough. If there was one person I trusted to hold a gigantic, pinching crab monster with, it had to be the calm and reliable David Fairclough. We grinned like kids at the camera, lifting the crab by its claws.

Afterwards, we were taught how to kill the beasts, before we gathered in a big lavvu – a Sami tent used by the people of northern Scandinavia – while the crabs were simmering in huge pots over the open fire. John Durnin could not remember my name, so I repeated my not-so-international name.

"Ragnhild."

"What? 'One-nil?'..."

Laughter spread on the reindeer rugs. It is quite easy, getting a new name. A name which has followed me since among my Liverpool friends. I take comfort in the fact that at least it is a victory, if not a big one, and it is better than what my Australian friends, who also struggle to pronounce my Viking name which is translated as 'Warmaid' or 'Warrior goddess', call me. So, Down Under, I had become 'Wrong hill' or, in the worst cases, 'Wrong Hell'. If I had to be named 'Hell' I would have much preferred it to be the right one, not the wrong one! So,

a small victory – the same scoreline that Liverpool won the 1978 and 1981 European Cups by – is far better.

March 2011: The spring after our visit to North Cape, I met David Fairclough at Liverpool's plush Hilton hotel. He walked in smiling, wearing a striped shirt and a dark blue suit jacket. His freckled nose and boyish smile makes him look young still. He gave me a hug and said it was nice to see me again. The feeling was mutual. It is always nice to meet the former striker. He is honest, straightforward, and easy-going.

Two elderly ladies in the hotel restaurant were sharing a sandwich and drinking mineral water with lemon. I asked one of them to take our photo. She asked me who I was with.

"He's David Fairclough, ex-Liverpool player," I told her.

A little later, I could hear her talking to her husband on the phone. She was whispering excitedly to her friend what he was telling her: "That's David Fairclough, he used to be called 'the super sub'. He used to come on with 10 minutes left and score!"

There are two things that have stuck above all else from Fairclough's career. Two phrases resound in the mind of old colleagues and fans: "super sub" and "St Etienne". I start with the latter.

"You know, I have followed Liverpool FC ever since I was a little kid, and I have some fantastic memories from Anfield. They are still strong in me. And I had never thought I would play an important part in a match that many define as the ultimate, or one of the two ultimate, Anfield experiences. It is a gift."

On this March day in 1977, none of the Liverpool players realised this match would be talked about 30 years later. There and then, they were just happy about the outcome and already moving on to the next battle. David tells me that almost every single day from that game onwards, someone has talked to him about the home match, the return game of the European Cup quarter-final at Anfield.

"It is astounding. Sometimes I think, 'It's not going to get mentioned today, the St Etienne game', but, before I finish the thought, someone appears from thin air and starts talking about the match. If you haven't walked in my shoes, you wouldn't believe how often people mention St Etienne to me. Things like, 'That must be the best goal you've ever scored, I remember where I was when you scored that goal', and so on."

People in Liverpool of a certain age still talk about where they were when David scored against St Etienne. Personally, I think I would have gone bonkers if I had to relive one moment of my life daily, on repeat, for years and years. Does he ever tire of talking about that match?

He laughs, draws breath and considers for a moment.

"I don't know. I get a bit embarrassed about it, but I don't get sick of it, because it's such a huge memory for people and I have to respect that. I'm playing my part in their memory.

"People still give me programmes from that day to sign, pictures from the event, any odd thing. Yesterday, the match was mentioned to me. The day before that, I was watching it on a video cassette in somebody's office. I have to live with the match all the time. I'm honoured, but also a little embarrassed."

For a couple of weeks, they had been building up for the big game. Everyone knew this was a big occasion. It had been hyped up by the media and, although it was the quarter-final rather than the last four, French champions St Etienne – Les Verts to their fans – were seen as potential European champions. Liverpool were trying to win a first European Cup and the French side looked to be a difficult obstacle to overcome, particularly as the Reds had lost the first leg 1-0 in France.

There was tension in the air, but the Anfield faithful were optimistic. They always believe in victory on the Kop.

The night before, the Liverpool team stayed in the city. They dined together and prepared mentally. The next day, it was business as usual. They tried going through the usual routines, but several players were a little more excited than usual on the short drive up to Anfield. They were greeted by an amazing sight upon arriving at Anfield Road. An unbelievable queue had formed there. It was a sea of people. Something different was definitely happening.

"That mass of people, and the atmosphere that met us inside Anfield was simply amazing. I don't think any of us had seen anything like it before. Yes, there had been the unbelievable night in 1965 against Inter Milan, but nothing quite like this. The atmosphere was very different from what it used to be – the air was tense with the excitement and the anticipation of the packed crowd was almost tangible."

Kevin Keegan scored in the second minute from an acute angle, making the task appear slightly easier for the Reds.

"When you equalise in the first few minutes, you think this is going to be easier than you thought. However, it wasn't to be, they were such a great team. St Etienne were just as good as us when the match settled down."

In the second half, Les Verts scored, to equalise on the night. It meant Liverpool had to score twice more. The atmosphere became more intense and nerve-wracking. Fairclough was on the bench. He was nervous, but desperate to get on and feel what it was like to play under such pressure in a crucial match. With 59 minutes on the clock, Ray Kennedy scored the Reds' second goal, but they still needed another to win. Then, with 16 minutes to go, Bob Paisley turned to his young striker.

"David, go out and see if you can make a name for yourself!"

That was often the instruction he got from Paisley before he was let on. Sometimes he would say: "Go out and see if you can get amongst them and grab us a goal!" In other words, simple instructions. There were no detailed tactical discussions.

The redhead – who would come to be known as 'The Bionic Carrot' – ran out on the pitch thinking: "I'm really going to make the most out of this one."

In his mind he went over and over his mantra as he ran into position: *"Just make sure you hit the target."*

With six minutes remaining, he got his chance: Kennedy's through ball opened the defence and Fairclough ran on, shrugged off a defender and slid the ball past Ivan Curkovic, the St Etienne keeper. There was bedlam, and not just on the Kop. People in all four of Anfield's stands completely lost it. David's parents were there. They were excited and happy, watching their son speed away from the goal, skipping through the air like a gazelle. Liverpool were through.

There are many famous photos of Fairclough jumping through the air with joy after scoring that goal. All eyes were on him. He was the undisputed centre of attention that night.

"Football life has changed a lot since then. Now, the players plan all kinds of routines that they go through when they score. Some suck their thumb, kiss their wedding ring and clench their fist, or they lift their shirt to reveal a T-shirt with some kind of message.

"Whenever I scored, I had no idea what would happen. Most of the time, I was in control. Sometimes I didn't even celebrate, I just clapped my hands and ran back to the centre line to get ready for the kick-off. Thankfully, I did celebrate the St Etienne goal, and it's been shown so many times through history."

After the match, there was chaos around the 20-year-old. Everybody wanted a piece of the man who had secured Liverpool's place in the European Cup semi-final. In the players' lounge, his dad Tom was waiting. Tom had been a Liverpool supporter all his life and seeing his son settle a European Cup quarter-final at Anfield was a dream come true. However, he was never boastful about his son's performance. Fairclough's parents stayed in the background while their son was making his name. They were down-to-earth people and never changed.

The striker remembers that they left Anfield and went out to the parking lot together that night. He saw his parents get into their car.

"See you at home," he said, all very matter-of-factly. Then, he drove home with his mate who lived a couple of doors down from him. While the rest of the Liverpool team went out and celebrated at a nightclub, the match-winner went home and watched Sportsnight with

his parents. He thought it would be too late to go out. It was 10.30pm by the time he got home.

"Why didn't you celebrate with the others?"

"It wasn't my thing, really. Besides, we didn't realise how big it was. I honestly thought it was just a moment in time, not a lifetime. It was a Wednesday night and I was hoping to play Saturday, so I just wanted to stay in shape, in case I was given a chance."

The Liverpool Echo wanted to come and take pictures of David relaxing the next morning, but he had no time to take it easy. He was due in for training at 10 o'clock.

Before that, the paper's photographer showed up and arranged a photo in which Fairclough's mother treats him to the luxury of a cup of tea in bed. Normally, it was nothing like that. If you wanted tea in the Fairclough house, you had to get out of bed!

"This was not the way we were. I was never treated as a superstar at home. We were a very down-to-earth type of family and my mum would never have allowed me to take off. She still doesn't."

He was a 20-year-old football pro and still lived at home in his parents' small council house. They lived in an area that was generally considered one of the roughest neighbourhoods in Liverpool. The house was very modest. He had just bought a small car. Before then, he had travelled to training by bus, whereas Kevin Keegan arrived in his smart Nissan sports car every day.

"It was very down to earth, not like the kids today. Now, I think, unfortunately, they get too much, too soon. They think they're good footballers before they've actually achieved anything. At this time, I only earned a fifth of what the other players got. That's just the way it was. You stepped up in the club. And I wasn't one of the big earners – it wasn't my goal to earn lots of money, either. I took it in my stride."

Just four months after the St Etienne triumph, which was followed by a semi-final success against FC Zurich and the club's first-ever European Cup in Rome, his father Tom collapsed unexpectedly and died of a heart attack. The day was July 15, 1977. It means that what is remembered as a great year for Liverpool became a terrible year for the striker. The trauma, grief and pain was so massive that it was impossible to bear for the small, tight-knit Fairclough family.

"I was 20 and lost my guide, my soundboard."

His eyes well up, his voice shivers slightly.

"You talk things over with your dad, and my dad had always had my best interests at heart."

He breathes in, long and hard.

"To lose someone I could confide in implicitly, it was bad timing. Not just for me, but for the whole family. We had so many plans. Now that I was making a bit of money I was planning to move the family out of the council house and things would have improved for all of us. But my career changed dramatically."

His story has me thinking about one of the worst days of my own life so far. It was the funeral of my own dad, who had also died unexpectedly and much too young. He had a massive coronary on the last checkpoint of an orienteering course and, ironically, there were three trained medics – two of them specialists in CPR – on his heels. But they could not save him out there in the woods. And a defibrillator was too far off. He was 61 and we had no idea he was ill.

A week after this tragic and very much unexpected death, I felt certain my legs could not carry me when we parked outside the small church of Kviby, my father's childhood village, a 30-minute drive from Alta. Even though we were there early, the parking lot was already full, and a steady flow of people – to this day I cannot remember who they were – trickled in past us. I remember thinking this had to be a nightmare, and that I'd wake up soon. I had no idea where to find strength to be at the funeral of my own father; my rock. I also wondered how on Earth I was going to manage the long walk up the red carpet to what I dreaded most of all, the proof it was all true: my father's coffin.

"I lost my father very early, too, and whenever I achieve something big, I can't really enjoy it because I feel sad that he's not there with me to experience it. Did you feel something like that?"

"Yes!"

He breathes heavily, struggling to find words. His voice is trembling and he fights back tears.

"We were very close. I just have the one sister, so my dad followed me everywhere. I was very sad when he died. On one or two occasions – well, always – when I achieved things, dad would be on my mind.

"It was very tough losing him and I think it made me a harder person. I don't think anyone helped me in my grief. My mum, my sister and I had to work it out ourselves. It was pretty tough."

I was surprised at his story. He had a whole football team around him. Surely they offered some kind of support?

"No. There was no guidance or support for me in that period. I was given a week off from training to arrange and carry out the funeral. I had to pay for it. Then I was back in training again. Move on!"

"Nobody talked to you about your father's death?"

He thinks for a moment.

"No. Bob Paisley never mentioned my dad. I think a little counselling might have helped, but the offer never came."

"That's strange.."

"Yes..."

I think back to my first days back at work. I was in charge of several live broadcasts every week. However, my boss had taken me for short walks in the sun, letting me cry on her shoulder. And I had a staff around me who let me talk and were good listeners to my grief and anger. That way, I managed to work as a radio hostess in my darkest hour, when the whole world seemed pointless. I cannot imagine what it must have been like to go to training day in, day out, playing games with a pressure to perform at your best every time – without any compassion.

"Was the environment really *that* macho, that tough? Or do you think nobody talked about his death because it was too hard for them?"

"I think it was the time when Paisley and Joe Fagan grew up that defined the atmosphere. They'd been through war and weren't the types to put their arm around you. You were very much on your own."

"But what about your team-mates? There must have been some on the team who were closer friends than the rest. Didn't they speak either?"

"No. I was among the youngest on the team and most of my pals were in the Reserves. People like Colin Irwin and Jeffrey Ainsworth tried to help me, but it wasn't the time for it.

It's a very selfish environment being a footballer. I've often wanted to say this: it's dog eat dog. It really is. If someone scrambles out of the door, others will be scrambling over you to get your place. It's not an easy environment."

"What does that kind of environment do to you, when you're in it for so long?"

"It makes you hard. Sometimes I feel I'm too hard on my son, but I only want what is best for him. It does make you hard. I'm a much nicer guy, more emotional, to people I don't see regularly – aside from my mother and my sister, of course. I'm happy to help people in need and do any kind of charity, but I'm harder on people closer to me. It's very strange."

"I think it makes sense. You usually take your frustration out on people you care for. Do you have a bad conscience for feeling this way?"

Tears are rolling down David's freckled cheeks.

"Well, football is a very hard environment, but I wish we could move on a little, because we all have different handicaps in life, obstacles along the way. For me, losing my father so young has been my biggest obstacle."

"It's like a wall falls out of your life," I add. "People who haven't lost a parent that early don't know what it's like. You can't describe it."

"No, you can't describe it. Suddenly one of the secure walls of your life is gone and you feel a little lost – and you probably will forever."

It strikes me how similar patterns and mechanisms form in a mind in mourning. Apparently, it does not matter whether you have lived your life as a football star, or as a journalist. Gender is also irrelevant – as is whether you were raised in a poor working class area in Liverpool, an infamous one at that, or in a newly-built middle class home in the north of Norway.

David bought his own house a little over two years after his father died. More as an investment, somewhere he might like if he moved out of the council flat. All the necessary furniture and equipment was there and he pretended he was going to live there.

"But my mum was alone with my sister. Sometimes at night, when I was at my house near the training field, I would ring my mum and ask her if they were still up."

If they were, he would get into the car and stay over at his mother's house. It took him a while to move out for good.

David does not hold a grudge against Paisley for how he treated him after the striker's father died, but he remains annoyed that the manager left him benched so often that it led to him being dubbed 'super sub'.

"There's no doubt in my mind that I should've played more for Liverpool. Only Bob Paisley and I know exactly what was said at the time and what I was told. I was constantly given excuses why I wasn't in the starting XI. He told me he had plans to change the team, and that I was part of these plans. I'm not saying this to slag him off, but I think he could have handled me better. He later admitted to it, more or less, but for a long while I was a guinea pig in that sense. I was very disappointed.

"Now people ask me if I feel I should have played for England, and I think I should have. I only played for the B team and the Under-21s. I would have loved to have had a full England cap and my chances would have been bigger if I could have showed off more and played more regularly for Liverpool. There are also a couple of finals I think I should've played in.

"I do feel I could have made more of my career, and it's partly my own fault – but I don't think Paisley helped me enough."

That being said, there was fierce competition for his place. Kevin Keegan, Steve Heighway, David Johnson, John Toshack, and later also Kenny Dalglish. Was his timing unlucky?

"I couldn't compete with Kenny Dalglish, but the others I have no problems comparing myself with. I had a little bit of everything as a player – I was faster than Heighway and could score more goals than him, I was faster and dribbled better than Johnson. Toshack was a better header of the ball than me, but he couldn't run like I could. And, even though he's one of my heroes, I could score goals he couldn't.

"I'm not trying to get under anyone's skin saying this. The point is, I was just as good a player as they were. I had more than my fair share of ability. We were all different, but I don't feel inferior to any of those I battled with for game time."

"Are you bitter you didn't have more playing time for Liverpool?"

"Bitter? Yes. Bitter is as good a word as any – and angry. I know I should have played more. I would rather play for the reserves than be benched.

"I was there to play football. Money didn't matter to me. I'm still mad at Paisley for not letting me play more. After 35 years, my anger hasn't cooled. It's a bit sad, really. Unfortunately, the only other person who could have explained why I was constantly rejected is dead."

Fairclough loathed being benched, just hated it. Back then, apart from in European matches, there wasn't a gang of substitutes waiting together. Only one was permitted. So, when named as substitute, Fairclough was alone. A lone wolf. Everybody else got to play, just not him. It is a little like being chosen last in PE. Only one left. Least wanted for the task. Yet, in some way, you are chosen – you are a part of the first-team, but an inch from being one of them. You are caught in the middle.

Ronnie Moran used to ask Fairclough if he had learned something, watching the others from the bench.

"No, it was rubbish!" he used to reply.

"I hated watching football. There was nothing worse. We worked hard all week in training and then came the message, the infamous phrase, 'Dave, you'll be sub'."

There are many reasons why Fairclough was ranked as 18th out of all Liverpool's players who "shook the Kop" when more than 110,000 supporters voted in a poll held by LFC TV in 2006. One of the biggest reasons is that he is remembered as the super sub, not just a sub.

Fairclough had a special ability to come on and settle important matches. He thinks Paisley realised this. One episode is imprinted on his mind.

Liverpool were playing Sunderland away in November 1976. At half-time, it was still 0-0 and David was angry, as usual, for being benched. He went to the toilet and must have looked pretty angry, staring at the Sunderland motif in the Roker Park away dressing room toilets, when Paisley came and stood next to him.

"Get your chin up, you'll be on a little later," the manager said in his typical manner.

The player did not believe him. However, Paisley kept his word. Fairclough did get on. Not only that, he scored the winner, the only goal of the match, within a minute of running onto the pitch. The day changed completely for *super sub*. His mood, too.

"I'll never forget that moment at the toilet. We did have moments like that, and this is one of the good memories."

"What has it done to you, spending so much time on the bench, waiting? What has it done to your ability to wait for other things in life? Are you more or less patient now?"

"I'm not the most patient person. My grandmother used to say that I had the redheaded temper. I can be really furious."

"You seem so calm."

"I know, but that's because I'm working on it. I was never the type to fight in a bar, but I've got such a competitive nature. That's why I avoid too many team events, they bring out the worst in me."

David went through good days and bad with his club, and chose to stay there until he transferred for a short spell at Toronto Blizzard and the Swiss team FC Luzern. He played for seven different clubs over nine years following his departure from Liverpool, but what did he learn most from his years at Anfield, the club where he spent most of his career?

"I'm tempted to say humility, good grounding and a sense of reality. As a talented kid it's easy to think the world revolves around you and that you're the best. However, when you come to Liverpool Football Club as a 16-year-old, you're at the bottom of the ladder; it's not all about you. You learn not to get on your high horse or believe you should receive special treatment.

"The lessons I learned early on at Liverpool were good habits. It was a bit like being in the Army – we had to clean baths, clean floors, clean boots. I enjoyed all that. I still like to be clean, I like places clean and things kept in order.

"We worked our way up the ladder. Nothing comes easy, you earn your little position in the club. So, the first thing I think of, looking back, is the grounding I got as a 16-year-old. I still don't like dirty baths, dirty sinks, dirty floors. All those little things haven't made me who I am, but they're a big part of who I am."

Having stayed 11 years at the club, there are many memories to choose from when trying to pick a particular favourite. David's biggest memory is walking through that very special door, time and again. The first time was the most intense.

He remembers when he was a kid walking along the car park where the players arrived before a match. He was a keen collector of autographs, so he spent many hours in the car park collecting scribblings from his heroes. He collected hundreds of them in books, on pieces of paper and match programmes. Some of them are still in boxes in his loft. You see, David Fairclough is a collector. But, back to the story: he often stood staring at the door where the players would come out, waiting.

"I'll never forget the first time I walked in myself. I was 15, arrived on my own, by bus. I was nervous, my heart was pounding and I made my way into the car park thinking, 'It's my right to be here! What will it be like going in?'

"My biggest Liverpool moment was when I opened the door to the main reception area and entered the heart of Anfield. It was always in the dark, the sun doesn't shine in there. I thought: "I can walk into Liverpool and nobody can say, 'Who are you and what are you doing here?'"

Every time he arrived at that Main Stand car park on the team bus with the rest of the team and gazed at the kids standing outside, waiting patiently like he had done to see his heroes, he felt great. Later, when he got his own car, he had a parking spot with a little number on it. It was a big thing, every time he drove in and parked in front of Anfield. It hit him: *I'm going out of my car and in there. Brilliant!*"

"Walking down that 25-metre long corridor, which has now been decorated with pictures so you get the feeling you're at Liverpool FC and not somewhere else, was fantastic. It was a massive kick the first time I went down there. I still get a buzz every time I walk through the reception door at Anfield."

Over the last few years, Fairclough has had a chance to feel that Liverpool's anthem "You'll Never Walk Alone" is not a cliché.

It was the autumn of 2010, just a week after Fairclough had entertained us at my book launch at Anfield, and just a week before he was supposed to go with me on a book signing tour to the north of Norway. He was at the gym when he suddenly felt ill, so went home to lie down for a bit. It turned out he had suffered a heart attack. It was a huge surprise. David and his wife Jan had always stressed the importance of keeping fit and eating healthily. Luckily, he got to the hospital quickly and was operated on in time.

The news that David had been admitted to hospital spread quickly among Liverpool's supporter community. I talked to him a couple of days after the operation, as he was supposed to have worked with me the following week. He said declarations of support and well-wishes were flooding in on Facebook, Twitter, the club's website, via emails and text messages. There were cards, fruit baskets and flowers arriving from all over the world.

"I was totally taken aback by how quickly people responded to my situation. I would have liked to have kept it private. But I was completely blown away by the massive support and by how many were concerned about me. A lot of people also expressed difficulties understanding that I, of all people, should be hit by this, and that is how I felt about it, too. I had never expected so many Liverpool fans to support me and wish me well."

It was too emotional for him to read every message, so his son Tom helped him reply to those who had written. The support helped him recover more quickly.

"I was deeply grateful and completely overwhelmed by it all. There were even Manchester United fans sending their best wishes, as well as people from other clubs. But 99 per cent were Liverpool supporters, of course. This showed me how football links you to others like a family.

My extended Liverpool family is just fantastic. It was a tough period, I cried a lot. But, luckily, I made it, and I'm back in good shape."

It was tough going through such a serious illness that had come on so unexpectedly. There was a lot of concern about David's recovery after his heart surgery and, as he has said, he would have liked it all to have been kept private.

"Is that part of the cost for being a famous footballer?"

"Yes, I think I don't realise quite how much I've influenced other people. I learned that when people took time to offer me support. My children were also very grateful for the support. Luckily, this is all over now."

Just one month after I met David in the Hilton, something horrible happened.

Jan, his beloved wife, suffered a brain aneurysm and fell into a coma. She had been his life partner through adulthood but on April 9, 2011, she passed away. They have two grown kids, who still lived at home.

It was unreal. I felt for him. David had let me see the vulnerable grief he carries with him, and has done for more than 30 years, and now this? It simply could not be true.

"Dear God, please let this be a nightmare that will end soon."

It was not. Thousands of cards of condolence landed in the Fairclough family's letterbox. David, his daughter Sophie and son Tom were kept busy opening all the envelopes. The whole house, all rooms, filled up with hand-written cards side by side, from all over the world. On every shelf, window-sill, mantelpiece, along the walls, on the floor. The first person to arrive at the door with flowers while Jan was in a coma was Steven Gerrard, who lives just down the road. The flower delivery men were busy for days, while the Fairclough quickly ran out of vases.

A few days later, David publicly thanked everyone through Liverpool FC's website. He thanked the Red world for the immense support he and his children had experienced after Jan had left the tight-knit family so abruptly.

He said:"What happened was an enormous tragedy, but the reaction from everybody at Liverpool was amazing. Fans have supported us in every manner, sending cards, letters or flowers. It is simply overwhelming.

"Jan had an enormous amount of friends and was respected in her own right as a businesswoman, but the way fans have responded and tried to support Tom, Sophie and me has been incredible. I can only say thank you.

" When I had my heart problems six months ago, I was flattered over all the response I had from fans and I thought my share of goodwill had been used up. But the reaction to Jan's death, so shortly after my own illness, was more than I ever expected. It has helped us all so much."

Before the Manchester City game at Anfield there was a minute's silence. It was for the 96 Hillsborough victims – ahead of the 22nd anniversary of the disaster – for the fallen soldier and Liverpool fan Mark Burgan and for Jan Fairclough. I was three rows down from the corner flag on the Kop and I cried. I cried my eyes out for David and his two children.

Just over a month after Jan's death, photographer Tony and I visited the Faircloughs to take some photos for this book. There were still cards everywhere, even though a lot had been taken down. It was difficult to remove them, too. There were greetings from a lot of old heroes, as well as current ones. Removing them felt a little like removing Jan, too. So, the cards still dominated every room. The funeral had been packed with people.

"Jan and I were soulmates, so losing her is very, very tough. She was loved by so many because she was that kind of person who gave more than she received. Always kind and interested in people. Now I am experiencing real support from the Red family, but this is also a result of real admiration for her."

David gave me an order of service from the funeral. In church, Kevin Keegan had been stood shoulder-to-shoulder with Sue Neal. The troops gathered around David's family. He told me it had been a good ceremony. I leafed through the order of service, read, looked at the photos. Jan was so beautiful. She was glowing. The family looked very happy together, like a four-leaved clover for good luck.

Why does someone always get the heavy burden?

thanks to all Reds fans for their incredible support through the good times and the bad times.
David Fairclough

Liverpool FC Career: 1975-1983 *Appearances: 154* *Goals: 55*

Jamie Carragher
Father and Son

"He has got it all. He is verbal, he has got commitment, passion, drive. He knows and understands what it requires of someone giving 90 minutes and Carragher has given everything in those minutes playing in the red shirt. I'd miss him in any Liverpool team."

Phil Neal

The sun is shining and there is a strong wind blowing. On the sidelines of the pitch, parents are anxiously watching the action. Some have brought camping chairs, others just stand around, discussing their sons' achievements.

One of the seven-year-olds out there has just signed for Manchester United and will be travelling there three days a week. Another kid has recently been accepted at Liverpool's Academy – James Carragher, son of Jamie. He has just scored his second of the day against a team of boys a year older than him. Now he is sprinting towards the line where the parents are stood. Still running at pace, he drops to his knees and slides over the grass while triumphantly raising his hands above his head. The score is 8-2 – that's what you call a comprehensive win.

It's the last match of the season. The opposition stood no chance against a team of seven-year-olds who have already won the league. No wonder the figure on the opposite line is smiling. Philly Carragher is dressed a little like Bob Paisley. Throughout the game, he has given little James Carragher and the others on the team encouragement and advice. He even bent down to tie a few laces before the match. Now they will get some well-deserved rest – the season is over. Time to pose for a team photo with the trophy.

Little James is all smiles, too. He is looking forward to telling his dad about the game. About the goals. About outclassing the other team. Because dad could not come. He is preparing to play for Liverpool the next day. A game that will give him an even firmer grip on second place on the list of most games played in the history of the club. Philly Carragher also brings his grandchild James to all Liverpool's matches, home and away, just like he took his sons to matches when they were young. They travelled everywhere to follow Everton. Jamie was only six or seven years old when he started going to away games to see the Blues.

Philly's most memorable trip was following Everton in Europe with his son Jamie, who

113

was about seven. Everton were away in the semi-final to Bayern Munich in the European Cup Winners' Cup.

"This was at a time when England and Germany both had problems with hooliganism, Philly recalls. "When we got there, the police asked if we had come for trouble, and James [he always calls Jamie 'James'] replied, 'No, we've come to win 3–0!'"

It was young Jamie's first European away game and, at the hotel later that night, he could be see wearing a blue and white scarf and a little blue and white hat while being interviewed by a German TV company.

"I wish we had that film!" Philly smiles.

The trips to Europe taught Carragher Jnr a lot about interacting with fans. The Everton stars were always accommodating and kind to their own on European nights. That made a lasting impression.

"It's not that hard to be nice. But it's easy to be horrible. At that time, a lot of people would borrow money or scrimp and scrape to be able to follow the team – and the team needed to show a little respect for the fans. I think James' experience in his childhood taught him that respect. I'm very proud of that, really. I genuinely believe people like James. I know they like him.

"I see what he's doing and how he treats people when we're out. He makes sure people feel at ease around him. He's not one to fool about. He's one of the lads, and still a really nice boy. It's a wonderful feeling, seeing your son behave so well and being so down to earth, not flashy and big-headed."

So, the Carragher family changed colour. As if by magic. Because when James Lee Duncan Carragher grew up, he was – like his son now – a very talented young player, scoring one goal after another. He was so keen to start playing that dad Philly had to lie about his age and say he was eight, when he was seven, meaning he often played against boys three years older. At a very young age, Jamie was a striker – and also played midfielder for a while before he developed into a defender at Liverpool.

Both Liverpool and Everton were interested in the youngster, but he signed for the Reds first. Later, when he was offered a place at Everton's youth team, he transferred to the club he supported, but quickly discovered that things were much more organised under the wings of Steve Heighway at Liverpool, so returned to the red half of Merseyside. The youngsters there were apprentices at Melwood and could admire the first-team up close in training.

Back then, there was no Academy in Kirkby, so everyone was at Melwood – and that is why Liverpool's training ground became the best place on earth for Carragher; the place that he now, towards the end of his career, dreads having to leave the most. It is part of his

soul, it has been his daily refuge and a greenhouse to his dreams ever since he was a kid and cleaned the boots of the big stars.

Philly used to go with Carragher, his eldest, and the two younger brothers, Paul and John, behind the house to practise shooting – with both feet – on the back wall. The house had no hot water before the future football star was born.

Indeed, the defender's life had a very dramatic start. He was born with his intestines outside his stomach and had to be operated on quickly. His first days were tough and his parents were terrified they would lose their little firstborn. During his wife's pregnancy, Philly had built an extension to the small two-up, two-down, so that now it also held a bathroom. After six weeks, the child was brought home and the house had a shower, hot water and a toilet. Father and son ended up having their first bathroom in a home at the same time.

For as long as the Reds' No23 can remember, he has been completely absorbed with football. Not that surprising, as from when he was quite small he used to go along when his dad was coaching Sunday league teams in Bootle. He followed them from the sideline while Philly was yelling out orders to his men using words that gave the youngster a whole new vocabulary.

Philly is quite a colourful person, if ever there was one! He fills every room with his personality. He is warm and inclusive, enthusiastic and very passionate. And occasionally, he admits, short-tempered.

Temper is a family trait. Jamie has inherited the short temper, too. I thoroughly enjoyed reading his excruciatingly honest autobiography Carra, in which he describes his own and his father's hot-headedness. I decided I would talk to him about this if I ever got the chance.

Luckily, Philly had promised me an interview with his son, and he kept his word. On the Monday morning, I met the man who also willingly met me for an interview for my last book. Incredibly, he recognised me, and greeted me with a warm smile when he saw me waiting on the grey leather couch in the Melwood reception.

I'll never forget our first meeting, which took place a few years earlier. I had come to Melwood without starry eyes and shivering knees as I was not yet the big fan of Liverpool that I am today. To me, Carragher was just a name and a shirt number and I was just doing my job. I had come to see the President of the Scandinavian Supporters' Club, Liverpool's No23. I was worried about one thing only – everybody had told me how difficult he was to understand, that he talked so fast. So I was wondering if I would be able to understand him at all.

Whoever told me that had clearly never spoken to his father on the phone, or late at night in a bar. I have. Philly is a fast talker! His son talks in a low gear by comparison. There was no language barrier between us at Melwood. But, back then, I was almost taken aback by Carragher Jnr's friendliness and politeness.

The previous weekend, I had taken pictures of his son in the sun. A series of photos of James wrestling for the ball in front of goal and then scoring; running towards me and sliding on his knees proper Premier League-style. I had made printouts of the photos for his father. As a mother, I thought that, if it were my son and I had missed a moment like that, I would have appreciated photos. I took them out of my bag and gave them to Jamie, who immediately lit up very proud and leafed through the pile. Then, he thanked me for them several times.

I told him I had been watching Philly on the sideline last weekend and it felt like I had been given a small glimpse of what Jamie's own childhood must have been like. He nodded and said his father had always loved football, just like himself. They live and breathe football.

Philly is manager of James' team, Bulford FC, just like he was manager of his son's team when he was growing up. You need your parents' support and help playing football at a young age.

"My father was always very competitive. We were all raised that way. We always want to do our best, but we always want to win. No matter what we do."

When Carragher was his son's age, he was once meant to play a match in miserable weather. There was much at stake; a team of boys two years older were coming in and they were so good they were reportedly winning games by 10 or 20 goals.

The pitch was muddy, Carragher was cold – he did not want to play. He faked an injury to get away and to get back into the warmth again. When they came home, his father was furious. Philly was so mad he threw Jamie's boots at his son and told him plainly that this was the wrong attitude if he wanted to go somewhere. Be a winner, always be the best you can be!

Whenever Jamie has thought about quitting, he has remembered that day when his father threw boots at him – it has helped him fight. But, back then, he cried his little heart out and felt it was very unfair. There is no doubt his father has had a tremendous impact on the footballer's career. He let his son start playing at a young age, encouraged him and travelled everywhere with him.

"He was always there for me, and I believe most top footballers have had it the same way. Their parents have been there for them.

"Michael Owen's dad was very similar. He was always there. He's a character, my dad, and having him around has made me who I am. I've certainly got my father's competitiveness – and probably his short temper, too, sometimes."

It has caused him some trouble on the pitch.

"Whenever the camera goes on me in a game I always look angry, or like I'm trying to sort something out. I think it's the fear of losing or not playing well. Always worried something will go wrong if you're taking it too easy, or aren't serious enough.

"People play football in different ways. Some play with a smile, but I'm different. It's probably the fear of losing. I've been like that since I was a kid."

The Carragher house could be pretty lively at times. It is not just Philly and Jamie who are short-tempered – his brother Paul is, too. The third brother, John, is different, though. He has a calmer nature. Any flaring of tempers were mostly stirred by competition in some type of game or other. So, if you met one of them for a game of cricket, on sports day or even swimming, you would almost certainly see the mood swings.

"But are there also advantages to having a temper?" I ask. "Does it help you in trying to reach your targets?"

"Oh, yes," he responds. "I'm absolutely convinced it's helped me. If you have a setback, you don't just give up. You go back and fight."

Jamie draws his breath, before continuing: "And it shows you can turn the situation around and win again. That way, you can prove to yourself or other people that you *can* win again. In football, there are lots of ups and downs, and I believe it's vital to have that drive to fight your way back up again. Many experience setbacks in their football career as well as in life and it finishes them off. They never come back. So, I think temper is a good thing."

However, sometimes, it can get him into trouble. In an FA Cup tie against Arsenal at Highbury in 2002, Carragher was fouled and jumped back up, furious. Just as he was complaining to the referee, he was hit by a coin thrown at him by an Arsenal fan. It made him flip out.

"For a second there, I lost it. I threw a coin back at the crowd. That was a mistake. I was sent off and that cost us the chance of getting something from the game. I had to learn from that.

"One thing is me being in trouble, but that affected the whole team. I was incredibly disappointed for having let the team down. We went out of the FA Cup as well. It wasn't good at all. So, I've been working very hard at this. That's why I don't show my temper so much on the pitch anymore, in terms of yellow or red cards. I'm more controlled on the pitch now. But, inside me, inside my whole body, anger can be raging. However, it looks silly when players lose it on the pitch. I normally get more angry with my team-mates than at the opposition or the ref – and, luckily, you're not carded for yelling at your own!"

It makes me think of the match against West Bromwich Albion in May 2009, when he got into a face-to-face argument with his then team-mate Alvaro Arbeloa, something I remind him of.

Carragher laughs: "People say you shouldn't do things like that, and I know. But when you're so competitive, it rages through your body, sometimes it boils over. That's what happened.

"I think Manchester United had just won the league and the score was 1-0. I was scared West Bromwich would score and I was just very frustrated. So, I lost control for one minute – but that's football."

I had never thought about it before, but football is like life in general: you get most annoyed at the people you care about. Have you noticed? How often can you be a happy bunny with other people but as soon as you come home, you vent your anger on your partner? And why does it make you more annoyed when your own kids spill food all over the kitchen than if other kids do? The fact that Carragher gets angriest at his own team-mates – could it be because he loves Liverpool FC so much?

"Yeah, I think if I'd played for someone else I wouldn't have been the same. But I'd still be something like that, it's just who I am. It means so much to me that Liverpool win and do well, so sometimes I boil over."

Everybody I have talked with tells me it is extremely important to have a father figure in football. Jamie is still followed closely by his father. They are tight-knit, like mates more than anything, Philly tells me. He will *always* get a call from his son within an hour after a match, even if Philly was at the game or not. Then Jamie will get his dad's judgment.

"I've never looked to give James negative feedback. No matter how he has played, I always look for something constructive. If I'm in my car, on the bus or on the train with the lads on our way home from the match, he'll give me a ring. I always find something positive to say.

"Of course, I've seen him play a few shaky matches – you're allowed to, having played more than 660 times for Liverpool! If I've seen him play four or five matches where he wasn't good enough, what's the point in me telling him? I'll let him know what positives I saw. You know yourself if you've done a bad job – you don't need others to tell you."

That is an important message to parents – always emphasise the positive, not the negative. It's so easy to pick on your kids. Philly agrees.

"Exactly! You have to teach them right from wrong, as with your kids now, they need it. But later in life, around 15, they know right from wrong. They're in a different phase and need you to build them up."

Philly Carragher has three football-playing sons and admits it is hard to find the balance as a passionate supporter of your children.

"You need to stay level-headed and not get too involved. A lot of parents get carried away because their child has signed for Liverpool at eight or nine years of age. It's hard not to, it's difficult to remain

calm. There is so much emotion involved in football. But, I say to the parents, 'Keep your feet on the ground. Don't get too carried away. The chance he'll make it to the top is so remote, but the chance you'll make yourself look silly is huge.'

"However, they get that carried away. Don't! Just look at statistics – how many have come through at Liverpool after Stevie and James? How many homegrown kids have made Liverpool's first-team since them?"

Liverpool's No23 married his childhood sweetheart, Nicola, and they have two children – Mia and James. The latter is, as I have mentioned, a promising football talent like his father. Now that he follows his son's development, the Reds icon understands better what his own father went through with him as a boy.

"Now that I can watch James play and win, or score, the joy is bigger than when I play myself.

"It's great going to the LFC Academy with him a couple of times a week. It's fantastic learning for him – and he learns from the other kids as well. But it's like in any match; sometimes you're disappointed when the kids don't do well and they get beat. So, I go through the whole spectrum of emotions watching James, just like when I play myself. And I probably feel it even stronger because it's my own son playing. I'm desperate to see him do well."

I know what Carragher is talking about. Last winter, my four-year-old son Elias was starting his very first cross-country ski race. Hundreds of kids had turned up. The slopes, four ski tracks side by side, had been prepared several days beforehand. We had been there to try some of the tracks before the race. As a proud mother, and former district ski champion, I was very moved, photographing my son being handed his first bib number. By the start banner, Elias bumped into his best friend and they set off together. I walked next to them, cheering for my son.

Then, something strange happened. I got so worked up that I instructed my son to overtake the slow kids on the slope. He had never passed anyone before – and "clear path!" was unknown territory.

Elias went ahead, while his best friend – who is also a decent skier, despite his age – was stuck behind someone slower. I was taking photos and cheering for Elias – and I admit I may have bumped into a few parents in my eagerness to follow him.

On a hilltop, before a fairly steep downhill slope, a woman held them back and made sure they went down safely, one by one, and did not run into each other. Up there, Elias discovered that he had left his best friend behind, so he wanted to wait for him. But what did his mother do?

"Just keep going, Elias, come on!"

So, he rushed off, while his friend had to wait his turn to run down. That way, Elias was past the finish line quite a while before his friend. I applauded him loudly.

While my son got his prize bag of sweets and other trinkets, it hit me: "What am I doing? Nobody times these kids! It is simply a matter of finishing, about having fun, about taking part. Yes, maybe it was even about attending your first ski race shoulder to shoulder with your best friend?"

As my pulse and adrenaline settled down, I was ashamed. Why did I get so carried away? It was certainly a wake-up call. My son had not even started organised sports. Even though he loves both football and skiing, there is no specialised training for kids in Norway before they are six and start school. It struck me that the important maturing process before taking up a sport would be my responsibility.

It is a balancing act for parents to support their talented child and to let them enjoy a sport. How does Carragher balance motivating and encouraging his son without being too pushy?

"I'm in the middle of the learning process, seeing as my son has only started playing football. Everybody treats their children differently. I try and be as positive as I can. But sometimes I can't help it and I have to criticise him, too, say, 'Maybe you need to do this or maybe that.'

"I think, as long as you're enthusiastic and have the right attitude, you'll be all right. We all play a bad game now and then, which is why you must support your child if they fail – no one wants to make a mistake. Sometimes you get too involved because you love your kid so much. I sometimes see parents shouting from the line."

"I've done that myself," I admit.

Carragher offers words of comfort: "Oh yeah? That's the way we are. We want what's best for our kids, but sometimes it's not a good thing. That's why I feel it's better for the kids to train at the Academy rather than playing Sunday morning matches. The Academy's a good place to be, with proper coaches being more involved in the kids' development and achievement than the parents. I think it's actually better for the kids."

Carragher is one of Liverpool's biggest celebrities. He is recognised and stopped for autographs and photos wherever he goes. What is it like to be there for his son in this circus?

"I don't say, 'We can't go there because of who I am and that I will be recognised.' If he wants to go to town and get a new football kit, I'll take him. I also go to the Academy, to his Sunday matches and his summer league. I always have to sign a few autographs, but I never turn James down. I want as normal a life as possible with my son."

"What's it like to miss out on his games?"

"It's difficult. But my dad will be on the phone with me through the game, keeping me updated on the score, telling me how they're doing and how James is playing. I desperately want them to win. James is like me – when they win, he's on top of the world and, when they lose, he's very disappointed and sometimes angry."

"Do you see anything in your son that you recognise in yourself?"

"I can't remember that well what I was like as a kid, or how I played at his age. But I definitely know he's got my enthusiasm and will to win, and he does get quite angry when they lose. My dad gave it to me and I've given it to my son. We're all probably the same, that's the genes.

"James is very competitive and he loves football. That's just like I was. He watches football in the morning. I used to collect sticker books and kits. He's exactly the same as I was as a kid."

Steven Gerrard has said that Jamie is absolutely obsessed with football, that he tapes everything and watches the clips over and over. What is it about football that fascinates him so much?

"I've been involved in football since I was a kid, I've always loved the game – reading about football, watching football, playing football. It's a massive part of me. I love watching all kinds of football, not just Liverpool FC. I've never really been interested in too much outside football, but I think that's helped me as a footballer.

"Many people my age look forward to the day they retire, finally get some rest. I just want to play as much as possible before I finish; I know I'll be devastated when I have to stop."

It's true what they say, then – Jamie Carragher is a right football geek. What plans has he made for the day the unavoidable is a fact? The day he is no longer in the team? The day when the youngsters take over?

The No23 says he has no plan A or B for his retirement. He will have to look at job offers and decide then – but he is certain it will be something to do with football. Quite a lot of people I have spoken to about the future of Liverpool FC see him and Steven Gerrard as a managerial duo, but I'll leave the future to itself.

The old players from the 1960s, '70s and '80s think everything was better way back when – what does he feel, as a representative of football in the present day? Tommy Smith claims only Carragher and Gerrard would have been good enough to play for the '60s team.

Carra smiles: "That's a compliment, really, because conditions were quite different in the '60s. The pitches were of a different quality and tackling was something else completely.

"I think good players today could have played in any era. I don't believe it when people say they couldn't have played now, I'm convinced they could. If the '60s lads had played today, they wouldn't drink so much, they'd have had better food, better coaches, masseurs, better doctors, better physiotherapists, sports scientists. All of this makes the game quicker now – but the human body is still the same as it was 20 or 30 years ago. It's just that we have better help off the pitch, making us run faster and last longer. I'm sure the old players would have done, too, given the same support network.

"I'm sure a good player could have played now, then, and in 20 years' time. And I'm sure the old players would have loved to play on today's pitches, which are just so much better!" He laughs again.

I have seen YouTube clips of "the good old days" and, on rainy days, Anfield and other grounds looked more like pigsties than football pitches. The thought of these mudholes brings Carragher back to his own childhood, playing Saturday and Sunday mornings. The way pitches have developed with the advancement of artificial grass; high-tech draining methods; heating cables; lighting and irrigation – all of this a welcome improvement.

However, it is not just technology on how to grow and maintain grass pitches through the winter that has developed lately. Technology is also used to compile the stats and analyse the game to improve the team. Sometimes after a TV match, I think: "When will the analysis stop? Should we not put this match behind us soon and look forward to the next?" Sometimes I feel football matches are analysed to death. But the defender does not support me in this view.

"I love information and the statistics, they help me see new things. Every manager does it his way. Rafa [Benitez] was very much into analysis and statistics, whereas Kenny [Dalglish] isn't. But it all comes down to winning. Whatever you do, if you win, it's declared the right method. And, whatever you do if you lose, it's wrong."

Nowadays, sports science gives you the answer to how far players run, how many sprints they have, and so on. That has changed the game, because now players in each position will have to run so much, or make so many sprints, to do well. If you start missing the targets, you may be in trouble, because the manager will know your current performance from the stats. These are important elements in football now.

When Dalglish said he was returning, some people were worried that he would lose his legendary status by not being able to adapt to the modern game. Has he taken on much of the new technology and analysing tools, or does he do things the way he used to?

"He does it his way," Carragher tells me. "And the modern stuff, what is it really? Some say sports science. However, the manager doesn't have to watch the fitness training or read the stats, he has someone who does that for him. He's the manager – his job is to manage the team, and Kenny does that fantastically well.

"I don't really think the manager's job has changed. Maybe there's a bigger squad now; maybe more people from different countries, maybe that changes it slightly. But you still have to pick 11 players, give them belief and bring out the best in them: man management. Other people do other jobs and together we make up the team you're seeing at the moment."

Carragher claims the two managers he played for before Dalglish – Rafa Benitez and Roy Hodgson – were more like coaches than managers. They liked being on the training ground and telling players what to do. He thinks Gerard Houllier was more similar to Dalglish: "Someone who comes to training, observes them and suggests one or two points, but leaves it to the others in the coaching team to carry out the training."

He underlines that there is no right or wrong way of doing it, as long as the team is successful.

It is no secret that Liverpool started doing better soon after Dalglish took over, even though they were exactly the same team to begin with. What did he add to the team to begin with? What is his secret?

Carragher thinks what is most refreshing about having the legendary

manager from the Boot Room period back is his fantastic ability to bring out the best in each and every person, as well as his good mood. He laughs and jokes with the players and makes them relax. Then he lets the support network deal with the more serious side of training.

"Kenny's like a father figure to everyone at the club. He knew a lot of the players beforehand through working at the Academy and as ambassador for the club. And, he is Kenny Dalglish. He has an aura about him. He's a Liverpool legend."

"I have a theory that everybody wants to be seen and acknowledged. Nobody really wants to be invisible. You say Kenny talks to everybody and is almost like a father to you all. What do you think this does for the players?"

"I think it's been very good for the players. If you look at some of them – their performance – they're playing really well under Kenny. The obvious effect is that he boosts confidence. They come to training every day now and enjoy themselves. I think that if you feel good and enjoy what you're doing, your achievements on the pitch will improve."

Carragher and Gerrard are the last high-profile players who are homegrown Liverpool talents. After many years at the club, they have reached the final phase of their professional careers. A lot of fans have scratched their heads, wondering when the next local hero will get a chance. This is also very close to Jamie's heart. He is overjoyed that Dalglish is trying out youngsters from the Academy in the first-team.

"It's great! We've had a few injuries and it's given them the chance. Kenny knows these players from the Academy. I've always believed that there are players there who were good enough. But, unless you give them a chance to show their abilities, you'll never know.

"If Jon Flanagan and Jack Robinson were never allowed to show what they can do, the fans wouldn't know if they were good enough for the team. They're here at Melwood now, thanks to Kenny – and thanks to themselves, too, because playing for Liverpool is not easy. People all around the world talk about you, especially on the internet. There are fans everywhere and they're very outspoken. So, it takes a lot to play for the team at that age. I'm so happy they're doing well and the rest of us must do anything we can to support them."

I have seen how Carragher has taken care of Flanagan during warm-ups before games and how he follows him closely and encourages him as they play. The young right-back has flourished and played with confidence. There is such a thing as youthful rashness – and maybe football should try taking better advantage of this boldness before it fades from the feet and minds of the young.

With decades at the club, and a total number of appearances only Ian Callaghan can better, I wonder what Carragher – as a person – has learned at Liverpool?

"The Liverpool way of doing things – always be humble, never boast too much about the club or myself. Never get above myself, but think about what's best for the team. That's what this club has always been about: team effort – and that includes the supporters, who are part of the team.

"If you want to do anything in life, and especially if you want to succeed on the football pitch, you have to work together, not on your own."

So, you need to think *team* before you think of yourself. But what other advice will he give his son, and others with a dream of becoming a professional footballer – in preparation for life at the top of English football?

"Try and enjoy it, really, because the youngsters at the Academy are very good and everybody there tells you how good you are. But there will come a time when it's not like that and people will criticise you. Maybe you'll get injured or you're not in the team. That's when you need balance.

"Never get too carried away, but realise there could be down periods around the corner. That's football – there are ups and downs, you'll need to pick yourself up. That's why my best advice is not to take off completely, not get too high or too low. Always just work to come back after a defeat.

"Now that I'm at the end of my career, it's easier for me to look back and realise the good things I've done and the mistakes I've made. I've never won the league and I would love to get that before I quit. It would have been a great way to finish."

Despite so many matches for the Reds, coming to training every day and working hard is still the most important thing for Carragher.

"For 20 years I've been doing the same, and the day I'm not doing this again will be really strange. I get in the car in the morning, I know where I'm going and I see the people you don't see on the outside of the club. We're only at Anfield every two weeks, but we're here at Melwood every day, that's why this place – and everybody I meet here 10 months a year – will be what I'll miss the most when I quit.

"The people who make the food; the receptionists; the people on the gate; the kit men – when I hang up my boots, I'm going to miss them most. Not the big events."

I must admit, I am slightly surprised by this. Certainly, the vice-captain holds the Istanbul victory very, very highly and he knows it is a match that most supporters consider their greatest Liverpool memory. Yet, it is the routines, the days of repeat, the days some might find dull and dreary, that he appreciates most.

I think that says something about the strong family ties of the club. Many of us longingly think back to where we grew up, to our childhood home. We want to visit, be nostalgic, feel the belonging, rest in familiarity and spend time with the people we love.

What is family life like for a big celebrity and dedicated footballer such as Carragher? How does he manage to make his wife, his kids and himself love this circus that constantly demands something from him?

"By winning matches," he smiles. "I can do this because I really only have football and family in my life. I don't go out a lot with my wife Nicola – there are too many people hunting for autographs, with camera phones and all that. There's not much chance to relax, so we stay at home or go to family parties.

"However, I do take the kids out; I take James to football training and Mia to dancing . I also take them to school and pick them up. I make sure I don't miss out on what the kids are doing – it's very important to me – but we don't have a lot of activity outside the family. We try to keep very private and do our own things at home."

"Phil Neal has told me his strong story," I tell him. "It was about not seeing how his wife, at home with two small children, was suffering from depression after they moved to Liverpool. She felt very alone. Neal says it's even harder for football wives today."

"Yes, I suppose it is. No matter where we go, my wife is aware that people are looking at her. They probably look at what she's wearing, what she looks like, and so she feels under pressure to look good, because people expect that of her.

"Sometimes she just wants to leave the house without make-up but feels that she can't, especially if she's with me, because of the pressure to look good. People look at her because she's a footballer's wife. As far as the kids are concerned, I don't think they really understand yet; they quite enjoy it when people say, *'Wow, is Jamie Carragher your dad?!'* Maybe it will change when they're older. However, at the moment, they seem to enjoy it."

In September 2010, Carragher had his testimonial at Anfield, the proceeds of which went towards his '23 Foundation', a charity he established at the start of 2009 which aims to help local kids. Philly Carragher and Mike Lepic run the foundation and they have daily requests from children from throughout the world for help. They donate signed shirts and photos as raffle prizes. On other occasions they have extended the running of a local school for two years.

Jamie spends a lot of time signing photos and shirts to children who are ill and need encouragement, while his father and Mike make sure they go where they are most needed. A lot of people who contact them wish to thank a hospital for saving someone's life or helping as best they could during periods of illness. As his own son's life was saved by hospital personnel, Philly's motivation and commitment to local society is strong.

With more than 20 years of service in the red shirt, there is no doubt about Carragher's strong loyalty to the club. This has made him incredibly popular with Liverpool fans throughout the world. How does the defender think club loyalty has changed from Tommy Smith's days 50 years ago to today?

"I think the game is massive now, there is much more public opinion from supporters and the press, from agents and managers. You have Sky Sports News and the internet, where everybody has an opinion about the club and players, whereas, previously, there were only a few to disagree with the choices made by a club or player.

"Now, people all over the world have their say. This creates enormous pressure when you make a career decision. Players are coming and going – but, hopefully, it won't be me," he chuckles.

"How did you feel when Fernando Torres left?"

"We were all really disappointed. I'm just thankful that the club had a plan because, at the time, he left, we didn't know. It was a shock. I thought he was going to wait until the end of the season, but Fernando will probably tell you at some point in the future that he really wanted to go the summer before, so…"

The club's press officer knocks on the door and politely asks us to round things off. Carragher continues where he left off: "Maybe it would have been better if he had left then, but, at the moment, we have to be pleased with Luis Suarez and Andy Carroll coming in. Fernando was a great player for Liverpool, you can't deny that. He did some great things, but we don't wish him too much luck at Chelsea… But, hopefully… I mean, after all, he's been a Liverpool player. We like our ex-players to do well when they move on. So, hopefully, he will do well, but not as well as Suarez and Carroll."

"Do you really want people who leave Liverpool to play for other English top teams to do well?"

"Well, I really don't want Fernando to do too well, as he went to one of our biggest rivals, Chelsea. But if a player goes to another league, we don't have a problem with them doing well. If they go to Chelsea, we don't want them to play too well, because it could affect us."

That's Jamie Carragher for you. As loyal to Liverpool as they come.

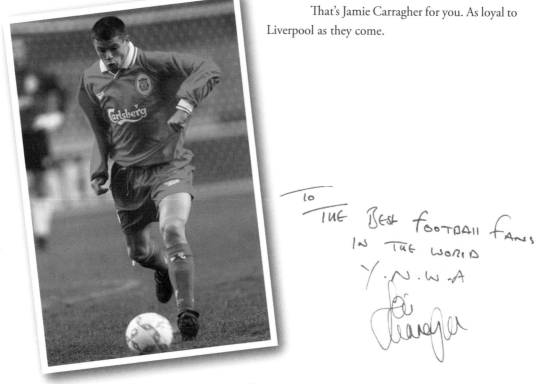

130

Liverpool FC Career: 1997- 🦅 *Appearances: 689* 🦅 *Goals: 5 (as of 3/3/2012)*

Ian Callaghan
Gentleman With A Capital G

"Ian playing all the way from the old second division to a European Cup final. That's some achievement. I am still trying to work out how he made 857 appearances!"

Jamie Carragher

There are no two ways about it: Englishmen are famous for their politeness and their tea. Phrases with *"please"*, peppering their surroundings with *"sorry"*, *"excuse me"* and *"pardon?"*. Every time you talk to them, they cannot thank you enough, whether it be in an email or in person.

That is not the way in the country I come from. We do not exhaust courtesy in word or deed in Norway. Do not get me wrong, Norwegians are friendly people. We are considerate and warm in our own way and, if you make friends with a Norwegian, you have got a friend for life. We are just not that nice in public, among strangers.

I remember I was getting off a bus with my two kids, a kids' bike, a pram and only two arms. But here was an almost chock-full bus of people, none of whom lifted a finger to help. I wondered if they actually found my battle to get out the door amusing, as they all sat there in their seats without considering lending me a helping hand.

I can say one thing with a 100 per cent certainty: if Ian Callaghan had been on that bus, even if he was in the back row, I would not have had to struggle off it without help. He would have rushed to my rescue.

I can almost picture his full head of white hair, shuffling quickly down the aisle, smiling his characteristic smile with that charming gap between his front teeth and his friendly face. He would have gallantly taken the pram by the handle and wheeled my daughter – who has an identical smile to him – safely out. His smile is one of the most beautiful in English football – the Cally smile.

Or, he would have taken my son Elias by the hand, lifted his black bike in the other and put them both safely on the pavement, nodding at me with a smile and wishing us a good day going back on board after making sure we were all safely off the bus. He might even have treated us to a chivalrous bow and a kiss on the cheek.

I had been looking forward to meeting Ian Robert Callaghan. No matter who I had

133

mentioned him to, I had been told the same thing – he is the nicest man you will ever meet, he is a true gentleman. So, I was not nervous when I welcomed him to the open-plan office floor at Sport Media, the publishers of my book. Chief editor Ken Rogers – who knows Callaghan from way back – introduced us.

I was surprised at how small Callaghan was. Everyone had described him as a monumental fellow. No one had mentioned that he was not a midfield giant by stature, but by his skills.

Nobody has played more games for Liverpool than Callaghan – a staggering 857 matches. The longer he was at Liverpool, the more he was referred to as 'marathon man', 'grandad' and 'evergreen'. On top of this, he went on to play for a couple of other teams after the Reds and ended up with nearly 1,000 games in his career, never picking up a single red card. He didn't get many yellow cards, either.

"How is it possible to play so many games and only be booked *once* by the referee?"

"To be honest, I'm not sure. The game has changed a lot since then, I'd probably have had more yellow cards today," he says, humbly. "The game is quicker now. The ball is lighter and zips around at a higher speed, so players have more contact with each other, also because the pitches are better.

"Just look at Anfield. The field is just as good at the end of the season as at the beginning. It wasn't like that when I played. We'd play on muddy pitches. Science hadn't designed these great pitches back then, so I'm sure I'd have gotten a few more yellow cards today. I was lucky, quite simply."

Not everyone would agree with Callaghan that it is easier to get yellow cards on a better pitch. However, regardless, the irony of it all is that the one time he did get booked, he should not have been.

It was a replay in the 1978 League Cup final between Liverpool and Nottingham Forest. They had played at Wembley on the Saturday and drawn 0-0, so the replay was at Old Trafford. Early in the second half, with the score at 0-0, referee Pat Partridge awarded Forest a penalty after Phil Thompson had tackled John O'Hare.

"The tackle was outside the area," Callaghan recalls. "But he fell inside it and they got a penalty."

John Robertson took it. The ball grazed Ray Clemence's fingertips, but he couldn't keep it out and Forest were 1-0 up. That's how it finished, denying Liverpool a first League Cup success and Callaghan the only medal missing from his collection. Instead, he finished the match – his last but one in a Liverpool shirt – in the referee's notebook.

The ball bounced between Callaghan and Peter Withe, a much taller Liverpool lad, who played for the opposition. The pair of them went up for the header and Callaghan hit Withe's rib with his shoulder. Withe went to ground. Partridge came over and booked Cally, to massive protests.

"It got a little nasty out there. We didn't agree with the penalty and a few challenges went in. As for the yellow card, even Peter said it wasn't a bookable offence. The club tried to get it annulled, but to no avail. It has become a talking point about my career – 857 games and one booking."

However, Ian has a little secret – it wasn't his first booking in a Liverpool shirt. During a friendly against Borussia Dortmund in Germany three years before that replay, he picked up a card. However, with it being a friendly, it was never recorded and has, hence, been forgotten about. Until now!

All the Liverpool legends I have spoken to describe Callaghan as a gentleman both on and off the pitch. So, I asked him if he thought that he should play like a gentleman, or was it simply in his nature?

"No, no! I didn't think about it at all! But I don't think that me *not* playing ugly took anything away from my game."

"You must have had great respect for your opponents?"

"I think everybody does. There aren't many players out there who deliberately try and injure you. I just got on with the game and never thought about being a gentleman or whether I'd be booked."

"Are you a gentleman at home, too?"

"You're formed very early through your parents. If I'm a gentleman, I think that's fine and that would be down to my parents and the way they brought me up. Besides, the big man himself – Mr Shankly – must get some of the credit. I spent a lot of time with him. He had a lot to do with the way I was brought up."

"Are you a door opener?"

"Oh, yes. I'd stand up on a train if a lady needs the seat. But I think that comes naturally to people."

"Not to everybody, it doesn't."

"Well it's natural to me. It's the way I was brought up."

Born in Toxteth, Callaghan grew up with his younger brother Philip, who never had any interest in the game at a time when the city of Liverpool was making its mark as an exporter of world-class football as well as popular music.

"Liverpool was unique in those days," Callaghan says. "28,000 people came to the Kop and the noise and singing was intense. Liverpool were on the up under Shanks and our music was hugely popular. The Beatles took the world by storm and many other bands from Merseyside followed, like Gerry and the Pacemakers. With the football and the music, it was just fantastic to be a part of that era."

"The rise of Liverpool?"

"It was! Football took off. LFC were in the Second Division in the 1950s. Then, this great man arrived at the club and changed everything. I was so fortunate to be at Liverpool at that time."

It was the unbelievable atmosphere that stands out in Ian's mind when he thinks back to watching Liverpool at Anfield. The legendary Billy Liddell was playing then and every time he was on the ball, the sense of anticipation on the Kop was palpable. Just as he was for so many other Scouse kids, Liddell was a hero for Callaghan and football became a huge part of his childhood.

Callaghan played for Liverpool schoolboys and was offered the chance to sign for either Everton or Liverpool. He immediately chose the red shirt – and, remember, this was before Bill Shankly took charge.

At the time, the team was in the Second Division and going nowhere fast, but Ian wanted to play for Liverpool. The reason was simple – the atmosphere at Anfield. He chose them despite his father being an Evertonian, though he never went to games at Goodison Park. Ian went against his father's Blue heart by signing for Liverpool. It turned out to be the best thing he ever did.

He left school at 15, got work as an apprentice and signed an amateur contract with Liverpool. He worked in the city centre and twice a week he would jump on the bus after work and go training at Melwood. Every Saturday he played for the juniors on the A, B or C team. Only when Shankly replaced Phil Taylor in 1959 was he offered a professional contract.

Callaghan was serving his time to be an engineer at this stage. It was a good job, so he asked Shankly to talk to his parents about his offer. One day, a huge, dark Ford Corsair turned up outside the block of flats where the Callaghans lived in Caryl Gardens, Toxteth.

It caused a commotion. There were not that many cars around in the 1950s, especially not in the working class areas. You took the bus if you were going somewhere.

The kids around the neighbourhood quickly realised who it was and were soon shouting: *"Bill Shankly's at Ian Callaghan's house!"*

The Callaghans took to him instantly – the incredibly charismatic Shankly was sat in their house, impeccably dressed in a suit.

"I was only small, so Bill Shankly promised my parents he'd look after me and give me plenty to eat."

It's fair to say engineering took a back seat after that meeting.

Cars were a rarity at the beginning of the 1960s, too, so when Callaghan was going to his debut against Bristol Rovers six weeks after signing professionally, he had to take the bus to Anfield. It was a 45-minute ride. He got to the bus stop at 1pm and needed to be at Anfield at 2pm to be ready for kick-off at three o'clock.

The queue of people going to the match was unbelievable, something he had not thought of. There was a long wait. Would he get there in time at all?

However, when he arrived at the stop there was a stir.

"Look! It's Ian Callaghan, he's going to make his debut for Liverpool today!"

Ian was pushed to the front of the queue and made it in time. He played the game and was involved in three of Liverpool's four goals in a 4-0 win, earning him applause on the Kop. He took the bus back home afterwards.

When Callaghan was put in the team at outside right, he took over from his idol – and Anfield's biggest hero – Billy Liddell, whose shots were so hard he once fractured the hand of goalkeeper Rolando Ugolini in a penalty incident, and in the '50s fans would turn up just to see him play. Instantly, I think that it must have been some pressure for a young kid?

The Scotsman's shots were so fierce he once fractured the arm of Nottingham Forest goalkeeper Harry Nicholson and, in the 1950s, fans would turn up just to see Liddell play. Instantly, I think that it must have been some pressure for a young kid.

"Billy was at the end of his career and I don't think, at 17, I fully understood what was happening. Only some time afterwards, when people said to me, *'God, you took Billy Liddell's place,'* did I realise. I was young and ready to get started."

"Could it have been a strength, that you were young and did not think so much about keeping the nerves at bay?"

"Yes, I believe it was, actually. I got a fantastic start in my first game, so I must have done something right mentally.

Callaghan got a standing ovation when he left the pitch after his debut, although it was 1961/62 before he became an established first-team player. He stayed in the team until 1978.

The '61/62 campaign was Liverpool's promotion season. With Callaghan in the team, Shankly and his men succeeded in returning to the First Division. Today, a lot of people believe that much of the recipe for success in football is in the ability to analyse the game down to the last detail: angles; percentages; length of runs; length of shots, and all the rest. But what were match preparations and match analysis like in Shankly's era?

"He always sent someone off to watch the opposition and we had a players' meeting on Fridays. However, he was more interested in how Liverpool were going to play.

"Let's say, for instance, that we were playing Manchester United, who had Denis Law, George Best and Bobby Charlton, all exceptional players. He'd talk us through how each of them played, especially if we were meeting them at home. Then, he told us how they were planning to stop us.

"When we went to Old Trafford, we knew they played terrific football and that we had to watch out for those three. So, in the Friday meeting, we'd go through how we'd cope with them.

"He was always very thorough in these meetings. He had back-up in Bob Paisley, Joe Fagan, Reuben Bennett and Ronnie Moran at the same time. They were people he listened to and had confidence in."

"After matches – did you go through it?"

"No, very rarely. He'd come into the dressing room and, if he wasn't very happy, he'd talk things through with individual players or all of us as a group. We played Saturdays, so, usually, we wouldn't be back until the Tuesday. Then he'd talk about the game. It's very different from today, where they go through videos and everything."

"Was it more personal, one-to-one feedback before?"

"Yes, I believe so."

"Was there a lot of yelling and screaming if Shankly wasn't happy?"

Callaghan laughs: "No, there wasn't a lot of yelling and screaming. It was mostly one-on-one. He was honest with us with what he meant and he had no problems getting it through to us.

"He was one of the best, if not *the* best motivator for any player. He made us go out on the pitch on Saturdays as world champions giving it our all. That's what he expected from us – that we gave a 100 per cent and were honest."

And sometimes he spied on the lads on away trips!

"He'd let us go out for a beer, as long as we didn't abuse it. But he knew how to handle people. He was very good at reading us. He could have prepared something for Wednesday, but have changed the whole routine when he noticed that one of his staff or players was jaded after a match and travelling. Maybe we'd just have a little five-a-side, or he'd even just send us to the steam baths.

"He brought something to Liverpool that I didn't know at first. Players who'd been there before him said how much he changed the training. He did everything with the ball; the players weren't used to that. Until then, it had been all sorts of running, etc. He changed everything."

Before matches, Shankly walked restlessly in and out of the dressing room, or to the sink to fill his plastic cup. He would be constantly sipping water from a plastic cup and would wear his nerves on his sleeve. At other times, he'd wander about with his hands in his coat pockets, stop in front of the mirror, comb his hair and look at himself.

In addition, he tested many of his one-liners on Liverpool trainer Albert Shelley, checking his reaction before he used them on his players or the media.

"Shanks was ahead of his time," says Callaghan. "We were fortunate he chose us. Certainly, the Liverpool fans, if you ask them today, they'll say there will never be a manager like him again. They just adored him. Even the Evertonians did, which is very rare!

"He had this charisma, he was extrovert, he had his way of talking to the fans. There will never be anybody like him."

"When you talk about him, he almost sounds like a second father to you?"

"That's one way of looking at it. I was young and spent a lot of time away from home; he was the boss I set my life after. For 14 years, Shankly held me under his wing and shaped big parts of my life. So, yes, he was like a second dad to me."

"I just have to read out some of the things he said about you, it's so wonderful: *He is a model professional and a model human being. If there were 11 Callaghans at Anfield there would never be any need to put up a team sheet. He typifies everything that is good in football and he has never changed. You could stake your life on Ian.*"

Powerful words, Ian!

Callaghan is looking for words. His eyes are almost welling up.

"God, I don't know." He takes a deep breath. "Our relationship was very special. I think it all boils down to that day when Shankly visited my mum and dad and promised them to take good care of me. He saw my background and obviously liked me as a person.

"Even today, I talk about our special relationship and how there will never be anybody like Shankly again. I was lucky and had 14 years with him – and I can honestly say I never had a cross word with him. I never asked him for a rise, but he gave it to me anyway.

"He kept his promise to my parents. Shankly formed a lot of my life – how to handle yourself, your attitude to things, respect for other people. He has been the greatest man ever for me."

The summer of 1974. The season had finished with Liverpool winning the FA Cup at Wembley by beating Newcastle 3-0 and Callaghan was taking time off with his family. Along with his wife Linda, a former Miss Liverpool, and their two girls, they were going to the Lakes. They had just put the bags in the car and were closing the door when the phone rang.

"Leave it, we're on our way," Linda said.

"Nah, you never know who it is. It only takes a couple of minutes," her husband replied.

Callaghan went in and answered the call. A journalist called Michael Charters, who worked at the Liverpool Echo, was on the other end.

"Ian, have you heard the news?"

"No, what?"

"Bill Shankly has resigned."

"I can't believe that!"

Callaghan could not understand, so they got in the car and drove off. However, over the course of that weekend, scores of people came up to him, as he was a very recognisable Liverpool player, to ask him about it.

"Everybody asked me why Bill Shankly had retired and I had no idea. I still don't know, only that he must have been tired and had had enough.

"Shankly had few interests outside of football, so I think he half-expected to be made director of the club. That didn't happen. It was sad, really, because football was his life. It was like a drug to him."

Bob Paisley, who had been Shankly's assistant, reluctantly took over, and Ian played for a further four seasons under him.

"Bob was a nice, quiet man and terrific to me as I approached the end of my Liverpool career. He let me go to America, in 1978, and play for five months at Fort Lauderdale, so my family could experience America.

"He allowed me go to Swansea, too, even though he didn't really want me to go there. He'd rather have me play in the reserves and be the old head helping the youngsters through. However, John Toshack had gone to Swansea as a manager and Tommy Smith had signed for Swansea, too. Still, Tommy and I were allowed to train every day at Liverpool with the lads despite being Swansea players, as though we'd never left. Then, we went down to

Swansea on Thursdays and played Saturdays. That says a lot about what he thought of us as players."

"That would never have happened today!"

"No, I don't think so, either. No, when you sign for somebody else, you get your boots and you're on your way."

When comparing modern football to the game in Callaghan's time, loyalty is one topic that comes up automatically. He is probably the most loyal player I have ever met – and am ever likely to meet.

"Did you think a lot about loyalty while playing or was it just there?"

"It just came. I was brought up to respect my parents. They brought me up the right way and, when I signed for Bill Shankly, he carried that on.

"I was fortunate, in the sense, that there wasn't a big squad with lots of subs to begin with. We often played two games a week and we were often on the road. It was fantastic. Loyalty probably came because we didn't have to experience going in and out of the team.

The only time I was out of the team was when I got injured. It was this way right through my career, until the end of my time with Bob, and then I knew it would be over soon."

"I appreciated what Liverpool Football Club did for me. I just loved my time at the club. I used to pinch myself getting into my car and driving to Anfield. The training sessions, the travelling, the matches – all were great for this fantastic club.

"I was a Liverpool lad and had followed the team since before I signed for them. Being a part of the trip from Second Division to the First was brilliant. To win the top league, the FA Cup final for the first time in 1965, the European Cup for the first time in 1977 and be on the bench in 1978 when we won the European Cup again, at Wembley, was fantastic.

"That '78 final was the end of my service for Liverpool. I made good money and got to travel all over Europe. What a fantastic life I've had."

Callaghan remains closely associated with the club now, as host at Anfield on match-days, and has been secretary and chairman of the Former Players' Association. Liverpool have been a very big part of his life, but was there never anything he missed as a player that made him want to move on?

"No, I never even thought about moving on. If you were a regular in the team, nobody approached you with a contract. And there was no speculation in the press. But players who were out of the team, or back and forth, sometimes moved on. I never had a period where I was unsettled at Anfield, so, I just loved all my years with Liverpool Football Club."

"I've never thought about it like this before, but do you see loyalty as the club also being loyal to you?"

"Exactly. The club and the two managers were incredibly loyal to me. Plus, they had an amazing staff in Joe Fagan, Ronnie Moran and Reuben Bennett. They all had jobs to do, contributing to making this club great – not to mention Roy Evans, who could have continued his playing career for a different club, but who retired as a footballer and became part of the staff, and finally manager. It's one of those clubs you never think about leaving.

"It really has been magical to me, still is. Being a local lad probably makes this magic stronger, a magic that lives on in admiration for those who carry the club now. Look at Stevie Gerrard, one of the best players in the world. And, if you ask me, he's probably Liverpool's best ever player."

"You rate him higher than Dalglish?"

"Yes, I do. It's a personal thing, and Stevie plays in a different era, where the pressure on footballers – especially profiles like him – is enormous. Yet, he handles himself fantastically, captains the club, and I think he's a very, very special player."

"Kenny played in a better side than Steven..."

"Yes, and Kenny was an exceptional player as well. People feel differently about this.

Some people would say Kenny is the all-time greatest. Others say Keegan. In my case, it's Stevie G.

"Players like him come along very rarely. He has the skills to do anything as a footballer – and he has done, too. No one player has turned games around in the way Stevie has.

"He could have left the club. He could have walked into any team in the world – and there was talk of him going to Chelsea. It never happened. Even at his age now, the top clubs would still want him. He'll finish his career here. And certainly Jamie [Carragher] will. They're both loyal Liverpool lads and, if you ask me, they've been the two best players in the last 10 years."

Callaghan loved training and the feeling of unity at LFC. At the end of his career, a lot of people said he would miss it, having been at the club such a long time. They were right. Even now, after all these years, he still misses the daily routine and the camaraderie.

"I had been part of a group and had travelled all over Europe. I missed that a lot. So, it wasn't Tuesday nights and Saturday matches that I missed most, but working days."

"You were there for a long time – what was it like saying goodbye to a lot of your friends, who quit before you, and building new relationships again?"

"There are always comings and goings in football, new signings who didn't make it and were moved on. I never really thought about it much. Players came in and adapted to our routines and our system of play. We all got on well, so, obviously, it was sometimes sad to say goodbye. Some became closer friends than others.

"Luckily, most of my close friends were outside of football. Once I had left training, or was back from a match, I had my own circle of friends. It was a different life than football, even though I never escaped the role as Liverpool player."

"Do you think having so many friends outside football made you last longer as a player?"

"Yes. I believe that may have been the case. We had our life with friends and family outside football. I definitely think that helped me. Our friends wanted to talk a little about football, of course, but my wife wasn't interested. She usually didn't go to matches, but went with us to some of the big games, home and away. It was actually quite useful that she wasn't so interested because when I was home I could think about other things, too.

"However, it was very difficult forgetting football entirely. The doorbell would ring and people came asking for an autograph. When I went to school with my girls, people wanted to talk football. If I went to the shop, the butcher wanted to talk football, so I couldn't get away.

"It helps having a family when you're a professional footballer. You have a base, other people in your life, and, at the same time, I was involved in their lives – my wife's cookery classes, the kids' school and leisure activities. A normal life."

"When I look at the number of matches you've played, I don't think anybody will ever beat your record for Liverpool."

"I don't know, never say never. Records are there to be broken and I've said this on numerous occasions: Jamie Carragher has the second most games now. If anybody did break the record, I would love it to be Jamie. A fantastic player, great ambassador for the game, local lad and lovely guy."

Love of the game, the routines and his team-mates were the key to Callaghan's marathon career. The players tried to eat well but did not have the scientific methods nor the knowledge of training or diet the players of today have. They lived their life freely outside of football, too: Callaghan used to like going for a pint with the lads on Sundays and they usually had a few beers after matches, but all within the rulebook. They led normal lives and did not think about lifestyle as much as players do now. The former winger believes they possibly think too much about this today.

"No matter how much science you put into a player, if he's not a good player, a diet won't make him one," he says. "Lads like Jamie or Stevie G won't be better players because they're more fit. Yes, they'd probably improve a little, but I think players are born that way. Stevie G was born to be a good player, just like I probably was. It becomes evident at such a young age.

"I played for the school under-10s before I was 10, and something about me got me trials for Liverpool Schoolboys already at 14. Then, you had to take it to another level. Shankly saw something in me, brought me to a new level and persuaded my parents. He must have told them what he saw in me. He must have seen I could make it as a professional footballer. And he was right!"

We laugh.

With a professional career as long as that of Callaghan – he had 18 seasons at Liverpool and left at the start of his 19th – it is not easy to pick his best memories. However, he settles on two.

"When you do something for the first time for this fantastic club, it's extra special. You make history for the club and for yourself. So, apart from my debut, winning the FA Cup for the first time in 1965 is my strongest memory. We had never won it before and it was my first time playing at Wembley. I managed to cross the ball for Ian St John to score the winner against our great rivals Leeds United.

"We won 2-1 after extra time and early on in the game Gerry Byrne broke his collarbone. We had no substitutes, so Gerry played three-quarters of the game plus extra time with a broken collarbone!

"I recently saw the match again when I was doing a job for LFC TV. Playing with a broken collarbone for that amount of time... he even crossed the ball for the first goal! It was simply one of the greatest feats in football. Later, with his arm in a sling, I had to help him put on his blazer before we left Wembley to celebrate."

Then there is 1977, when – 17 years after his first-team debut – Callaghan was a sub when Liverpool played Manchester United in the FA Cup final at Wembley. Ian came on for the last 26 minutes. However, Liverpool were beaten 2-1, ending dreams of winning an unprecedented treble with the league title already in the Anfield trophy cabinet.

In training the following Monday, Bob Paisley suddenly ran beside him. It was the day before the team were going to Rome to meet Borussia Mönchengladbach in the prestigious European Cup final – Liverpool's first.

"Do you want to play on Wednesday?" asked the manager.

"Of course I want to play!"

"Well, you're playing."

Then, he was off.

Not that long ago, Tommy Smith told Callaghan that Paisley had confided in him that he regretted not playing Callaghan from the start in the FA Cup final the previous weekend. Paisley felt he had made a mistake. He never told Callaghan, but admitted it to Smith. Callaghan believes that is why he got a chance in Rome.

He remembers the hotel in Rome and what it was like getting to the match. What stands out in his mind is the sight going to the stadium and when they got onto the pitch, seeing the amount of Liverpool supporters who had travelled over. A lot of them had been to Wembley the Saturday before and were hugely disappointed. Still, they had gone to Rome by any means possible only a few days later.

"Winning the European Cup for the fans was fantastic, it really was. It was one of the most fantastic occasions in my career, being in the team that won the European Cup for the first time for Liverpool.

"We've won it five times now, but the first time is always very, very special. We made history for both the club and ourselves. I feel very privileged to have played for Liverpool, but especially privileged to have been on the pitch that night."

Callaghan looks at the time. It turns out he should have been at a lunch date quite a while ago. He was probably too polite to tell me. Time flies in the company of a true gentleman.

The Greatest Football Fans In world – It was my pleasure to have played for them

Ian Callaghan

Liverpool FC Career: 1960-1978 🦅 *Appearances: 857* 🦅 *Goals: 68*

10

Bruce Grobbelaar
Warrior And Clown

"We always get together and he has a few laughs and jokes with everybody. And everybody loves him. Bruce has a great reputation in the game of football."

Alan Kennedy

The vehicle in front of you hits a landmine and three, four bodies blow out the side of it, right before your eyes. It could have been you. Friends of yours going through swift position after an air attack. Three or four metres ahead of you, a friend is shot. Not you. A helicopter dives towards the ground, trying to pick you up while others are shooting at you. The guy next to you is shot through the leg with a machine gun. It could have been you. There are so many things that could have happened to you, but didn't...

Bruce Grobbelaar pauses for breath before telling me one of his scariest experiences, when he was 17, a member of the Rhodesian army and in a far, foreign land. More precisely, Mozambique.

He was told he would have to make his own way back after an ambush. He heard over the radio that the enemy was on its way, so he was abandoned with just three other men. The border was 25km away. It was always about getting out of trouble. His four-man unit ran towards the border, but they would never have made it there in time. Finally, they managed to contact a helicopter, shouting *"CasEvac,"* into the radio. It meant somebody was shot and they needed an escape.

The helicopter technician was his cousin. Thank God for family in the air force, and thank God the helicopter came and picked them up. Their lives were saved, once again, when he thought it was all over.

149

September 11, 2010. Bruce David Grobbelaar is balancing on a straight chair on the first floor of a restaurant, mimicking his own spaghetti movements from Rome. The ones that psyched out the big Italian stars on their own home ground in the European Cup final in 1984. Earlier that day, he had added charm and glamour to my book signing in a little bookshop on the south coast of Norway. They had been very optimistic and ordered a lot of books, but now they were all sold out.

At the turn of midnight, it was my birthday, and Grobbelaar had somehow found this

out. He gave me a musical card from himself and the girls – his wife Karen and their little daughter Rotem, who were at their home in Corner Brook, Newfoundland. He had also been gift shopping, and surprised me with a lovely brown leather card holder. Sparkling birthday drinks were served by the driving force at Marna Cafe – Thomas – and the walls resounded with birthday songs.

I enjoy my birthday. And I like having my friends around me to celebrate. It is not primarily the attention, but having so many people I care about around. This year, I had to work as it was the book launch tour. But, as we say at Liverpool, *You'll Never Walk Alone.*

The next day was reunion time. Grobbelaar and I were going to guest TV2's Premier League show in Bergen. I had not been back there since my debut as a TV journalist almost 15 years earlier. The former Liverpool keeper had worked with the famous TV host Davy Wathne during the summer's World Cup in South Africa and now he had been hired as a 'stunt reporter' for the Norwegian TV channel.

It felt strange going into TV2's headquarter again. Much had changed since TV2 was a brand new channel and I was a young, insecure wannabe journalist and I was one of the first girls in the channel's sports division. These days, the girls are leading the show, where the witty Wathne once gained his reputation.

We were taken through make-up, and when I got there the stylist was delighted: "Yay! Finally – my first girl for the Premier League studio. Hurrah!"

While Grobbelaar and I were in the make-up room, Wathne came in and greeted us heartily. Going into the production studio, there were more familiar and friendly faces – colleagues from my one year as a not-quite star reporter. We smiled and hugged each other. They used to be editors, video-mixers and journalists; now they make up a highly professional production team for high-speed live broadcasts with a variety of elements. It is fascinating to watch them work. You definitely cannot be too sensitive, or scared of tempo, if you want to work in TV.

After my bit in the studio, Grobbelaar was up and I watched the match and comments from the production studio. I have great respect for the people who cover live football rounds, like Soccer Saturday on Sky Sports. This is advanced multitasking, all the matches running parallel and all the graphics, replays and snippets of analysis ready for whenever they need to cut back to the studio.

Grobbelaar, with arms longer than most, was born in Durban, South Africa, and moved with his parents to Rhodesia when he was only two months old.

Dad Hendrik Gabriel Grobbelaar played baseball and football. He was a goalkeeper. His mother, Beryl Eunice, was a hockey keeper, so their son was born to be a goalie. Mum would bring her kids along when she played hockey. The girls on the sidelines took care of his sister. Since Bruce was a boy, he was tied between two poles at the back of the goal. He could only run three metres back and forth, so most of the time he would sit and study his parents in front of the goal.

Little did he know that one day he would be running for his life through the forest as a soldier, and see such cruelty that he would never forget. He also could not know that the time spent observing his parents' goalkeeping skills would help make him one of the most famous people to ever stand between the sticks for Liverpool.

During his childhood in Rhodesia, now Zimbabwe, he would try everything. It earned him a place in the national team in three different sports at a young age.

His dad worked on the railways and his mother was a bookkeeper in a shoe shop. Every weekend, the three children would follow their parents and watch them play matches. Afterwards, they would go to a bar, but kids were not allowed in. So, they brought their swimming trunks and played in the pool outside while they waited.

Suddenly, one day, his father left. Grobbelaar was 10, his baby brother two and his sister 12 years old.

"My father decided he wanted a new life, and he left us," he recalls. "My mother had to look after us and support us all by herself. So, we always lived in a flat with no room to play. I used to go down to my old school and kick a ball about there. We were typical boys, always looking for a goal to play football, and, if there wasn't one, we put up two rocks and make one. I was often the goalie, because I loved diving after the ball."

Grobbelaar lived in the so-called avenues and nothing much happened. When he was 13, he ran away to live with his father, who had settled in a little farming community 200km away. Bruce jumped in an African taxi and arrived there at four in the morning. He was not in bed until six o'clock – his dad had been furious and had taken his belt and given him a proper hiding, telling him never to do something like that to his mother ever again.

His father still worked on the railways, he worked hard and had a new wife and new children.

"What was it like seeing him again after such a long time?"

"It was okay. I knew my father. He had been a good sportsman, but, unfortunately, had lost a leg to gangrene." He ponders on this for a moment, then sighs: "Yeah, he was my father. You've got to keep strong bonds with your father. That's what I tried to do."

He ended up staying there for three months before returning by train to his mother, who met him at the station.

"Mum was the backbone of our family. She kept us together and sane. We could have gone off the rails otherwise and done stupid things like a lot of kids in the avenues. If you lived in the avenues and you didn't have much, stealing and doing drugs were quite common. Luckily, I didn't go down that track. We led normal lives and I only ever wanted to go to the sports clubs."

Sport took him. Bruce played for Rhodesia's national cricket team at Under-13s, Under-14s and Under-15s level. He was also in the national team in baseball for Under-13s, Under-14s, Under-15s and even at senior level before he turned 15. He was that annoying kid in your class who could play any ball game better than everyone else. He was eventually offered a baseball scholarship in the United States of America, but that was after he had left the army and had long decided he would not go back to school.

It was going to be football for Grobbelaar, the all-round jester from Zimbabwe. And it was really all down to chance.

At 14 years of age, he was playing with a couple of mates at his old junior school. Bruce was in goal as they played a game in the penalty area. Nobody noticed the car that was parked by the road behind the goal. They played for 30 minutes and then took a break to get some water. When they started again, a man came up to them along the length of the pitch, wearing black trousers and a white shirt. He turned out to be Dave Russell, the Scotsman who coached Salisbury Callies Under-14s. They were the only white professional team in a black league, the league at the highest level in Rhodesia. Back then, Grobbelaar was goalkeeper for Raylton, a team in the white league. Now he had to choose between the white league and the black, and he picked the top black league. It was a much better standard, largely because there were more players to choose from.

Russell wanted to sign the kid who was diving so energetically after the ball in the junior school ground goal. But, to begin with, Grobbelaar's mother would not let him sign the contract. Only when the club promised to pay the affiliation fee and travel expenses to matches plus two dollars for every victory and one dollar for a draw, did she agree. Back then, that was quite a lot of money for a 14-year-old who would cycle 5km to training and 5km back – making him pretty fit.

He started in the Under-16s team but made his senior debut at the age of 14 years and 11 months.

"We lost 3-1. Not a good start, but it didn't scare me."

Salisbury Callies were a Scottish team with all-white players, playing in the black league. They were the only white team there and they played to get a bigger audience and greater publicity. They had played in the white league previously, but had won everything, so wanted a bigger challenge.

Grobbelaar went into the black townships with his new team. For a 14-year-old boy it was a big experience to go into the townships and play in front of 30,000 people.

"Did you see a lot of racial issues at the time?"

"Yes, very much so. This was the start of the Bush War. It started when a car was stopped on a farm and the farmer and his wife were murdered. We knew there were a lot of problems on the farms, but we thought it was mainly in the rural areas. There was racial tension everywhere. That's why there were always extra police when we played the black teams. And even when we played the coloured teams – the half black, half white teams – there were big racial problems.

"It was the same all over the country. You noticed different feelings and attitudes in the various tribes. As whites, we had to learn about what they went through. As a 14-year-old, I learned a lot about how Africans think and how their emotions worked. We learned to speak their languages and we learned not to be so confrontational.

"The football matches would break down barriers between people. The matches stopped the confrontational tension and racial issues... unless we, the white team, won. Then, we needed a police escort out of the townships.

"I got valuable insight into the various tribes and cultures. You knew where in the

country they were okay and loyal to each other and their employers (the farmers) and where they weren't. So, when I was in the military and was sent out to protect the farms and we got into conflicts, this was useful knowledge. In between it all, we would go into town to play football and then back into the military again. It made me grow up a lot quicker than a normal teenager."

Grobbelaar quit school and joined the army. He fought in the Bush War, an uprising against the big farmers. In the military he was sent to watch farms out in the bush. When talking about the most horrid experiences he had, he talks quickly and in a monotonous voice, as he does about that time he was rescued at the 11th hour in Mozambique.

"That time, all four in my stick survived. During my two years, I lost two people." He pauses. "Not bad. I was their stick leader, corporal, and I lost two guys. But the new guy was never as good as the old one – he had to be trained."

They were always in groups of four soldiers, so they could be picked up by a helicopter if they got into real trouble. In 1976, they were in the small Katia Tea Estates in Honde Valley. They were two on either side of the road, eating a little, before going into ambush position.

"I told them, 'Not long now, lads!' I had only signed for a year, and I told them that one day I was going to play for Liverpool FC. They said, 'Yeah, right', and laughed, 'We're going into ambush tonight – you could get shot!'"

At first, he had chosen Derby County as his dream club – but then found out they did not play baseball after all. That was just the name of their ground! When he first saw the Liver bird he thought it was a funny looking bird, so he chose Liverpool as his favourite team in England. All because of that red bird! He laughs thinking about this.

At the end of 1976, he only had 32 days left of his military service, but the government assigned another six months' service and, later, yet another six months. He ended up serving in the army for two years, despite only signing up for one.

"What has the war done to you as a team player?"

"As a goalkeeper, I felt I was in a unique position. The area around my goal belonged to me, just like I felt about my stick and the areas we protected during the war. As a squad leader, I had to look after my team in the same way I felt I was taking care of the defence. If someone did something wrong, you told them. If they did something right, you encouraged them. It was just like during the war."

Grobbelaar learned a lot about team-building during his time in the army, which came in very useful on the pitch. I say to him this must be rare in English football today, coming from such a background. However, the goalkeeper disagrees.

"I bet there are people with war backgrounds here today, too, who have been involved in war one way or another. Some probably went through the Bosnia crisis and, with the number of international players, I'm sure quite a few lived in countries with hostile neighbours, in South America and in Africa. There are players who are in danger of being kidnapped when they go back to their home countries because of their high profile and because the rebels might want something from the government. It happens. Like when Togo's national side was shot at in Africa for driving through Angola."

The Bush War intensified. So, as quickly as he could, Grobbelaar went to South Africa to get out of the country.

"When I came out of the military I thanked God and everybody that I came out unscathed. The only thing that wasn't quite sound was my mind...

"We went into a lot of places without a passport. We saw shocking things, which is normal in war. When you come out, you thank your lucky stars that you're alive. You must love every day like it's your last. That's probably the attitude I had in my early career."

I wonder if that is why he brings joy, fun and buffoonery wherever he goes. At a pub in Florø, Norway, he stood with his forehead against the wall, while pressing his left-hand fingertips against the floor and stretching his right hand towards the ceiling, to measure the distance between them, and then he asked me to do the same. Afterwards, he told me this distance is the same as your height. He tested his fun fact theory on me, and it was correct. It was correct for my husband, too, but not for himself. He took a sip of beer, planted it on the counter, then proved the length of his arms was longer than his height, measuring again.

I have spent a lot of time with Grobbelaar and there is rarely a dull moment. He is quick with a witty comment. However, he is, first and foremost, a practical joker. The other Liverpool legends describe him as good fun, full of ideas and mad. And all for a reason. So, I ask him if his sense of humour and general good mood developed as a method to tackle his previous experiences? He replies in earnest.

"Listen, you need a good mood. This world is a messed-up place. But, if you can keep sanity in your family and you can bring joy to them and your friends, that's the best thing you can offer.

"Yes, you can go through hard times. I've been through a few with Liverpool, too. It's like my mother said – and I'll always remember this – *'Life is full of disappointments, it's how you get over those disappointments that make you a better person.'* It's so true!"

For Grobbelaar to eventually end up playing for Liverpool is quite some story. He went back to his native town of Durban to get away from the war and played football there for 18 months, but the South African army wanted him to sign him up as he was a specialist in the army field.

However, Grobbelaar did not want to return to the military ever again, so he went to the UK instead, only to discover he could not get a work permit. His next stop was Canada, where he kept goal for Vancouver Whitecaps, and, after two years, he went on loan to Crewe Alexandra. It was at Gresty Road where Tom Saunders and Bob Paisley saw him play and, in 1981, they asked the keeper if he would like to play for Liverpool. The dream he had kept alive in the bush when he was on post fearing for his life had come true.

He was put up in the grand, white, dignified Adelphi Hotel in the centre of Liverpool. Paisley said he was to go to Anfield the next day by cab, adding that if there were a lot of photographers and journalists outside, he was to stay in the taxi and tell the driver to take him back to the hotel where he would get a phone call with new instructions.

It was March 16, 1981, at 11am, when Bruce arrived at Anfield in a taxi. In front of the main gate – this was before the Shankly Gates existed – there were a lot of photographers, so Grobbelaar did as he had been told and asked the slightly puzzled driver to take him right back to town where he came from. At 2:30pm, Paisley called the hotel and said he could come back up to Anfield because everybody had left. So he did, and signed a contract that was dated March 17 – the following day – because he needed to leave the country and fly back again with a work permit to get a residence permit.

Peter Robinson, the Liverpool Secretary, gave him a plane ticket to Paris. He went straight to the airport in Manchester and flew to Charles de Gaulle. However, he couldn't get through the airport with his African passport – he needed a visa to enter the country. Nor could he fly back to England after only staying in transit in Paris.

He was desperate. So close to his dream of becoming a professional footballer for Liverpool but stuck in transit! As he pondered his next move, he happened to see a little lady with a South African-looking passport in her hand. She told him she had obtained a 24-hour shopping visa "at a counter over there". He had a way out. Slap-bang, the stamp was in his passport, giving him an entrance ticket to Paris, where he stayed over at the home of an eccentric Hungarian called 'The Dentist of Paris'. The next day, Grobbelaar went back to Liverpool and completed his move.

He went on to replace Ray Clemence – a goalkeeper many felt was irreplaceable – and make 628 appearances for the club over a 13-season period. Only seven men have played for Liverpool more often and his run in the side also included a spell between 1981 and 1986 when he appeared in 317 consecutive matches, a feat only bettered by Clemence and Phil Neal. Liverpool's double-winning goalkeeper also has a European Cup winners' medal in his collection, with his 'spaghetti legs' performance in the 1984 penalty shoot-out against AS Roma in Rome the stuff of legend and an inspiration to Jerzy Dudek in Istanbul in 2005. For Grobbelaar, though, there were bad times as well. Heysel and Hillsborough were two of them.

After the Heysel tragedy in 1985, when 39 fans died and many more were injured before the European Cup final, Liverpool's goalkeeper lost interest in football and went away on holiday.

Heavy clouds lingered in his mind.

"Bruce, if you walk away from football, the idiots – the mindless few who did it – are winning."

He considered quitting, but a lot of people tried to persuade him to continue playing for Liverpool. His days as a soldier in the Bush War kicked in: if this had been a war situation, what would he have done? You get over the disappointments and keep going. So, he did.

Unfortunately, his career was to meet with another ordeal only four years later, when 96 Liverpool supporters lost their lives at the 1989 FA Cup semi-final against Nottingham Forest at Hillsborough.

A few minutes into the game, the ball went out for a goal kick and Grobbelaar went over towards the stand to get it. Behind him, in the Leppings Lane end, were Liverpool's travelling supporters. It was at that moment — a moment he'll never forget — that he saw faces squashed against the metal fences that were penning the supporters in. Somebody shouted: "Bruce, can you help me out of here?"

"I asked the steward and the policewoman on my side if they could do something, but the game carried on and I could hear the screams and the creaking of the fence. People had started lifting others over at the back and on the sides, and I was thinking: 'What's going on?'"

It was six minutes into the match the ball went out on the left and Grobbelaar ran to the referee, pointing to the people who were pressed against the fence. A major tragedy was unfolding and the referee took both teams off the pitch.

"I've been asked many times since, 'Did you know what was happening?' We knew. People came crying into our dressing room, 'One dead, two dead, three, four, five dead', but we didn't know the full extent of the accident until we were on the bus going back to Liverpool. Every hour, more and more were reported dead.

He will always remember the infamous 'The Truth' headline in The Sun the following week alongside false accusations that Liverpool supporters had robbed the dead and urinated on them.

"That was disgraceful," he grimaces. "It's the most despicable thing I've ever seen in a newspaper. I sat down and did an article in the Daily Express condemning what The Sun had written."

Many Liverpool supporters boycott that newspaper to this day and the story is seen by many as playing a significant part in denying the victims of Hillsborough, their families and the survivors the justice they deserve. He also firmly believes that the article he wrote in the Daily Express played a big part in his 10-year long nightmare in the English court systems following his departure from Liverpool.

"I'm sure that if I hadn't written that article against that tabloid, the accusations they made of throwing games in 1994 would never have gone to court," he says.

Grobbelaar was caught on camera by The Sun accepting £2,000, allegedly to throw a match for Southampton, his club at the time, and allegedly admitting that he threw a 1993 match against Newcastle that Liverpool had lost 3-0. He has always maintained his innocence – and, in November 1997, he was finally cleared of conspiracy to corrupt.

I wanted to get his side of the story on the match-fixing allegations. Grobbelaar had his testimonial in 1992. It earned him a lot of money and he donated around £300,000 of it to local charities. He had published his first book, *More Than Somewhat,* at that time and believes Chris Vincent, his former business partner, read it. Vincent contacted Grobbelaar and asked him if he was interested in investing money in a game farm, a resort for wild African animals. He went to Zimbabwe to have a look at it and thought it was a good idea. He says he invested £450,000 in the resort, but claims the money never made it to the owner.

Two years later, when he was at Southampton, his old business partner turned up again and proposed a good deal for him with some businessmen from Hong Kong, if he was interested. They would give him a certain sum if he would throw a game.

"I feigned interest and kept quiet. I should have gone straight to the police, but I didn't, I wanted to collect evidence and I didn't know he was taping our conversations. If you listen to what was recorded, you can tell I'm not guilty. But, if you only listen to a few bits, you'll think, *'Bruce Grobbelaar is guilty.'* Most people got to hear two-and-a-half minutes of the six-and-a-half hours that had been recorded. The prosecution never showed the whole tape to the public. If they had, they'd have known why I ask about my money. £450,000 is a lot of money, and that's what I was after."

One of the matches that was produced as evidence against him was Liverpool's 3-0 defeat to Newcastle at St James' Park. Andy Cole scored a hat-trick in the first half. Only 10 days before that game, Grobbelaar had two cartilage operations on his knees, yet his manager, Graeme Souness, wanted him in goal. He played in jogging bottoms that day, which he rarely ever did, because he did not want the opposition to see his bandaged knees.

On November 8, 1994, he was at Gatwick Airport when two reporters from The Sun showed up and told him they were printing accusations of match-fixing on their front page the next day. During what Grobbelaar feels was a witch-hunt in the press, he was accused of corruption together with Hans Segers and John Fashanu from Wimbledon, and the Malaysian businessman Heng Suan Lim. After two trials, the jury couldn't agree a verdict and they were all acquitted in November 1997.

"How did the Liverpool fans respond at the time?"

"I felt the fans were mainly on my side. Of course, there were some who didn't really like me as a goalkeeper, and said there is no smoke without fire. Everybody says that, but

I knew I was innocent. I've never harmed football in any way whatsoever and I knew that would come out in the end."

"How on earth could a goalkeeper fix matches on his own? Wouldn't he need somebody at the other end of the pitch, too?"

"That question was asked in court all the time, and I can repeat what I said, 'I can't. I could let in three goals, but there are 10 men in front of me who work to score goals. Unless you've got someone else in on it, it's impossible.'"

After being acquitted, Grobbelaar launched a civil action to take the tabloid to court for libel. He wanted to clear his name. He won the case and The Sun was told to pay damages of £85,000 in 1999. The newspaper later had the verdict overturned in the Appeal Court but when the case ended up in the House of Lords in 2001, the Law Lords reinstated the High Court jury's earlier verdict that the paper had libelled him. However, they reduced the damages awarded to Grobbelaar to £1 and ordered him to pay The Sun's legal costs of £500,000. He went bankrupt. He breathes heavily: "I'm certain that because I wrote that article against the tabloid after the Hillsborough tragedy, plus refused to write other articles for them, they pushed the case through what ended up as a marathon run in court. What can you do? Nothing, really. A 10-year battle in court turned to nothing. All I've done is lose a little dignity and all my money."

So many years of pressure. Accused of betraying the team you love, that you dreamed about in the midst of your life's worst misery as a soldier. A small conflict in your workplace could suck the energy out of you, but for 10 years! It must have been so draining.

"It was exhausting. But remember, at the back of my mind I was focusing on the fact I had done nothing wrong. *'Stay there. Stay there. You've never done anything.'* If I had been prosecuted, I was looking at nine years in jail. But it took 10 years to actually go through it all. Which is worse? Being in jail, or this? If, at the end, I had been prosecuted, would I have got a suspended sentence because it took 10 years to clear? How would that have worked? Were they trying to break me down? How do you break somebody who has done nothing wrong?"

When your life is in turmoil it is easy to take your frustration out on those closest to you. For Grobbelaar, it was a huge burden on his family. His eldest daughter was a young girl who had to live through a time when she had the paparazzi following her every step. His other daughter was just a child when it all started. She did not understand what was happening and, later in life, they had to explain it all to her.

"It was not a good feeling," he admits. "But we were made of sterner stuff and, in the end, they've come out very, very well."

In Great Britain, personal bankruptcy is normally for one to two years; Grobbelaar's bankruptcy went on for four years because of the legal fight. However, the financial issues are not over. The trustees from his bankruptcy still want the money and are now trying to get it from his ex-wife.

"Has it made you bitter?"

"No. I've lost three houses and all my money. So what? You have to start again – and that's what I've done. Besides, you learn who your true friends are at a time like this. Harry, a friend I used to live with in Durban, once said, 'Bruce, in times of trouble, you'll find out who your real friends are. I bet you won't even count them on one hand.' It was very, very true."

"Did people turn their back on you?"

"To put it differently: they stood back and only came back after the battle with the courts had finished. So, I know who my true friends are."

161

"What about your old team-mates, the ones you had fought with to win all the trophies and medals? The ones you were wrongly accused of betraying?

"I can't talk for them, but I do believe they were there for me." He pauses. "A lot of them were asked to write affidavits, and some of them did."

He pulls his moustache, one of the characteristic traits of the man in the green shirt between the white posts. His eyes glitter. They are always smiling, even when Grobbelaar, as now, is serious.

"I'm still welcome at Liverpool Football Club. If the club thought I'd done something wrong, I'd never have been welcomed back. The same goes for the Former Players' Association. So, I believe they supported me."

Grobbelaar got married again in December 2008. In 2009, his third child, Rotem, was born. Today, he lives with his wife Karen Phillips-Grobbelaar and their little girl in Canada.

"Everything I have gone through has made me stronger, made me realise that nothing is more important than family. I've got a beautiful family. Money can't buy that. It can't."

162

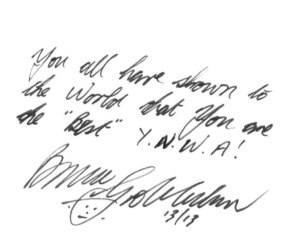

Liverpool FC Career: 1981-1994 🦅 *Appearances: 628* 🦅 *Clean Sheets: 267*

11

John Barnes
Water Off A Duck's Back

"It was such a pleasure to see Liverpool and John Barnes rushing down in full flight. On the wing, beating people, creating for people. It was great to be a Liverpool supporter at the time, because there was so much ability in the team and John was at the top. You couldn't meet a more down to earth guy. A lovely, lovely man."

Phil Thompson

May 20, 2011: A crowd of people with just-out-of-bed hair and trainers in fancy colours fill the reception of the Hilton hotel in Liverpool. The Sound City Festival is on and a non-stop flow of artists and bands are seeping in through the doors and up the steps to the registration desk. I am in a floral dress, literally on the edge of my seat, waiting for John Barnes, one of the few Liverpool players I remember from my own childhood.

Fashionably late is a well-known expression. I get a text from Barnes, telling me he will be 30 minutes late. In the meantime, I go up to the top floor, to the executive lounge, that the hotel has been kind enough to let me have at my disposal. I have learned this much – this city is proud of its football legends. The ex-players of LFC are well taken care of here. That is probably part of the reason why so many of them, who were not originally from these parts, or even this country, still live on Merseyside, just like John Barnes.

In the lounge, photographer Tony has rigged up his mobile studio. At the end of the long room, with a great view over the Albert Dock and Liverpool ONE, hangs his black backdrop. While I sit there, pondering what approach to take for the photos together with Barnes, I see a man outside, past his prime, going from waterhole to waterhole in the fountain in the alley down below that leads people from the new, popular shopping centre to the dignified dock area.

The fountain has a number of columns with water welling up at various heights. On this occasion, it is raining and the force is at its minimum. The water trickles out and in the middle of it all, this man, walking slowly. Obviously, he is already soaked and in no rush. A strange sight. I ought to think that it is a good thing; grown ups can also be playful, and dashing through the fountain is always so tempting for children, an almost magnetic force of attraction. But there is just melancholy and hopelessness to this man's slow march through the water.

Before the half-hour is over, I am back in the reception, where I wait almost another 30 minutes before he turns up. With his hair cut short, he's wearing a white T-shirt with grey letters forming 'G-Star' on his chest, a pair of jeans and matching white trainers. Or 'trainees', as Scousers tend to call them.

Barnes is in a wonderful mood. He fires questions at both Tony and myself. In no time at all, he knows how many children I have got, where I am staying in Liverpool and why Tony is a Liverpool fan, even though he grew up in Malaysia and is living in Stoke.

Liverpool's former No10 speaks almost like a machine-gun. I bless myself for having brought my sound recorder, as I would never in a lifetime have been able to scribble down half of the words fired through the air amidst gesticulations. He hits the table every so often and enthusiastically answers all my questions. This man is intense, fully present, very knowledgeable, passionate and efficient.

Barnes learned to play football at an early age, playing with his father, who captained Jamaica's national team and later became president of the Jamaican Football Association. So, John grew up playing football. He played all the time from when he was about four years old. He loved it.

His strongest childhood memory is also related to football. He was eight years old when his father went to the Olympics in Germany in 1972, and came back with what was John's first pair of football boots – adidas 'Gerd Müller'– named after the legendary West German international striker.

"I just loved German football," Barnes states. "West German football."

The World Cup Final in 1974 at the Olympic stadium in Munich was between West Germany and the Netherlands. In the audience, watching on a big screen at Jamaica's National Stadium, was Barnes, wearing his Gerd Müller boots and a German hat to express his support for the West Germans.

"Everybody wanted Holland to win, it felt like I was the only one who supported West Germany – and they won! It wasn't until I moved to England as a teenager that I learned people back then didn't support Germany very often because of the war. But they hadn't bombed my country! Being from a diplomat family, I realised I couldn't say that I loved Germany. So, even though I still loved the West German side and knew the whole German squad by heart, I understood that I had to say my favourite was Pele and my favourite team Brazil. However, deep down, my heart was always for Germany. West Germany."

John Charles Bryan Barnes grew up with his two sisters, Gillian and Tracy, his lawyer mother Jeanne and his dad Ken (Roderick Kenrick), who was a colonel in the army. When John was 13, his father became military attaché in London. His family lived in Golden Square in a stately neighbourhood near Piccadilly. When Barnes was 17, the rest of the family went back to Jamaica. The teenager's football skills had been discovered and he had signed for Elton John's club, Watford.

He did an amazing job there and helped lift the team all the way into the top division. They made it to the FA Cup final and Barnes was so impressive that he played his way into the English national team during just his second season at the club. On June 9, 1987, he signed for Liverpool for £900,000. The rest is history. Barnes' career in a red shirt has made him one of the greatest Liverpool legends of all time.

Unlike his mother, who had three children in three years, Barnes has spread his descendants out over a quarter of a century. When I met him, he was planning the baptism of his youngest, Alexander. His oldest, Jamie, is 25 and working as a doctor on Merseyside; Jordan, 22, is an investment banker, and 18-year-old Jemma is going to medical school, just like her brother did. In addition, John has three daughters: Jasmin, who is 14, Isabella, who is six, and four-year-old Tia.

So he has a fairly large family and has, on the whole, lived a very active life since hanging up his boots as a professional in 1999. By that time, he had also spent a total of two years with Newcastle United and Charlton Athletic. The father of seven now works as a football expert for various TV stations around the world. His youngest was born during a Liverpool match and, on live television, Barnes was joking that his son would be called Fernando – as Fernando Torres had a great game for Liverpool. In the studio, they patted him on the back, saying: *"Nice one, Barnesey!"*

"Imagine if I had called him Fernando, and now he's left the club! That's why I tell the fans, *'Don't fall in love with players, love the team'*. Just look at me, people used to love me and now I don't even come to the ground anymore. In the old days, you had players like Kenny Dalglish, who stayed at the club for 20 years, Rushie and I were there 10. People shouldn't worship individual players like back then. I promise you, given the right circumstances, no matter who they are, they'll leave the club. No matter the kind of support the player has at a club."

Barnes believes the biggest problem in modern football is that individual players are so powerful that they can become bigger than both club and manager. Except for Sir Alex Ferguson and Dalglish, he feels most other managers are too weak. It is not their fault. It is how football has changed.

"Nowadays, players go to the papers and say, 'I should have played!', and the fans will call for the manager's head because this player didn't play."

He mentions the examples of Roy Hodgson and Graeme Souness.

"Roy is obviously a good manager – look at what he's done at West Bromwich Albion – but the Liverpool fans didn't want him. I will never accuse any player of not trying their best under Hodgson, but these things happen subconsciously.

"The same thing happened to me during Souness' management, as it did with a lot of players. Before a match you obviously want to give 100 per cent. However, subconsciously, there's a different conversation, *'If I don't play well today, am I going to get booed? Or will the fans call for the manager's head? Do I really have to perform?'* I'm not actually thinking this, mind you, it's in my subconscious. So you convince yourself you gave it 100 per cent, but it didn't happen.

"Things changed at Liverpool when Kenny Dalglish came back. *'If I don't perform, they're not going to boo Kenny. So I perform.'* That's why there was a change in his first week as manager. He didn't change any tactics, but already in the first game after his return as a manager, against Manchester United, you could see a different attitude in the players."

Barnes says it is all about the players' feeling of commitment, desire and effort. All you can expect of a manager is to maximise the potential of each player. Ferguson, Dalglish and Arsène Wenger maximise the potential of their teams. Given the right environment, John claims, all players in the English top teams can perform, because they are not bad players. But, in conditions that do not suit them, they cannot perform at their best. It's all about giving them the right environment and support to see what they can do.

Barnes himself could not have been more fortunate with the environment that met him at Liverpool. Dalglish was focusing more on the manager's role, having initially been player/manager, and Ian Rush had gone to Juventus. The duo that had been terrifying defences for years was gone. Waiting to take over were John Aldridge, Peter Beardsley and this newly-signed Jamaican. Ray Houghton arrived shortly afterwards. The pressure of expectation was almost tangible – and everybody thought: *"Will this work?"*

From day one in training, it all clicked. Snap. Barnes, perhaps surprisingly, feels it was more luck than by design, because they had not worked on playing together like they soon were. It just happened.

"The best thing about Kenny is that he knows a good player when he sees one – and

he knows how to put a team together. He often doesn't make the big, tactical moves, he just knows which players will function together. It was the same way with us."

Dalglish's great team of 1987 to 1990 was created with the new arrivals and developed little by little by the people who were in it. It was not the individual players who changed the environment, but the type of player they represented. It was a crossroads for Liverpool, also in style of play.

In the old days, the midfield was like a machine, with players like Sammy Lee, Graeme Souness and Terry McDermott. According to Barnes, the 'new' Liverpool was not as strong in midfield – they did not have that hard-working machine, nor did they have as good a defence – but they played a new style of football that is considered by many to be some of the best football in the history of the club.

"Was it a kind of magic?"

He laughs: "Just luck!"

"No skills at all?"

"Sure, we had skills, but individual skills are different. There are a lot of examples of teams that have had fantastic players with amazing skills, but it still hasn't worked. The balance of the team hasn't been right. You may have 11 skilful players on the pitch, but if there's no balance in the team, it doesn't work. In our team, this balance was perfect."

This optimum balance took Liverpool to a runaway league championship in Barnes' debut season. His performances on the wing that year were outstanding and made him a big hero on the Kop. Indeed, his best Liverpool memory is also from his debut year.

Barnes was looking forward to a massive celebration after winning the championship, but it didn't happen. Ronnie Moran just came into the very modest changing room and left all the medals for each player to pick one up. There was no song and dance. No celebration at all. If you want to be hungry for success, you have to forget about the past – and this particular league campaign had ended a few minutes ago. It was history.

So, Moran just put the medals on the physio bench in the dressing room right after the match. No fuss. No tribute speeches. The players did go out to celebrate, but they knew their feet were being kept on the ground.

"The attitude has to be, 'We work hard to achieve success and are driven towards getting that success again. When we do achieve success, we forget about it, because you need to be hungry to repeat that success.'

"It's not a typical British trait. In England, we like to build up players before they've achieved anything; you can be just average, whereas in America you have to prove your worth. Just look at the Big Brother culture, the celebrity culture we've got in England."

"Ah, yes," I say, "It's awful. And then there's Strictly Come Dancing…" I cannot help myself, because Barnes has danced his way through that programme and earned great praise from the judges, so I'm told, for wriggling his hips to the salsa.

He bursts out laughing. "At least you must have achieved something in your past to be invited on that show! But if you're on 'Strictly' and expect to be something big later, you're in trouble.

"The American basketball star Dennis Rodman once said: 'In America, you have to be someone to get on the red carpet. If you get on the red carpet in England, you can become someone.' So, you can become famous without doing anything.

"You've got lots of kids out there who want to be famous, they don't care what they must do. In most countries you have to do something or achieve something to be famous. That's why we don't produce excellence anymore in England – not on the sporting field or anywhere – people just relax and do absolutely nothing. They're on TV all day long and turn into superstars."

Barnes pours himself a cup of coffee. I am thinking how silly it would be meeting with such a reflective guy without touching on the subject of importing African players to

Europe. Large numbers of African youngsters are brought into European football today, it is big business.

He has thought about the African players in English football. He feels in some way, it is giving a child the chance to make money, where they may otherwise spend a life in poverty. Barnes has travelled a lot in Africa to play, promote and not least comment on football. He has also worked with charity for Africa. What he is most concerned with is how the clubs can give something back to the community where the player is from.

"As a club, you are taking advantage of the difficult situation of the local community by picking up certain players, and I think the clubs should ask themselves, 'What more can we do to help this player's local environment?' If a kid from a war zone, or a place with no pure water, goes over to an English club and sends money home, that's another matter. We should also work up structures to help the community, in addition to helping that one talented footballer. We ought to set up an institution or a programme for the local kids in their own village."

"Are they taken care of well enough at their new clubs in Europe?"

"The good ones are, definitely. The less fortunate are thrown back to the wolves, or they're just not looked after. But I'm more interested in what we can do for the country they are looking to recruit players from."

Barnes has warmed to the subject of the African kids, who have a completely different background and upbringing than him. But throughout his professional career, he has still been confronted with his Afro-American complexion.

"At the time I was playing, racism was an accepted part of football. There was racial abuse from the terraces. The press, nobody, said a word."

Racist abuse was something that Barnes suffered during his career, I have learned that much from talking with the other Liverpool legends. Barnes was the first high-profile black player at Liverpool.

He says the worst incidences of it happened before he went to Liverpool. While he was a success at Watford, there were racist, nasty calls and chants from opposition fans, especially from Millwall and West Ham United. The chanting was offensive and bananas were thrown at him. When he got to Liverpool, it highlighted the whole issue of racism. When the Everton fans threw bananas at him in one of his first Merseyside derbies, it made the front pages.

It is in human nature, wanting to be loved. We want to be seen and we want people to like us. If you fight with family or close friends, it is painful, frustrating and stressful; it drains you of all energy. To be so publicly harassed in front of tens of thousands of people must be incredibly difficult to deal with. How did he perform under circumstances like that?

"Really, racism is like everything else in life. It depends on your perspective of it, your perception. Nothing can belittle me or undermine me because of my colour. It ran off me like water off a duck's back. Nobody could make me feel inferior or angry because they didn't like me as black, or because they felt superior to me. I don't feel superior to anyone in any way. I was completely comfortable with who I was and, therefore, the chanting didn't affect me at all."

Growing up in a lovely and resourceful middle-class home in Jamaica had made him strong and impregnable. He believes that if, on the other hand, he had grown up a black boy in London at the same time, he might have felt disempowered. If you see your parents cannot get jobs because they are black, or that you as a child do not get the same opportunities as the white English kids, it will affect your self-confidence.

"In such circumstances, you would feel like a second-class citizen. But my mother was a lawyer, my father was a colonel in the Jamaican army and my sisters became doctors. So, I didn't feel inferior.

"I came to London as a teenager and all these white working-class supporters with

no jobs were chanting nasty things about me, and I was thinking: 'What are these people actually trying to do? Are they trying to make me feel inferior?' It's all about how you let things affect you. I could have handled it differently. I could have been a young man who went out against racism. I didn't."

I am surprised by his strength, his reflections on racism, and his ability to rise above something that went on for many, many years. Personally, I think that would have eaten me up and destroyed me.

Mental strength is a lot of things. This tells me that power of the mind really can make you achieve the most unbelievable, even during great mental stress. It also told me how important it is for parents to arm their children with confidence, which can protect them against evil.

Barnes tells me there is a big difference to being racially abused on the pitch and if it happened to him in everyday life.

"If I walk down the street and someone racially abuses me, that's a whole other ball game – that's personal. In football, I felt it was different; I was racially abused by West Ham fans, but they would have cheered me if I'd played for them. When I played for Watford, Liverpool fans abused me. However, when I played for Liverpool, it was the Everton fans who abused me. My point is, the abuse wasn't personal, so I didn't take it personally."

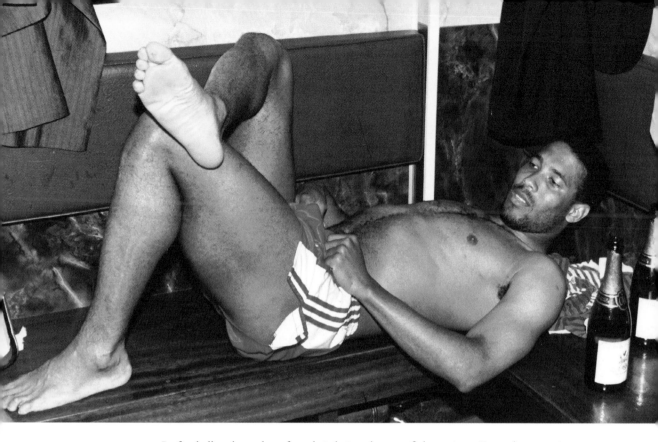

In football today, a lot of work is being done to fight racism. Since the sport is so popular, the authorities and a lot of organisations have campaigns such as *Show Racism The Red Card*, *Kick It Out* and *Let's Kick Racism Out Of Football*. They use football as a way to fight racism in society. Barnes feels it should have been the other way around.

"First, we must fight racism in society, otherwise it will never go away from football. You must get rid of racism in all walks of society. Football is just one area.

"You cannot just look at a microcosm, like football is, and say, *'We'll get rid of racism here.'* We can't get rid of racism in football just by saying we want to, or by threatening to throw people out the grounds for making racist chants. That'll just shut them up for 90 minutes, but they'll be just as racist afterwards."

Even though the problems have mostly been driven out of the football grounds, we cannot pretend that they have disappeared completely, because they have not.

"What is the percentage of black managers in the Premier League?" he asks.

"What is the percentage of black directors in the boardrooms? How many black football journalists are there? If you look at who dominates prison statistics or shop workers, you'll see a different equation. In our time of political correctness, it's no longer the case that unless you're a blatant racist, racism doesn't exist.

"When Emile Heskey was abused in Macedonia, England called out, 'Ban

Macedonian football!' What we have to understand is that in Macedonia, they weren't used to black players – that's why they react these days the way we did in England in the '80s. One of the same journalists who condemned that episode was on our plane home from an international in Brazil in 1984. Back then he didn't say anything about what had happened there."

Barnes is referring to what happened after England beat Brazil at the Maracana in 1984. Barnes scored what some people will tell you is the finest goal ever scored in an England shirt. He collected the ball, dribbled past six yellow shirts and slotted it past the keeper into the back of the net. However, on the plane home from Brazil, there were England 'supporters' from the right-wing extremist group The National Front. Incredibly, they were let on to the plane with racist banners and were allowed to abuse Barnes and Stoke's Mark Chamberlain – the two black players in the team. The extremists loudly declared that Barnes' goal should have been disallowed, because it was scored by a black man.

"Nobody said anything, and the journalists didn't mention this at all. Fifteen years later, in a drive to get rid of racism in football, the same journalists all of a sudden condemn it. Why didn't they say something back then? Because now it's popular to speak up against racism. It wasn't at the time."

The most fascinating part about talking to Barnes is that you cannot predict what is coming up next. Suddenly, he says that, having experienced it himself, he could understand racism 100 per cent. He explained it with the course of history. If we look back 300 years, and up to about a 100 years ago, black people were dehumanised. That is why some people still think they can do and say whatever they like about them. There is a lot of inherent racism in our culture, not least in our language.

"Just look at the way we express ourselves. We still talk about something scary or sad as 'darkness', and when something bad happens it's a 'black event', a 'black day' or a 'black conscience'. Why? Why isn't it a 'white day' when it's a bad day? Why are you as innocent as 'white snow'?

"And I ask my children: Who play the angels and the Virgin Mary in the school plays? The sweet, blonde girls with blue eyes. And why do the sweet, little blonde girls get to be angels? Because that's the way we see life! That's how life is in the West."

I felt a little like a schoolgirl, sitting there with my blonde, long hair and green eyes. A lot of what Barnes

was telling me I had never really thought about before. I believe I have a very conscious anti-racist attitude in general. I try as best as I can to promote tolerance and equality to my children.

But, then, there are all these tiny unspoken things we grow up with. There weren't many people who had a different complexion to mine in Northern Norway when I grew up. There were some who had been adopted, like my best friend Silje, who originally came from Korea.

I think back to the triumphant feeling I had when I got the part of the princess in a play. They brushed my blonde hair and I changed into several of my grandmother's old gala dresses on stage, getting my fair share of solo time. I basked in the attention, just eight years old.

Barnes also made me reflect on little details of what I experience in my own life. I can recognise some of what he is talking about – although, naturally, on a different scale than what he has experienced.

Most of us have probably at some point felt we were treated unfairly because others were prejudiced against us, against who we are. Perhaps it could be useful for the rest of us to acknowledge that feeling and realise that we can learn something from it about how we behave and how we judge other people? It takes one to know one.

A woman, writing official books about Liverpool and their players, is news. No woman has done this before me, yet I had not reflected on that when I started my book projects about Liverpool. However, at a supporter event in Liverpool, something happened that made me realise this. Even though I had not given a lot of thought to the fact I am a woman doing this job, one comment that afternoon made me understand that a lot of others probably had.

I told Barnes about the event that was held in a fine restaurant on Merseyside with 200 Norwegian supporters. I had spoken about my book projects and had interviewed both David Fairclough and Roy Evans on the stage. Afterwards, a handsome fellow of about my age, came over to the table and said:"What you did on stage there was really quite good."

"Thank you. Have you read Liverpool Hearts, my book?"

"No, I must admit, I've been wondering why on Earth I should read a book that a woman has written about Liverpool?"

"Right…"

I just stared at him for a few seconds while it dawned on me that if this young man, who grew up in our so-called equal society, had been thinking like this, he would not be the only one. For the first time, I realised that my gender was probably barring me from a lot of potential readers. It was absurd. Why should I not be just as good a journalist and writer simply because I am a woman?

"Exactly!" says Barnes. "You're in a very similar position to the one I was in. As a woman, you must not take it personally. I don't, because you can't control whether somebody abuses you or not. That's my philosophy in life: nothing is personal. I have no control over whether you like me or not.

"When I find myself in discussions with Liverpool supporters, I thank them for saying good things about me and saying that they love me. But, then, I tell them, *'It's not me you love, you love John Barnes, player No10 who did a great job for Liverpool. If I hadn't played well, you wouldn't have loved me.'* So, neither praise nor abuse is personal.

"I've got to be who I am, not the one you want me to be. I'm in control of what I do, what I want in my life, whether you like me or not."

Liverpool FC Career: 1987-1997 🦅 *Appearances: 407* 🦅 *Goals: 108*

12

Alan Kennedy
Life In The Fast Lane

"Barney is a left-back who always managed to score goals in big finals. He used to argue all the time, because his left foot wouldn't always do what it was supposed to do. He worked hard. A great person."

Ian Rush

 Rome, May 30, 1984: Liverpool were on the verge of winning the European Cup for the fourth time in eight seasons. Joe Fagan's side had just played AS Roma in the Italian champion's own Stadio Olimpico, but the winner was yet to be decided. The match had finished 1-1 after extra time – Phil Neal getting Liverpool's goal – and with Uefa having scrapped their old policy of finals going to replays, the European Cup final was going to be settled by penalties for the first time. What's more, it was also Liverpool's first ever penalty shoot-out in a competitive game, meaning that Fagan, in his first season in charge, was the first Reds manager to select five spot-kick takers.

He was smoking like mad as he considered his options. Dalglish was out, he had been subbed. Nicol, Neal, Souness and Rush would take the first four, but who was going to take the last penalty? He looked around and narrowed it down to two players: Bruce Grobbelaar and Alan Kennedy – neither of them renowned for their penalties. He took a long drag of his cigarette and went over to Kennedy.

"Are you all right?" asked Fagan.

"Yes, I am okay," Liverpool's No3 replied, not realising that he had just accepted the responsibility of taking the last penalty. When the penny dropped, he was scared stiff. Luckily, he was the last one to go. It gave him a glimpse of hope. If his team-mates did their job, and one of the Italians missed, he would get away without having to take one.

He had such luck.

Steve Nicol, who was up first, for Liverpool, missed – but so did two of Roma's stars, Bruno Conti and Francesco Graziani. They had been psyched out by Grobbelaar's spaghetti-legged antics in goal. When Graziani blasted Roma's fourth penalty over, Liverpool's keeper celebrated wildly. He knew that Liverpool, now 3-2 up in the shoot-out, needed just to score their final kick to win the European Cup. Then, he realised who

179

was taking the fifth – Kennedy – a man who had never taken a penalty in a competitive game for the Reds.

The tension inside the stadium was palpable as Kennedy walked towards the penalty spot. He could see Liverpool supporters hiding their faces in their hands. Now, it was all down to him. This was pressure. Could he hold his nerve?

A spring day in Liverpool, 2011. Spring is the time of year when the city of Liverpool is at its absolute best, if you ask me. Not much rain, lots of sun, and there are often surprisingly high temperatures. The Norwegian TV channel TV 2 came with me to see Kennedy. Both he and his old team-mate Phil Neal are having their photographs done by Tony.

Kennedy and Neal are great friends of Norway; they are among the most active after-dinner speakers at Liverpool FC events in my country as well as regular faces you meet in the Anfield lounges at home games. They had come to see me directly from a morning meeting at Anfield. It was time for a cup of coffee and some mineral water at the Matou restaurant, but first they both give me a big hug. Afterwards, my husband and kids come in, too, as they also wanted to meet their Liverpool friends.

Neal sticks his tongue out to Elias, who is spying at him from behind the couch. He quickly gets a tongue back and a sly smile. The two of them go out on the roof terrace to play football. The terrace has a spectacular view of the Liver Building, the Liverpool Museum and the Mersey. Before my five-year-old goes off to play football with his friend Neal, he has an impromptu Norwegian lesson with 'AK'. Kennedy tests the little bits he has learned on his trips to Norway. A very patient Elias then says a few phrases out loud, which Kennedy obediently repeats. Elias sips his coke and laughs at the unfamiliar pronunciation. There are smiles all round.

Kennedy's mobile rings non-stop. He is a man in much demand. Besides, he is in the middle of a divorce from his wife Jane, who has been at his side throughout his footballing career. She is the mother of his two sons, Andrew and Michael, and has also been his secretary. Now, he has to fix all practical matters himself, and it has been quite a change.

He was busy enough as it was. He has bought an iPad to help him keep track of all his appointments, inquiries and jobs, but some things are harder to master than scoring in European Cup finals. He looks a little puzzled by it. He wants to show me pictures he had taken with his Norwegian girlfriend along the Mersey but cannot find them. Instead, quotes pop up in his mailbox. He reads some out.

"Everybody on the planet wants to be happy."

"I disagree. I don't believe everybody wants to be happy. Some want to be miserable," I countered.

He carried on: "'No matter how much people long for happiness, they are – first and foremost – longing, because they believe the longing will make them happy.' Interesting."

"That *is* interesting. Are you happy, Alan Kennedy?"

"Yes, I'm happy right at this moment, but that doesn't mean I have to remain happy… something might happen! Maybe there's a parking ticket waiting."

He reads me another quote from his inbox: "Love is not about finding the right person, but creating the right relationship. It is not about how much love you start out with, but how much love you have built at the end."

He navigates the screen and continues: "'Whether it be health, money, love, relationships, material things, work – no matter what, happiness is the bottom line of it all.' There we go…"

Kennedy looks out the window towards the Mersey. He looks thoughtful and a little tired. Below us, a man is drawing using charcoal.

"It's very interesting how he goes from one picture to the next," Kennedy muses as he cranes his neck to keep track of the local artist.

A few weeks ago, Jan, the wife of his old team-mate and friend David Fairclough, died after suffering a brain aneurysm. It was very sudden and her death has sat heavily with him.

"These days, I think a lot about what life is all about. It was so hard when Jan died. I used to go to her business, and I can't imagine David and the kids without her. Being in the middle of divorce makes me extra vulnerable. I'm alone now and have only myself to think of, but it's so painful that Jan has gone.

"I try to focus on work, but I realise I should try and enjoy life more. This summer I'm going on holiday for the first time in a long while. I'm going on a cruise and it only includes a bit of work. Then I'll visit a friend in Australia."

The Mersey gleams in the daylight. We talk about how the city has been developed towards the waterfront. I had been to Liverpool many times before. But I had not been aware of the beautiful sandbanks along the Mersey that show at low tide. Not until the new Mersey ferry ticket office, the restaurant, and the Liverpool Museum had been built.

"Reclaimed land!" Kennedy says, giving me a smile that makes his eyes narrow. His face bears trace of having smiled a lot.

"While sitting here, you may also reflect on how much water is under the bridge in your life, too."

He breathes heavily: "A *lot* of water."

By all means. His career has been a dream come true.

"Since I was five, or even younger, my brother Keith and I only ever wanted to play football."

Keith is two-and-a-half years older and they practised kicking the ball with their left foot, because a good left foot would get you into the team. Alan Phillip Kennedy remembers the form he had to fill in at 11, between junior and senior school. Under 'What would you like to be when you grow up?', he carefully put: 'Professional footballer.'

"Unfortunately, I couldn't spell 'professional'!" he laughs. "And, so, I figured I'd better brush up a little on my English first and learn how to spell it. 'Footballer' was easy enough to write.

"I knew I wanted to be a footballer and a lot of my teachers said, "You've got a chance." However, nobody thought of becoming professional at that time. I was the only one in my school who wrote it."

This was the early 1960s in the North East of England and many people wanted to work in factories, in construction or at a pub. There were plenty of pubs back then.

But not Alan. He wanted to be a professional footballer, except for a moment around 16 when he thought he might need extra qualifications to lean on. By then, his brother Keith had established himself in Newcastle's reserves and had played some games for the first-team as well. He had made it, so it was only a matter of trying to copy him. However, his brother told him how tough life was and the money in football was nothing to write home about back then. In the early 1970s, there was a recession and people only got to work three days a week. Alan dreamed of going away and looked at people like George Best and the glamorous side of football. His favourite player was Bobby Charlton of Manchester United and England, one of the heroes of the 1966 World Cup.

"These were people I desperately wanted to emulate. I attended a professional footballers' dinner some 10-to-12 years after the World Cup triumph. I had just signed for Liverpool at the time and I met Charlton. He was walking one way, I was going the other. I just had to talk to him, it was the first time I'd ever seen him in person. 'Hiya, Bobby!' But he just walked straight past me."

"Oh, he didn't say hello?"

"No. He didn't know who I was. I thought, 'I've just got to go over to him.' I had a beard then, so he probably wouldn't have recognised me. I plucked up a little extra courage, went over to him and said: 'Hi, Bobby, I'm Alan Kennedy.' He said: 'Hi Alan!'"

Then came the confession that Bobby was his favourite player. The legendary international thanked him and asked him why?

"Because you scored fantastic goals from 25 to 30 yards, with your right foot, left foot and a few headers, too."

"What position do you play?" Charlton asked.

"I play full-back."

"Oh, you're not going to score a lot of goals there."

"I'll try and score some important goals, in big games."

Alan was going to do exactly that.

Kennedy played 359 matches for Liverpool and has decided two European Cup finals. His professional football career spanned 20 years. It started at Newcastle, then he joined Liverpool, before a spell at Sunderland. He made appearances for 13 other clubs – including Hartlepool, Wigan and Wrexham – and was still playing at non-league level into his 40s.

Growing up, neither he nor his brother could know they were one day going to make a living from football. In 1962/63, they played in the same school team. Kennedy the younger was only eight. His brother Keith was very good; physically strong and one of a group of players that the future Liverpool defender found fantastic.

The star in the making thought of himself as a physically weak outside-left. One who might be able to do something if he got the ball as he was fairly quick. However, being just eight among 11-year-olds is in itself a challenge. He now looks back on that time, when he went up against the big lads and played some tough games, as an important part of his upbringing in football.

"Everybody in that group should have made it, but only my brother and I went all the way. Wind the clock on 10 years and my brother was a professional and I became an apprentice at Newcastle. I was probably more determined than anybody else there, possibly including my brother. He had the skills to go further than me. Keith was always my sports mentor. I looked up to him and what he achieved. He was playing for Newcastle's first-team, I wasn't."

The Kennedy brothers were both left full-backs, which made them compete for the same position as teenagers at Newcastle. The problem was that the management had to choose just one of them. Unluckily for Keith, they chose his brother. That is how the younger Kennedy later became a star at Liverpool and Keith went to Bury.

"I felt for him at the time, but he stayed at Bury, who were in the Third and Fourth Division then, for 11 years, while I signed for Liverpool in 1978. We learned a lot from each other. Sometimes, we played against each other, like when Liverpool played Bury in the FA Cup in 1980."

It was strange meeting his brother like that. They both got the captaincy for the game. The Kennedy brothers were hyped up, competing against each other as they were.

Bury gave little brother Kennedy and Liverpool a difficult time. They held their own and almost scored, while the Reds looked short of ideas. Then, a certain super sub came on and changed the game. David Fairclough scored twice and Liverpool won 2-0.

Keith's testimonial came up on May 19, 1982, and Alan helped organise the match by getting Liverpool's first-team to play against a team of Bury legends. A crowd of almost 6,000 people showed up at Bury's Gigg Lane for a match that was played the day after Liverpool had completed their 1981/82 campaign with a 0-0 draw at Middlesbrough.

"It was a lovely gesture from the players to go there. Grobbelaar, Hansen, McDermott, Rush – the regular first-team showed up. That would never have happened today, but the

playing nowadays, I've got to play like I did when I played for Liverpool. I don't think about how old people are, but I think that they remember me as I was in the team 30 years ago.

"The feeling you get when you enter the pitch is just amazing. I can't feel the cold, or the rain, I only feel that I'm wearing the shirt of Liverpool Football Club. That I'm representing the club.

"There are so many memories from my time at Liverpool, such as coaches and managers saying certain things. But, to me, the camaraderie is the strongest memory. People like Jan Molby, Michael Thomas, Ian Rush and John Aldridge – all these great players. To think I played with some of them for Liverpool and I play with some of them for the legends team... they're all quality players and great lads to be in the dressing room with."

Alan says that, no matter what you do in life, quality is very important. Liverpool were fortunate to have such a high quality team who knew they could trust each other.

boys made a day out of it. They even had to get to the ground themselves and, as it was the end of the season, they could not stay away from the pub! When they ran on to the pitch, you could smell alcohol. But, truth be told, that probably just made the match even more entertaining."

The 8-7 scoreline in Liverpool's favour suggests he's right!

"It was a fantastic turnout, from players and the crowd alike, and Keith is so grateful for it all. He still knows some of the players and he still talks to the world's greatest McDermott."

The Kennedy brothers are still close and they are also close to their sister Beverley, who lives in Scotland. She used to come to Liverpool to cheer for her brother when he was in a red shirt. So did Keith – and, if Kennedy the younger had a chance, he'd go to see his brother play. They were a close-knit gang, the Kennedy siblings. They still try to meet up as often as they can and keep memories going that way. Their meetings are often emotional. They lost both their parents much too early. The former Liverpool full-back does not want to let go of his family or his football passion – life has revolved around football, even after his professional career was over.

"Football is still my entire life. I love playing, watching football and watching my sons Michael and Andrew play. Unfortunately, Michael plays in the USA, so I don't see him

that much in a year. But, as often as I can, I'll go to see Andrew play for his local club."

Kennedy is one of the most popular after-dinner speakers in Liverpool. In addition, he hosts one of the Anfield lounges on matchdays. He also organises exhibition matches with ex-Liverpool players in England and abroad and plays himself. The fear it might all end makes him accept a large number of jobs.

"I've been to four countries in three days. I was in South Wales Friday, drove over to Scotland Saturday, then back to catch the plane to Dublin at seven and I spent Sunday there. We had a match. Sunday night, there was a dinner and I entertained before flying back to England the next morning. I loved every minute of it and the best part was the match. I love playing with the Liverpool legends. It's so much fun."

When he returned, there was no time to relax. Another job was waiting for him the next day.

Life in the fast lane got in his blood as a Liverpool player; matches and travelling all over Britain and Europe. Liverpool Football Club was in the fast lane and Kennedy thrived upon it.

During his Liverpool heyday, they had a strict regime. The Monday training session after Saturday's game was hard work. Tuesdays, sometimes a training match, unless they had a European game on the Wednesday. Then, they trained again on Thursday and Friday and played on the Saturday. Sunday was a day of rest – and maybe a trip to the pub for a beer. Everything was structured through the week.

"That's why in my life now I still need to structure everything. I've got to write it down and plan every weekday. But, now, I've suddenly started thinking, *'When am I going to have a day off?'*"

He hates turning jobs down, but must admit he has to sometimes.

"I've got everything more or less planned for a long time to come. Not everything will happen, but I feel my life has become very one-dimensional. It's all about work. Maybe I need someone to tell me it's time to relax a little. But…"

"It's time to relax a little now, Alan!"

"Yes, I hear what you're saying, Ragnhild, but I'm sitting here thinking about all the appointments I've got today. Tonight, I'm going on the radio talking about a huge sports dinner next week which is raising money for a deserving cause. I'm working on that project with former Everton player Ian Snodin. We're arranging a Reds and Blues night. When I finish my radio visit at eight, I'll drive out to Tarleton, 20 miles from here. I play football there every Wednesday with some fantastic fellows. We're not allowed to swear, so I need to keep my mouth shut. They're around 15 super lads and I've known them for years. They play decent football and they're all younger than me."

"Do they make you feel younger?"

"Definitely. The training helps me keep a certain standard for whenever I am playing with the Liverpool legends, because it's still just as important to win and to entertain. Last week, we won 4-3 outside Dublin with the oldest full-backs in the world, Phil Neal and myself. John Wark was there, too; our average age was about 56 to 57 years. We let three in, but that was the keeper's fault, obviously!"

I have seen several Liverpool legends matches during the last few years. The first time, it was exciting to see all those people my mates, boyfriends and father had talked about.

However, honestly, after having seen a few, the novelty wore off, at least for me. I suspected the lads were taking it too easy. They looked so slow out there on the pitch. It is a little like driving on the autobahn in Germany. You get used to the high speeds. There are people who have opened the car door, doing 20 miles an hour on their way into a petrol station. They have lost their sense of speed and believe the car is at a standstill. Maybe it is a little like that with the legend matches. Do we lose our sense of speed watching so many games from the Premier League and suspect the legends are just loafing around in their show matches? However, the truth is, they are all doing their very best. At least Kennedy swears they do.

The game in Dublin did not start off very well for Kennedy. He had not played for four months and had a shocker. He kept losing the ball and could not keep up with the pace. One of the other lads jokingly shouted: 'Alan, we're in red!'"

"I know we are!"

"So why aren't you passing the ball to us?"

Kennedy could see Neal on the bench, shaking his head, ready to take over. So, he ran like mad up and down his flank in the second half so nobody would take him off the pitch. Finally, he was subbed, reluctantly. But, then, another player got injured. He went back on.

"I hate it when someone says, 'You only lasted 70 minutes. You should last for 90'." He smiles.

"Are you bad at exits?"

"That's a very good way of putting it. My whole life has been about football. Any holidays I've had, all the trips I've been on; it's all been connected to football."

Even family holidays were about football. He once took his kids and his wife to Spain on a long-awaited holiday but had to do a radio programme every night for the entire week! Every night, he had to go to a friend's house, where they had an ISDN line, which enabled him to go live on air in England. People thought he was in the studio in England, but he was really on a 'family holiday' and should have been with them.

It reminds me of my own honeymoon with Jostein. The first week, one of the albums of my husband's band – Dadafon – was mixed. I think back to all the trips to a small hotel nearby that had an internet connection so he could listen to the different mixes. The unrest, the interruptions of the otherwise idyllic days. It did not take that long, but it lay murmuring underneath, stressing us and splitting up the days. It was not the recipe for romance and magic.

I have been working as a radio host for many years myself and, to me, a week of radio shows every night does not sound like holiday. At worst, it is an illusion, at best, a cover-up to work for a week in Spanish surroundings. Had I been Kennedy's wife and the mother of his children, I would not have been particularly pleased with the whole radio deal, to put it mildly.

"I did it because I got paid for it. At that time, it was important not to lose my radio show, or I'd lose my wages. But it affected the whole trip, naturally. We couldn't go out to relax until after the show. So, yes, everything in my life has been about football.

"I think it's been a very good life. Some people say maybe I should slow down a little.

However, if I do, I don't think I'd be as satisfied as when I'm living in the fast lane. Though, it may just have been to the detriment of my family…"

He continues: "As I'm now going through a divorce from my wife, whom I've been with for almost 30 years, I'm thinking more about how I've chosen to live my life. My choices have probably cost me my marriage. At the same time, it has given my family and I the opportunity to see the world."

"You're saying football has added quality to your life and your family's life, but that it probably cost you your marriage?"

"I've been too preoccupied with work and accepted too many offers. But, I must add, that it's better having too much to do than too little. I like working and I like my job. I'm a public figure, with my lectures and meeting other people. This has given me confidence. If you look at family life in the middle of it all, then, yes, in many ways it has cost me my marriage."

"What's Jane like? Does she like football, or is she like Phil Neal's wife Sue, who hates it?"

"I think there is a balance in a marriage and there has to be give and take on both sides. If he's happy working and doing his job and making money, I think the wife should be supportive. Jane was very supportive when I was out there working.

"Then, when I was around 35-36 and had a knee injury, I had to consider what to do next. Nealy stayed on in football as a coach and manager. I didn't. I became a youth team coach on my own and launched the Alan Kennedy Soccer School. To be fair, my wife was a fantastic support and did all the paperwork and gave me all the help you need in a relationship. But it was hard work – and, on top of it all, she had to bring Michael and Andrew up."

Kennedy decided to call time on his soccer schools eight years ago and concentrate on his work on the radio. Now, he was the only one working. He would have the whole day off and leave the house at half-three in the afternoon, do 90 minutes of radio and come back home at nine. The job, and his time schedule, left little time for conversation.

"I think Jane felt the relationship became a little strained. She missed time with me and I could only give her time on my own terms, or the job's."

"Looking back, I don't blame her. I did my best to make a career that would give our sons a good childhood. One of our sons went to private school because he was bullied in the public school. That meant we needed a tuition fee, £6,000 or £7,000 a year. That was extra money for the family and I had to work a bit harder."

It was also an extra burden on their marriage.

"So, yes, I worked more to pay for my son's private school, but I was exhausted. I wanted holidays, I needed time off. However, if I left for two weeks, it meant I'd miss two weeks' wages. So, I stopped going on holidays. Jane went away with friends, but I worked non-stop. That was part of the reason why our marriage broke down.

"There were other reasons, too, of course. Now, I'd rather go on holiday than work. But, back then, I needed the money and would rather work than take time off. I'm going on my first holiday for years now. However, if another job offer comes along… no, I'm serious. I will do it."

Kennedy has learned a lesson from all the work and the fear of not making enough. But it is not the only lesson he has learned. He had seven years as a player for Liverpool and has worked as club ambassador and Anfield host for years. What has he learned most as a person from his time at the club?

"Humour! In the North East, where I'm from, they've got very funny comedians. Think about all the hilarious people from the Liverpool area – we're talking great people, comedy sketches – and I think humour can help in any situation. I'd have liked to see people smile and laugh more. But there is one thing Scousers are dead serious about: supporting their football team. Whether it be Everton or Liverpool, they're so passionate."

The last few weeks and months have put things in perspective for Kennedy.

"Bill Shankly said, 'If you are first you are first. If you are second you are nothing.' He also said that football isn't a matter of life or death; it's a lot more important than that. It's not, really. The recent situation with the very, very sad death of David Fairclough's wife, I'm thinking about what's really important in life.

"One minute, you're elated with Liverpool's fantastic 3-0 victory over Man City, the next, you hear that Jan has lost her fight for life. It puts it all into perspective when everybody's grieving. No, I think about what is really important in life. You just have to try and pick yourself up and try to get on with life.

"It must be so hard on David and we all sympathise. These are sad times. In the middle of it all, I'm picking up what's left after my broken marriage; we'll just have to see what the future has in store for me."

It is good to know that happiness comes easily to Kennedy. And the most fantastic thing he knows is playing football.

"Football is the best thing that ever happened to me. Every time I pull on the red shirt, even now – ooohhhh – nobody knows what's going through my body just then. This would only happen at Liverpool Football Club. The club is so special. When I'm

"We made our share of mistakes. Now that we're old, we make a lot of them, but we still feel that we're back at the club when we play legend matches.

"It's hard rating the strongest moment, because my whole life has been about football. I've been lucky enough to be in the right place, at the right time, so lucky that I've played for Liverpool, because the club is very special to me. Had I achieved the same for Man United, I don't think I would have enjoyed it as much. It's about Liverpool's standards."

Kennedy will never be forgotten. He did decide two European Cup finals, after all. They are the biggest games he has played, but not the ones he enjoyed most. There are other matches where he felt he played better and had more control than in the two finals that made him so famous.

"In the 1981 final against Real Madrid, I scored a goal completely out of the blue, but maybe I shouldn't even have played at all. I had a fractured wrist and was not supposed to play for weeks. Luckily, the manager believed in me as a full-back. Bob Paisley would rather play me than Avi Cohen, Colin Irwin or Richard Money. There were plenty of takers for my place at the time. I hope I managed to repay him the debt of gratitude for letting me play."

The former full-back knows that the 1984 final could have gone both ways for him. He still does not know why he was picked to take a penalty, but he scored and will remain in the history books for eternity as the man who got winners in two European Cup finals.

"We beat Roma at their home ground. We beat a Real Madrid side that many had described as the best, or one of the best teams, in Europe. That Liverpool team was so good I think we could have beaten any team in the world. Even Brazil."

When we had finished our lunch, he looked out on the Mersey again: "Sometimes you ask yourself, 'What has been your greatest moment? Is it family-oriented? Is it about football?' To me, it has to be about football.

"People ask, 'But what about when your sons were born?' Yes, they were great moments, but you can't really compare that to my sons being born, which was the greatest family moment. So, I have to say my biggest achievements have been in football."

On our return to Norway from Liverpool, the Lund Ansnes family discovered that John Lennon International Airport offers a 'fast lane' to get through security for an extra fee.

Money will get you anything these days. Sometimes, they are kind enough to let families with small children through the fast lane. We were lucky. While packing up our Macs; baby food; milk powder; liquid goods; emptying the pram and folding it; removing our jackets and sending four pairs of small and bigger shoes through, as well as balancing all our hand luggage – including a guitar – on the luggage belt, a familiar face appeared. Who came up behind us in the fast lane? None other than Alan Kennedy. Not that our family was manoeuvring particularly quickly through security.

He was, by chance, getting on the same plane as us to Trondheim. It is a small world. Even in the fast lane. We were even sat right behind each other on the KLM plane.

"I try to tell myself, 'I'm still going up in the world. I still want to be that footballer who plays and plays.' However, at the moment, I feel I have to take a step back. Not back, but take a step in the right direction.

"Listen, you've got to make life happen. At the age of 56, I have to make sure I last another 20, 30 years – and I have to stop drinking so much black coffee."

He leans backward in his seat to rest.

"I realise now that I've put everybody else before my family, and work before them, too. That will change in the future."

Hello! To all the best fans in the world I love you. All the best

Alan Kennedy

Liverpool FC Career: 1978-1985   *Appearances: 359*   *Goals: 20*

13

Roy Evans
The Boot Room Secrets

*"I thought he was a great manager and a great person, and a bit unlucky at the time.
A Mr. Liverpool through and through. Player, coach, manager."*

Steve McManaman

A small room with no windows, black wooden pegs on the walls, boot hangers. There are several rows of boots, around 40 pairs, marked with names like 'Kenny Dalglish', 'Ian Rush' and 'Phil Neal'. This way, the staff know which boots to pick for a match.

First-team players' boots were packed first, then the reserves. Some days, the stench of sweat would be particularly bad. There were a couple of small, grey, plain cupboards for the coaching staff at Liverpool for coats and personal belongings. In one of them, there were always a couple of cases of Guinness, a couple of cases of Harp, a bottle of whisky and some glasses – not crystal, but proper, simple glasses. Washed once a week. The crates of ale, and two or three big wicker skips to carry the kits to away games, worked as seats for those who did not capture one of the two chairs that stood by the small table.

On the wall, smiling, are pictures of scantily dressed calendar girls from Playboy or Penthouse. Roy Evans always put the annual calendar up. The ladies on the wall were sometimes addressed by the boss himself: Bob Paisley would come in after a disappointing match and say: "You played better than us today!"

The calendar girls used to make the visitors to 'the Boot Room' smile or laugh. In other words, the most feminine element in the room functioned as an icebreaker. Many people came to visit. The opposition's coaching staff always stopped by. Sometimes before a match, almost always afterwards. Celebrities from film, television and music would also come in. Rod Stewart was a regular. He often took the Boot Room staff's kids out with him on to the pitch to play football after the game.

"The Boot Room was really a little, poxy room," Evans tells me. "Its legendary status is nothing to do with the room whatsoever, because it was nothing. It was the people who gathered there who made it special. Shankly didn't start the Boot Room tradition, as some people think; it was Paisley and Joe Fagan. Shanks was rarely there, but the opposition would come in."

Roy smiles as he thinks back.

It was almost like backstage at a concert arena. When 10 or a dozen people were inside, it was chock-a-block. They needed somewhere to entertain visitors after a game without having to answer thousands of questions from fans before they had collected their thoughts. Win or lose, they would talk the game through in there. They needed somewhere to meet and, since there was nowhere else to be left in peace, they chose a cubbyhole used for boot storage. Their beer and whisky was shared generously with all their exclusive guests.

"We were the most successful team at the time. It never ceases to amaze me how we always asked the questions to the managers who stopped by over the years: how did they work; how did they prepare for matches; what training sessions had they had during the week; what did they eat on the bus home, etc? We tried to learn off all of them and, to this day, I can never understand why they didn't ask us anything, as we used to win all the time. Perhaps our opponents felt we wouldn't have told them anyway. Why didn't they want the answer to what made us so successful?

"I know what Joe Fagan would have said if they'd asked. He'd say, 'Because we've got the best players who perform week in, week out.' Still, it's all in the details, what makes one team better than the other. I'm amazed they didn't want to spy a little, like we did."

The Boot Room was not cute or cosy. To quote Evans: "It was not the place you would bring your wife for dinner." The room was, in reality, also the coaching staff's office, where they wrote their thoughts and kept their notebooks.

Every Sunday morning, they would come in to wash the boots and hang them back on their pegs. They also washed the glasses after yesterday's debriefing and entertainment, and treated players in on their day off for whatever injuries might have occurred.

This was an era when Liverpool's coaching staff took the kits home with them. Ronnie Moran and Evans took the responsibility, taking it in turns to make sure those famous red shirts were washed. That is, their wives Mary Jones and Joyce Moran did, while Fagan made sure the socks were washed. Often, they would shrink in the laundry and that did nothing for comfort. It was bad business to have shrunken socks. They stopped sending the kits to a laundry because some would disappear. Inexplicably, the shirts of the most popular players seemed to disappear most often. Funny, that. So, the boys handled the washing themselves. After pre-season tours, Evans would always return to his wife with a ton of sour-smelling kits as a homecoming present.

Those Liverpool kits were used over and over again. They did not get new ones for every game. The players had two long-sleeved and two short-sleeved shirts each, and some changed to a dry kit at half-time. They rarely swapped tops with an opponent, and even more rarely gave one away.

"Ronnie would go mental if they did. He'd be saying something like, 'Why on earth are you giving your shirt away!'"

Importantly, the Boot Room boys were all on equal terms, but very different people.

"If we'd all been like Shankly or Paisley, it wouldn't have worked," Evans admits.

"Not that we all got along all the time. Sometimes, maybe Bob could fall out with Joe on the night before a game. We usually had a drink at the hotel. Fagan would claim he was going to bed, but 10 minutes later he'd be back and say, 'Come on, let's have a quick drink, but don't tell the boss!'

"It happens. Strong personalities don't always get along and don't always agree, but they were a terrific bunch. Even if Shankly had a bit of an ego, it was his natural way, and everyone served the club. It wasn't about them, they just wanted the job done in the best way possible. Joe even said he took the manager's job just to make sure the rest of us kept our jobs. That's the way they were. They weren't thinking about themselves, but about the team. We were wonderfully different in so many ways, but managed to pull together and do the right things."

31 July 2011: It was a warm summer's day in Oslo, the capital of Norway. However, not even the sun and a big Liverpool supporters event, warming up to the game between the Reds and Valerenga IF the next day, could disguise the dismal, sombre atmosphere. It had been only nine days since a horrible terrorist act – the worst atrocity in Norway since the war. The government block had been bombed and a large number of dedicated and politically-active young people with bright futures had been killed at a youth camp on the island of Utoya.

Earlier that day, Liverpool's Managing Director Ian Ayre laid flowers and a note from Liverpool Football Club outside Oslo cathedral: *"To the people of Norway from Liverpool FC and the people of Liverpool. You are in our hearts and minds at this sad time. You will never walk alone."*

He had then went on to the residence of the American ambassador and his wife; a beautiful, spacious residence in the centre of Oslo. My husband Jostein and I were on our way there, too. Earlier in the summer I had received an invitation with ornate lettering from the American ambassador to Norway, Barry B. White and his wife Eleanor G. White, inviting me to a reception for Liverpool owner John W. Henry in connection with the pre-season match between VIF and LFC.

As we walked past the guards and up the driveway that half-turned before revealing the beautiful, big white house, we saw the flag was at half-mast in the ambassador's garden. Inside, we were served champagne, the ambassador and Mr Henry both said a few words to their guests, and Ambassador White joked that, if there were any Manchester United supporters in the room, they should leave immediately. Mr Henry said his wife Linda Pizzuti and their young daughter were there, as well as his parents-in-law and his daughter from a previous marriage. He introduced Ian Ayre and Director of Football Damien Comolli. Mr Henry spoke warmly about his family's love for Norway; this was their second visit in two years.

A little later, food was served on silver platters. Egil 'Drillo' Olsen, coach for the national team and former manager for Wimbledon FC, had left his wellies at home and was out on the huge balcony with his wife. Evans, ex-Liverpool player Vegard Heggem, secretary of the official LFC Supporters' Club Scandinavian Branch – Tore Hansen, my husband and I found a place at one end of the balcony. Mingling is not a problem in company where everyone is interested in football. But I had brought a signed copy of my book for Mr Henry and his beautiful wife and I was too shy to go over.

"You, shy?!" Evans laughed heartily. "That's the biggest load of nonsense I've ever heard. You're not a bit shy!"

The majority of people at the reception were men, so when Linda smiled at me for the second time I mustered up enough courage to go over to her. We talked for a long time about all sorts of things. We talked about her projects for the club, she asked my advice, and I told her about writing Liverpool Hearts and my new book Liverpool Heroes.

Ian Ayre joined us after a while. Then, Mr Henry came over and I told him about my honeymoon with Jostein; the starting point of my first Liverpool book project. Our flight was on the day of the Istanbul final. Mr Henry laughed and told me it was the funniest Istanbul story he had heard so far. I can say this much about the new Liverpool owners, they seem genuinely interested in what people tell them, as they ask a lot of good questions. Henry asked Evans which young players he believed in most and listened eagerly to the former manager's opinion.

After the reception, we walked slowly towards the city centre, to where the evening's event would be held. We walked along the street in an usually quiet part of town when, all of a sudden, we could hear screeching tyres right behind us. It was like something out of a film – we were in the middle of a car chase!

"Stay away from the crossing!" Evans shouted, and pulled me away, in case the cars skidded on the road just ahead of us. On their tail, police cars with blue lights flashing. The cars took a hazardous U-turn and suddenly sped back to where they came from.

The white-headed man from Bootle has seen more car chases in his life than I have. He loves music, hums a lot and is fascinated by the life of musicians. He has played many rounds of golf with Brian Johnson from AC/DC. Musician and songwriter John Miles is a good friend of his. In his time at Liverpool, he saw football stars and musicians get together and find common ground.

Very early in his career, Evans was offered to be part of what was to become a legendary coaching team at Anfield. He was a player at the time. However, when I ask him, he cannot remember the exact years he played for Liverpool's first-team.

"I played for about 10 minutes altogether," he chuckles in his trademark dark, hearty laugh. Evans laughs a lot and is always ready with a witty comment. "So that's the end of this interview?" More laughter.

Evans was a Liverpool player for eight years, but he only made 11 appearances for the club. Eight of them were in 1970, one in 1971 and a couple more eventually followed during the 1973 Christmas period. By then, Evans was 25 and at the end of the season manager Bill Shankly surprised everyone by retiring. Bob Paisley had reluctantly taken over as boss and Joe Fagan and Ronnie Moran were staying with him on the coaching staff. Evans was still hoping a career as a regular for the first-team could follow, so he was somewhat taken aback when Paisley called him in for a chat.

"Would you like to take the reserve team as a coach?"

"No. I want to play football. The best part of football is playing it."

"But won't you just give it a try?"

"No."

"We want you on the coaching staff because we like your attitude at the club. And, in all probability, you're not going to be a regular in the team. You might get the odd game, which is great, but we'd like to keep you here. We like your character."

"No."

Different people tried to persuade Roy to take the job, but with no luck. Do not underestimate the power of words, though. Finally, it was his father in football, the one he always listened to – Joe Fagan – who pulled him aside and said:"Look, Roy. At the end of the day, it means you get the chance to be part of the staff and you'll be working closely with the rest of us. You know us, you know how we work and we'll be helping you. We know it might be difficult sometimes because you're only 25, but we'll listen to your opinions, as sometimes your opinion will be better than ours."

This time, Roy listened. He talked it over with wife Mary, as well as his father, and decided Fagan was right. .

"It was the best thing I did for my career. I could have gone to a different club in the First or Second Division and played for many years, but I had always wanted to be involved in Liverpool Football Club, ever since I was a young lad. This was just on another level and different from what I had imagined my Liverpool career to be. I got the chance to develop and move on in the system."

He learned a lot from Fagan in his first years as reserve team manager and later he took a lot on board from Moran. Evans got an insight into how to pass on what he knew without being over the top: about teaching people to play their position with confidence and be true to their personality. He learned a lot about balance – sometimes supporting players and sometimes giving them a kick up the backside.

"It doesn't happen that much now, but back then we would often have someone from the first-team playing for the reserves if they'd been left out of the team or had been injured. If they'd been left out, a lot of them didn't want to play for us, so it was my job to put my arm around them and say, 'You're going to play for my team and not ruin the game for the others. We're doing well in our league and want to win. And the only way for you to get back in the first-team is to play well for us'."

In modern football, you are either in the first-team squad, the reserves or the youth team. In Evans' time you could go from one squad to the next in a few weeks. And, then there was Kevin Keegan, who came from Scunthorpe in the Fourth Division. He spent pre-season with Evans and the reserve team. When the season started, they never saw him again.

"That is how good Kevin was."

"He gives you a lot of the credit for that. He told me you gave him the confidence to go straight into the first-team."

"Maybe I did a little. One of the most important things working with the reserve team was building confidence in the young players. Kevin had confidence, great ability, and great athleticism. Yet, it could have been frightening coming to a big club. That's why I was the type to put my arm around people, talk to them. Ronnie Moran was the sergeant major. It was the perfect balance."

The reserve team usually played Saturdays, as did the first-team. So, Evans did not often get to go with the first string. However, if the reserves did not play, he was always there and they asked his opinion on matters, such as: *"Who would you pick for the team?"*

He had a say as much as Fagan and Moran. They valued his view.

"They would say, *'You're slightly on the outside, you might see a different point from us that just might make a change. Other times, you may be wrong, and then we'll tell you. Never be afraid to have an opinion – football is all about opinion. We have a little more experience than you, but we are all in this together and, with your young man's energy and enthusiasm, we make a decent team'.*"

Evans quickly earned the nickname 'Mr Nice Guy'. John Toshack was a player he and Moran worked their motivational magic on. Evans put his arm around Toshack, Moran would kick him up the behind. Toshack scored 96 goals in eight seasons for Liverpool. They got the best out of him, as did Fagan, who was master of telling the absolute truth, and Paisley, who had a gift of picking the right player for the right game.

"Rumour has it that Paisley could pick out an injured player from miles off."

"No," replies Evans. "No one could see injuries, really, because we had no physiotherapist back then. We had doctors we could consult, and I was the first one to take a course in injury treatment. However, it was the balance in the backroom staff that was important. I don't think the 'Mr Nice Guy' quite describes me – just ask the lads who played for me. We gave the rough with the smooth. We had to balance the whole team and the staff."

"The sugar and the whip?"

The ex-Liverpool boss bursts out laughing: "That must be a Norwegian saying, but, yes!"

I blush, but also start laughing at the metaphor.

"No! I invented it just now. I'm the queen of making up expressions," I add, shamelessly. "I'm from the top of Norway, after all."

Evans says that, as coach or manager, you sometimes wonder why a player did what he did. You never give them stick for making a decision, but you can if the player failed to make a decision on the pitch. That is a lot worse than making mistakes. You have got to be positive about what they are trying to achieve; "say what you mean" was an important element of the Boot Room era.

"Every team will say that if they can't speak their mind or be critical, they're wasting their time. If someone criticises you and you think he's right, hold your hand up and say: *'Yes! You're right!'* However, if you disagree, let him know, because the staff can go in later and analyse which player was right that time.

"We expect players to go out and win every week and if they don't have an opinion about how the games should be played, then we're asking for the impossible."

If you go to Anfield, or are lucky enough to be let in behind the walls at Melwood, you will see that one man is worshipped visually, as the club symbol, above everybody else. That man is Bill Shankly, the man who got Liverpool into the top division, who renovated and lifted the standards at Anfield and who had a close relationship with the fans. In comparison, there isn't as much visual worship or honour bestowed on Bob Paisley, the only manager to have won three European Cups in the history of football. I wonder what somebody who spent 34 years at the club and who knew them both well has to say on the matter.

Evans says it is a difficult subject to discuss.

"Shankly was the one who came and changed the club, something we must never forget. He was also unbelievably charismatic. He lived with the fans, talked to them, said the things they wanted to hear – sometimes wild things like football being more important than life and death – but the fans loved it. He could say anything and people would believe him.

"Bob, on the other hand, was not as eloquent. He struggled verbally and could forget players' names and just call them 'doings', but he would still always get his point through."

Shankly lifted people – the fans, players and possibly even himself – with his words. It was all a matter of confidence, which he had in spades. He also brought the belief and confidence that Liverpool could beat any other team. He led Liverpool to promotion, a first league title since 1947, a first FA Cup success, into Europe and to a first Uefa Cup triumph. That being said, Paisley and Fagan were part of Shankly's success, and deserve credit for it, too.

"Bob was the most successful manager in the history of English football, yet he was never knighted," says Evans. "Personally, I don't believe in knighthoods, but that's my personal political belief, no disrespect to anyone who has got a knighthood. But I believe Paisley will always be remembered and loved by the fans. He wasn't as charismatic as Shanks, didn't say wild things or shout at the fans how good they were. He just did his job; it was the same way with Joe Fagan. If possible, he drew even less attention to himself. Joe wasn't after any fame in football, he just loved the game. During his years as boss, he won the Treble (the league, European Cup and League Cup) one year. Joe did a remarkable job for the club, in his own way."

Because Shankly mapped out the route in the first Boot Room era, and because of the

man he was, he will always be remembered and admired. But it would make Evans really sad if future fans forgot the rest of the Boot Room boys who are also part of the club's foundation for success.

"Statues or not, the most important thing for me is that people remember us, though statues help. Young Liverpool supporters have easy access to the last 40 to 50 years through the internet. I think people will always remember Shankly and Paisley regardless, but it would be nice if they also remembered Fagan, Moran, Kenny and possibly me. Now that Kenny [Dalglish] is back at the top, there's no risk people will forget him – and he seems to love being back."

"What did you learn most from life with the Boot Room boys?"

"Humility," Evans replies immediately.

"Or maybe that's the wrong word. Respect. Respect for other people. Because we all respected each other, and respected what the others tried to do.

"We went to a lot of other clubs to play and a lot of them had better and posher reception rooms than our Boot Room. However, I will never forget one time when we had beaten a team in the cup and their manager was under pressure. One of their coaches came in and said, 'You battered us today and were a much better team, but I wouldn't have chosen the team my boss did.' Joe Fagan said: 'Excuse me, but if you've got a complaint with your boss, tell him, not us! We don't want to hear it. Respect your boss, he's the one you work for!'"

Evans believes it was right and proper that, as a thank you for loyalty to club and manager, they were all promoted in due course until they became Liverpool manager. None of them had coaching badges or the certificates that are required today.

"Me having no education, I had to use my brains," Shankly is supposed to have said. In Evans' early days at the club, Ian St John was at the end of his playing career. He told Shankly he needed to go away and get a coaching certificate. However, Shankly huffed and asked what good that would do? None of them had the certificates, but they all had the knowledge. Shankly and Paisley would sometimes go down to Lilleshall on a four-day coaching course and return after half-a-day, saying, *'We've seen enough, let's go home!'* He was a restless soul, Shankly. He couldn't sit still for more than five minutes.

When I wrote the book Liverpool Hearts, I was surprised by how many fans had

chosen the team after the two tragedies that hit the club in the 1980s. Evans experienced both tragedies first-hand and those two terrible events are without a doubt his hardest Liverpool memories.

"The days after Hillsborough and Heysel were dark, dark days," he says.

Evans saw more casualties than most in Belgium on May 29, 1985, when Liverpool played Juventus in the European Cup final. A wall collapsed after a crowd disturbance and 39 supporters died. Many, many more were injured, yet the match went on, after a delay.

Joe Fagan was the manager and Phil Neal the team captain. Neal still regrets not being stronger, not refusing to play in those horrible circumstances. While people fought for their lives, they were playing a match that meant nothing to them after the tragedy.

Liverpool served a six-year ban from European competition after Heysel. Neal insists that, if they had refused to play, Uefa would not have been able to ban them. Evans believes the stadium in Brussels wasn't up to standard for such a big game.

"So many thoughts have haunted me in relation to what happened that day. Yes, there was trouble between the supporters but I believe the stadium wasn't good enough."

The players' wives were quite close to the stands that collapsed and could see people dying nearby. Evans' wife Mary was there, too. She saw a lot of blood and lifeless bodies.

She will never forget all the shoes lying around at the front of the stand, nor the people who walked around shoeless in the midst of the tragedy. Mary and the other wives were held back in the stand after the game and they were spat at on their way to their bus.

Evans also saw the human tragedy up close. He was functioning as the team's physiotherapist at the time. Mark Lawrenson suffered a dislocated shoulder when the game eventually kicked-off and they had to get him to hospital. It was full of people who had just lost their loved ones. The corridors were filled with seriously injured supporters and here they were in their Liverpool FC tracksuits. The police told them to cover their tracksuits.

"Whoa, I'm not covering anything up," I told them. "This isn't Liverpool FC's fault. Liverpool are not to blame for everything."

They got stick from Italian fans both on their way to the hospital, inside it and on their way back to the team bus. It was a terrible atmosphere and a lot of things were said. Evans only has sympathy for them.

"You have to understand and accept people's reactions because they were beside themselves after the tragedy."

The Voice of Anfield through 40 years, George Sephton, was in a suit and Liverpool tie that day and describes his way out of the stadium as his most scary experience ever; he walked between furious Italian fans, as he looked for the team bus.

How about Evans? Was he scared? He thinks for a while, before saying: "No, not really. Normally, you would have been, wouldn't you? But so many people had died… I had a great respect. We'd already seen the worst – dead bodies where the wall had collapsed and a hospital filled with people in deepest despair. The match was irrelevant.

"It became Joe Fagan's demise in football. He couldn't do any more after that. This match nearly stopped all of us from wanting anything to do with football ever again. None of us had joined football to be part of such a tragedy."

Mary Evans sat next to Fagan on the plane back. He was due to step down as manager anyway – Dalglish replaced him – but it was an awful way for him to end his time at Liverpool. Evans was also having doubts about continuing.

"When we came back home we were thinking, 'Do we let them dictate, the few who had misbehaved?' After all, the biggest tragedy was that the stadium was so run-down and bad. It was a scandal. There was indeed trouble between supporters. However, if the wall hadn't collapsed, I don't think anybody would have died, though a few might have been hurt.

"You have to dig deep down in your soul sometimes and think about what football should be and if we want to be part of it. I think that, as we got back on track, a lot of us thought that football would carry on regardless. We had to continue, too, and do the best we could."

I brought the whole Lund Ansnes family to the Kop for the 22nd Hillsborough memorial service in April 2011. It was the first time my children Elias, who was five, and Elvira, who was almost two, had been on the Kop.

We were way up in the gods and all around us people were in deep mourning and despair. The victims and their surviving families have still not had the vindication they deserve: nobody has taken the blame for the 96 Liverpool supporters who were crushed to death at Hillsborough on April 15, 1989. Many young people and children were crushed to death because they were often let down to the front to get a better view; down where the stands ended in metal fences in front of the pitch.

It is deeply moving, how thousands of people in the stands can be so quiet. It made a deep impression on the entire family, even the little ones, to hear people sob with grief, to hear the tribute from Rafael Benítez, who was moved to tears while accepting the gratitude he got by way of chanting and applause for his contribution to the Hillsborough Justice Campaign. It also made a strong impression on us hearing the ministers – Catholic and Protestant – take turns to read out the names of all the victims while candles were lit for every one of them. It took a long time to read out all their names. The tragedy still makes a huge impression, even on the outside world. Just after the ceremony, I was interviewed live on Norwegian national radio.

In honour of the surviving families, and because there is still no justice for the 96, the club keeps these memorial services going. Evans tells me what he will always remember is the reaction from Dalglish and his players in the days and weeks that followed. They ensured there was a representative at every single funeral.

For Evans, the day had started as "a regular semi-final". He got up, had breakfast, took a walk with the boys and they had a light training session. Then, it was time for lunch before they set off to the stadium in the sunlight. Once the game had begun, Evans, sitting on the bench, was so focused that he was completely at a loss when supporters started coming onto the pitch.

"We didn't understand what was happening. Was it a crowd invasion by the fans? The police stopped the game. We took the lads off the pitch and were quickly back in the dressing room. We thought it was a pitch invasion and that they'd clear it up and let us back out within 10 minutes. So, we focused on the game, gave the players feedback on the good start they'd made and said they had to go back out and continue like that.

"Then we started hearing what was really happening out there. It got worse and worse. The match was abandoned. Only then did we start concentrating on what was happening outside."

Evans' 14-year-old son Stephen and Dalglish's son Paul were in the crowd. They had gone to the match with Alan Brown, executive chairman of the Merseyside branch of the Official Liverpool Supporters' Club. They had to go through the Leppings Lane end, the stand where the tragedy occurred, to get to their seats on the opposite side. They were obviously very, very worried about their sons. After a while they managed to get in touch with Alan and he confirmed that Stephen and Paul were okay.

The players and staff still did not realise the extent of the tragedy as they left Hillsborough that day. It took days before they understood. On the bus home they had listened to the news on the radio. They started seeing the outline of the worst tragedy in English football in modern times. It was the beginning of an extremely tough time in the club's history.

"Young lads, usually focused on playing football, suddenly focused on helping people who had been struck by tragedy. It was an extremely difficult time for them. However, to a man, they coped incredibly well, each one in his own way. Some were more outgoing than others, but nobody backed off. Even the directors came to Anfield to help. It was an overwhelming community feeling – everyone helping to the best of their knowledge."

It made an unforgettable impression on Evans that everyone at the club was there. The squad, Dalglish, all the coaches, the press, even the local sports writer from The Sun, Mike Ellis, came in every day to help. He had not written any of the lies about the tragedy, but he got a lot of stick from angry people. Still, he was big enough to come in every day.

Everybody joined the support network: the cleaners; the people who cooked; the sponsors – absolutely everybody stood together to keep Anfield open and help those who had lost someone.

The club had representatives at all the funerals. The coaches and players went to several funerals a day in the following weeks. This knit them together with a lot of the grieving families and some have kept in touch ever since. Many still meet during the annual memorial service at Anfield.

"I wonder if the surviving families will ever have peace?" Evans says. "The club will never forget what happened and we'll never forget those who died. But I do wish they could find justice and peace sometime soon."

For all the European Cups, championships, FA Cups and everything else Liverpool have won, Evans believes the two tragedies have shown what is truly important in life. He hopes football fans around the world have learned from the two disasters.

"I hope that fans from now on will watch football and say it's something to look forward to, it's not a sport you go to in fear of your life. At least these two episodes changed crowd behaviour. There are still disturbances from time to time, but I hope we'll never see anything as bad as what Liverpool experienced at Heysel and Hillsborough. I hope the next years will be all about football happiness and the enjoyment of winning."

One of the families that was hardest hit by Hillsborough was from Kirkby. They lost a dad and husband that day. Evans went to the funeral and kept in touch with the relatives of the victims. They are still struggling to get on with life.

Liverpool won the FA Cup final against Everton the following month and Evans took the trophy home with him after they had been out celebrating. The next day, he took it to the Kirkby family. Kids rushed to him when he parked the car and got out with the FA Cup. There was great commotion. He knocked on the family's door and the kids inside went crazy when they saw what he had brought.

"Foolish or not, I told the kids they could borrow the trophy, but that I wanted it back within 15 minutes. Some people say that if you bring something to Kirkby, you'll never see it again. Then, I went inside and talked with the family. They'll never get their dad back, it was just a gesture from my part. I would probably have been told off by the club had they known what I was doing, but, 15 minutes later, on the dot, the kids were back with the trophy."

There is a time for everything, even for old Boot Rooms with whisky stowed away. When Graeme Souness became boss at Anfield, the old meeting place was replaced with a bigger and more modern reception room, to some people's resentment. It wasn't the decision of Souness to get rid of it – the club had to install a bigger press room at Uefa's request for Euro '96 and that was the best space available.

"It's a misunderstanding that it was the Boot Room itself that created magic and power in that era," Evans says. "It had nothing to do with the room, but with the people in it! So, when people criticised Graeme Souness for removing the old Boot Room, that was a load of bull. It wasn't his decision and they had to have a more modern and functional room for a meeting place."

Liverpool performed poorly under Souness after he took over from Dalglish in 1991. Dissatisfaction grew in the team and, in the summer of 1993, Evans was officially given the title of 'assistant manager'. Souness had experienced heart problems the previous year plus widespread criticism for selling his story to The Sun. The 1993/94 season wasn't going well, either, and, after an FA Cup defeat to Bristol City at Anfield in January 1994, his time as Liverpool manager was up.

"I felt very sorry for Graeme, I was convinced that he would do a good job. People say he changed too much too quickly by trying to do things in a more continental way. I don't necessarily agree, because what he did was according to modern football demands. When

you hear about other clubs' modernisation, you've got to tag along. But, perhaps he changed some of the ethics of what Liverpool had."

"Can you give me some examples of the changes he brought about?"

"Eating habits, for one. He was right to try and change that, but I don't think the players were quite ready for it. Graeme had been to Italy and had learned about the effect of pasta and carbohydrates. What he tried to introduce were really things people value today in relation to diet, training and how to take care of yourself as a player."

Souness hired a dietician, who once asked Steve Nicol what his first drink was after a game.

"A pint of lager!"

" Okay, how about your second drink after a match?"

"Another pint of lager!"

Evans cannot help laughing when he thinks about this expert who desperately tried to teach the boys about dehydration, fluid balance and the importance of giving energy back to the body right after physical exertion. In time, this became the norm, and these small moves made the players better.

Souness also tried to introduce statistics and new methods for medical treatment.

"All of this was probably a little too early for Liverpool FC. The players used the new methods as an excuse not to achieve. But, to be fair to Graeme, he had an enormous will to win. I've never seen a man more upset than him if we didn't win. He saw it as a huge setback, he really wanted to win."

The generational change the club was going through at the time did not help. A lot of important players held their testimonial matches in Souness' time, and Liverpool's biggest star, John Barnes, was riddled with injuries. Following Souness' departure, Evans got a call from Peter Robinson, the chief executive. He was asked to come down to the house of majority shareholder and chairman David Moores for a chat. He did not know what they would say. Many thoughts went through his mind – would he keep his job at the club? Would they ask him to be caretaker manager until they found a replacement? Or, would they ask him the biggest question of all: if he would become the new boss at Liverpool?

It was the last question that awaited him.

"Would you like to become the new manager of Liverpool? What have you got to offer? We like the way you work."

It was a short interview. Straight to the point. They wanted to appoint from within again and give Evans his chance.

210

Chairman John Smith's prediction in August '74 had come true. Evans had been appointed reserve team coach and Smith said: "We haven't made a deal for today, but for the future. One day Roy Evans will become our manager."

Now he had been chosen as the 14th full-time manager of Liverpool, after being with the club for 28 years.

He walked out the doors thinking: "God, I'm the new manager of Liverpool! What will it be like?" He was certain about one thing – there would be huge differences between being assistant manager and manager for one of the biggest football clubs in the world.

Responsibility is the biggest difference. Even while Souness was boss, Evans had a lot of responsibility as assistant manager, but he did not have *the* responsibility. Suddenly, it was his job to take care of all aspects of the team. Football is a result-oriented sport. The fans judge you by results. If the team played badly, you will get the blame, the players less so. For some reason it is always the manager's fault if the team fails. How did that feel?

"It was part of the job, and you have to understand why it's like that. The fans are so loyal to the club, so dedicated. The fans have a right to criticise you if you don't win. The supporters were pretty decent, but it wasn't nice when they screamed my name out in anger. Luckily, it's not easy to have a go at someone with a name like Roy Quentin Echlin Evans!" he laughs, before adding in all earnestness: "I had four-and-a-half years as boss. It was fantastic, but I have regrets that we didn't win the Premier League. We came pretty close – but as everybody knows, that's not good enough. Being fourth, third, third and fourth is pretty good, most people would say that, but at Liverpool you've got to be on top of the tree."

Liverpool finished third in 1997/98 and Evans went to Barbados for a breather. It had been a disappointing campaign – Champions League qualification had been missed – and before he left he had several discussions with the club about who they could bring in to assist him and lift morale.

It was felt the club needed someone with international experience. They had held talks with John Toshack, who enjoyed success as manager of Real Madrid. He said he would love to be part of the team again, but was honest enough to say he was a number one manager. He could not come back to the club as number two under Evans, who admired him for being true to himself and his own ambitions. So, they looked for others.

Evans himself came up with the idea of Gérard Houllier. He had been a language teacher in Liverpool and was part of the management team when France won the World Cup in 1998. Houllier spoke the language and knew Liverpool. Evans was convinced he could be the right man, so they went to visit him in Paris. During the conversation,

someone suggested: "What about joint managers?" It did not ring well in Evans' head and he told them he did not think it would work. He had to be called something else. Director of Football, whatever, but not joint-manager. Houllier, however, took to the idea.

"I was stupid not to underline clearly that I was going to be the only manager," he admits. "I should have said, 'Call him a Director of Football, or any other title, and we'll try to do the job together, but we can't do the exact same job.'

"However, sometimes being a fan of the club does you no favours because, ultimately, I want what's best for the club. I wasn't strong enough that day to say, *'No, that's not what it's going to be like. If Houllier comes in, he will be anything but a joint-manager.'*

"I don't think they would have disagreed with me. My own doubt about the right course was what ruined it for me and I brought about my own downfall. But, it's a football club, and sometimes you have to live by the sword."

The period as joint-managers was not easy. It started fairly well. Evans was in charge and there was input from Houllier, but the problems soon started. The players would ask: "When does the bus leave?"

"Half-twelve," Evans said.

"Twelve forty-five," Houllier said.

Petty little things, insignificant details, that eventually got on everybody's nerves and left the players questioning who was *really* in charge? Is someone in charge at all?

Evans felt that he was in charge up until the day in November when he quit. He had shared the managerial seat with Houllier since July and it was too crammed. Frustrations had built up until it felt intolerable to continue.

"All these little things made the players start doubting the whole idea of joint managers, and it showed in their performance. Maybe I was too honest, but, for the best of the club, I knocked on Peter Robinson's door and said: 'Listen, this can't go on.' I knew what Robinson would say; Gérard wasn't going anywhere. He had come to stay. It had to be me stepping down."

Robinson offered the man with almost 35 years of service at the club a place on the board, but Evans was not interested. It was the football itself that was his joy in life, not talking about it.

"I felt terrible. I thought a lot about whether it was stupid of me to leave the club. I did it because I felt it was the right thing to do. The frustration and collaboration problems had grown big and the board members weren't stupid. They talked with the players. Most things that happen will find their way to the board. They knew it wasn't all rosy.

"I didn't fall out with Gérard and there were no massive arguments. The joint-manager thing just didn't work. It wouldn't have worked if you shared the manager job with your best friend, even."

"You had 34 years at the club, and then all of a sudden out in the cold. What was that like?"

Evans sighs: "Well, I'd been an active part of it, though. I knocked on that door and let it happen. I respect Gérard. He was in the game and tried his best. On my part, I should have been stronger, refused to share the manager job, and maybe things would have been different. Nobody can do the exact same jobs, it just doesn't work. In our case, it lasted three months and then my time at the club was over."

The press conference to announce his departure was very emotional. He brought the man he had chosen back in time as his assistant manager, Doug Livermore, with him to tell the international press he was retiring from the job. It was impossible for the man who had spent most of his life at the club to hold his tears back. Afterwards, he and Doug went straight to Southport and drowned their sorrows.

Some emotional weeks followed. Grief and anger little by little grew into bitterness: *"Why me? Why did I do that?"*

Then, protective thoughts started to sneak in: "I don't care about the club anyway!"

"I was really bitter for a few months. But, if you're not careful, you could end up a bitter and twisted person. I had to turn my head around; I'd had 34 great years at Liverpool and they had the same amount of years out of me. You can't just get caught in your regrets.

"Of course, I wish we'd won the Premier League and the FA Cup. That didn't happen and you've just got to move on in life. If not, you lose the love of what was such a massive part of your life.

"Now, I can go back to the club and just be a fan. Now, I can be critical. Now, I can criticise the manager," he laughs.

The Boot Room boy from Bootle can put the boot in if he wants, but he rarely does. That's not the Liverpool way.

214

You've always been The Best through the good and the bad times Hope there is more good times to come

Steve McManaman
His Own Agent

"You don't get many in the game today who run as much as Steve McManaman did. He could win games with his pace alone. Terrific player! He was a favourite in my team because he was different. He gave us such a different aspect. When Macca played well we always had great success."

Roy Evans

 It was the beginning of September and the whole family was returning to Liverpool. Throughout the summer, I had felt a little homesick for the city I had been lucky enough to spend three months in during the spring. Both then, and on previous visits, we had enjoyed ourselves so much and felt so at home that we had started looking for a flat. In the summer, an offer had finally been accepted and now we were on our way to fit up our Liverpool home.

It was a fantastic feeling. Furnishing a place from scratch, with nothing brought in from previous years, and no negotiations between two people about what belongings of sentimental value should stay and what needed to go. I was so happy we owned a flat in Liverpool even the trip to Ikea was painless. We had shopped 'til we dropped and could not pack it all up quickly enough. Finally, we would have our own child-friendly place to spend good days with the kids without struggling to make them feel at home.

The day after our shopping spree, the flat was turned into complete chaos. There was cardboard and bits of furniture everywhere. I was thinking to myself that he must be a genius, the Swede who made the whole world assemble their own furniture after paying him for it! In the middle of all this I got a message: Steve McManaman had agreed to be interviewed the following Friday. Great news!

The week flew by. We worked 24/7 to set up our Merseyside residence and topped it all by travelling with 'The Irregulars' in their hired double-decker bus to Liverpool's away game at Stoke. By Friday, and my meeting with McManaman, I was completely knackered. I sat waiting a few minutes prior to our engagement, just staring at the wall. It was the first time for days I had been awake without doing anything at all. It was so nice I did not even worry when it was 15 minutes past our appointment.

217

The transfer window had closed a little more than a week earlier and I sat there thinking, philosophising over the opinions people had expressed during the last two transfer windows – the ones I had followed most closely.

There had been high-profile departures from Anfield that had something in common with the experiences of the man I was hopefully about to meet; there were often emotional outbursts when a well-liked, skilful player left Liverpool of his own volition, a player in the fans' hearts.

When McManaman chose to leave Liverpool and go to Real Madrid, people had shouted *"McMoneyman!"* and worse. Possibly they felt the worst part was that he used the Bosman ruling to go to another club for free after he failed to reach an agreement with Liverpool over a renewed contract. Even though the club got nothing for their star player, he got a good deal for himself in Spain.

As a relatively new football supporter, I must say, the last days of the transfer window, especially deadline day, is one of the most absurd things I have observed. Speculation, drama, beloved players turning into hate objects and jubilation over getting rid of one of your own – all wrapped in sums that are almost incomprehensible.

And transfer deadline day can feel so different. In January, I had an aching stomach and a hammering heart, stuck to my computer following Sky live, interrupted only by following social media updates or other news sites. I slept uneasily at night and was anxious for days. Fernando Torres had left us at the 11th hour. The Liverpool hero we had worshipped more than anyone to recruit our little son as a supporter. When the window had closed, I sat there, heartbroken, wondering what to tell my little boy the next day. How do you explain that someone has become an enemy overnight?

This time around, I had been completely calm. *'In King Kenny we trust'* is a slogan that is painted on and sewn into banners on the Kop. I could not have agreed more. I trusted Dalglish and director of football Damien Comolli with all my heart. The manager has the instinct and the talent to put a team together, as he proved during his previous period in the hot seat. With his experience combining with Comolli's breadth of outlook and "modern know-how." I could feel comfortable. And, backing them up, Fenway Sports Group, the new owners who were willing to invest in new players.

I was very happy with the summer transfer window, although I was sad to see Raul Meireles leave. Not just because my little boy had a No4 shirt, but because I thought he had been a good player for us and a colourful personality. There really should be more mohicans in the Premier League!

At breakfast the next morning, it was our painful duty to update our five-year-old heir about the new Liverpool FC landscape.

"Elias, Meireles has gone to Chelsea," his father said, pouring himself a coffee. Jostein's voice was calm. Placid.

"Why?"

"Well, he wasn't good enough to be in the team, we've bought so many other good players now."

"Oookay."

We sighed with relief.

When McManaman arrived half-an-hour late, he apologised profusely. He had been for an eye test that took longer than expected. I had to tell him the truth: after a week of working on the flat and entertaining two children, the waiting had been a wonderful break.

McManaman continues to train as much as he can. He has a gym in his house in Hale and a personal trainer who makes sure he keeps fit in the best way for him.

Besides, with daughter Ella adapting to school life and her little sister Lara, almost two, at home and his wife Victoria pregnant with a new baby, he needs the energy. After some time abroad, McManaman returned to England when his eldest daughter was ready to start school. They have settled about an hour away from Kirkdale, where he grew up. If you stood by Everton's ground and walked towards the Mersey, that's where he used to live – a 15-minute walk from Goodison, 20 minutes from Anfield.

"It was a very working class area and still is. I had a happy childhood there."

He went to St John's school – where his dad had gone 20 years earlier and was in Tommy Smith's class, no less. At school, McManaman started really playing football. He also used to go see his dad play at a high level of amateur football.

"Dad was a versatile player, midfield – both right and left. He also played wide, he could play anywhere, really. He was the star man in the area, but there was little opportunity to become a professional in the early 1960s."

His father, Dave, was born in April 1945. He was originally known as David. However, when Steve's younger brother was born they also called him David, so his father turned to Dave. Steve also has a sister, Karen, 18 months his senior. Their mother Irene was a blonde, pretty lady. She looked after herself and Steve says she was a wonderful person.

"What was your mother's role when you grew up?"

"She was the boss of the house, you know!"

"Yes, I know!"

We both laugh.

"Like women were in working class families," he adds. "The fathers went to work and

the mothers controlled everything at home. However, my mother worked as well, she was a receptionist at a health centre. When we were very young, her job was as boss and peacemaker at home. She was the one who brought control to our lives and made all the decisions. When I was 12 or 13 and we moved, that was her decision. *'We should do it now!'* If we wanted a new front door, that was her decision."

Unlike Tommy Smith, Dave McManaman was an Everton supporter. He took his son to games from an early age. The two of them would always go together.

"You've probably heard it a thousand times, but I started going to matches as soon as my father could lift me up and carry me through the turnstiles. I went to Goodison with him until I was around 15 and Everton were trying to sign me; they gave me free tickets and invited me into the dressing room with the Everton players before the games."

Behind a lot of football stars there is a dedicated and wise father. McManaman says no one has been more important to his upbringing as a professional footballer.

"I owe everything to my father. He's a fantastic man and a wonderful football teacher who always told me the right thing at the right time. Dad was never a shouter or a moaner. He used to stand on the touchline and throughout the match, good or bad, he would never say a word. Afterwards, he would give me a critique of what I'd done right, what I'd done wrong. We'd have a talk about it. But everything he said to me was correct. Everything. So I went off and practised what he'd said. It made me the footballer I became."

"I'm amazed. Your father was so keen and so into football himself and, yet, managed to stay so calm?"

"It was incredible, really, and I admired him for that. Because I see all the, excuse my language, *'idiots'* on the side of pitches watching their children play now; shouting and moaning at their kids and ordering them about. It puts the fear of God into them and you can see their confidence ebbing away as they're playing, too scared to do anything.

"I used to hear people shouting and that when I played, too – but never, ever my father. I knew we'd speak after the game. To be honest, I often knew what I'd done wrong, so I knew what he was going to say anyway. My football knowledge was pretty sound. So there were never any problems between us."

"What you're saying is, you and your father were on the same wavelength?"

"Very much so, yes. We talked a lot. It's silly, really, but yesterday I spoke to him and he advised me about playing in a charity match at Derby County's ground, *'Make sure you do things right, make sure you run, make sure you're quick...'* It's still the same, even though I've retired and it's a friendly game, but it was televised. I spoke to him again going home, *'Well done, you looked sharp.'* It does not necessarily mean that much to me anymore, but

it still matters to him that I've got the right attitude playing."

"Was that the routine? That you spoke to him on the night of a game and then again afterwards?"

"Yes, I did – and I still talk to him all the time. I'm a commentator for ESPN's broadcast to the USA and, so, I often go away to work. My driver picks me up and sometimes my dad travels with me. We see the game together, chat, have a laugh and a joke."

Blue to the bone, yet Steve and his father chose to jump at Liverpool's offer of a contract rather than signing for the club in their hearts. The whole process around signing for Liverpool made a big impression on young McManaman and he describes it as his strongest memory from his time at the club.

Steve stood out as a very special talent at a young age and several clubs wanted his signature. Liverpool scout Jim Aspinall visited the McManamans at home and was desperate for the young teenager to sign for the club. It was 1986. Aspinall visited a few times, but other talent scouts came calling, too. He had to think of something, so he invited McManaman Snr and Jnr to come for a drive with him and he took them to see Dalglish at Anfield.

The McManamans had no car at the time, they could not afford one. When they got to Anfield, Dalglish was in his office. The Liverpool boss got up from behind his desk and shook hands with Steve and his father. Kenny was still wearing his red Liverpool training kit.

"I just thought, 'Wow.' I was gobsmacked. Kenny told me it would be good if we joined them. He said he thought this was the right club for me and that, hopefully, I could play for the first-team one day. As you know, Liverpool's first-team were very good back then, but so were Everton's. He just said all the right things."

On the side of his desk was a pair of football boots, the likes of which McManaman had never seen before.

"There was this pair of gold boots unlike anything I'd ever seen in my life," he recalls. "Kenny had used them playing for the Intercontinental Cup in Tokyo against the Brazilian team Flamengo. Puma boots, in a funny gold colour, with white heels. They were like a pair of boots from outer space! I thought they were quite cool, and Dalglish said, 'Take them, they're yours.'

"In the car home, I held the shoes in my hand and decided to sign for Liverpool Football Club."

His dad was equally impressed. Even he, a true Toffee, made the decision just after the meeting with Dalglish – his son had to sign for Liverpool.

Thanks to the Aspinall's clever idea of taking the young talent to meet the boss himself at Anfield, McManaman chose the city's red team instead of the blue.

"When somebody wants you that badly, you don't think like a pure football fan any more, but you try to get control of your life and look at how the future will be – who gives you the best conditions, who'll pull out all the stops to get you? At the time, it was Liverpool, it was Kenny Dalglish and it was Jim Aspinall. When you meet Kenny Dalglish at such a young age, it makes an impression.

"He was the iconic footballer in England at the time. I don't think you can overestimate the importance of meeting managers who say, *'Look, I want you to join us, we think you might have a bright future.'* You can see Alex Ferguson still meets with young boys and their parents, it means a lot."

"Bill Shankly did the same," I add.

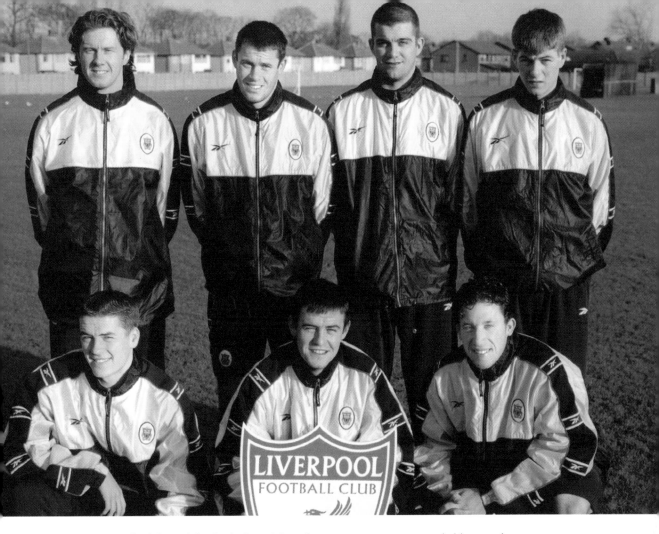

"Yes, all of them did it back then. A lot of young signatures were probably won that way."

Even though McManaman represents the more recent history of Liverpool FC, he was part of the set-up as an apprentice which involved him having to clean the older boys' boots. Today, emerging talents train at their own Academy and such things do not happen any more at the big clubs.

"The boot cleaning did me the world of good. I wouldn't have changed anything, looking back. I was mixing with the first-team as a 16-year-old, cleaning John Barnes' boots and others and putting their kits out. We travelled with them and ate with them and learned a lot! It was an exceptional grounding, building a relationship with the first-team so early on in our careers. It influenced me and shaped a lot of my career. It drives you on.

"Now that the kids and first-team are separated between the Academy and Melwood,

it's not the same. It was perfect back then. We cleaned the stadium, we worked in the offices in the afternoon. All these tasks certainly kept you grounded and the players of my time are all very down to earth lads. If you look at players now – not necessarily at Liverpool, but other teams – they are pampered and behave like spoiled teenagers before they've made the grade. Things come very easily for them. They really think they've made it at 16, but they haven't."

McManaman told me all the stars at Melwood helped him. The young ones trained on their own pitch with their own coach, but the coaches would talk. If they felt some of the young apprentices played particularly well, Dalglish, Roy Evans or Ronnie Moran would call them over and they would then get to train with the first-team. This was to see how they were and how they were getting on.

"Just that, being called over at 16 or 17 and suddenly getting to try a higher level and a quicker tempo. It was incredible. When I made a mistake, Barnes, Whelan or whoever would guide me. I went home smiling, proud to have been training with the first-team. It was very motivating and created a strong desire in me to develop. I have only good memories from that time."

It was at Melwood where McManaman met his two father figures in football – Evans and Moran.

"They were there throughout my time at the club. They didn't have to say much, but what they did say stayed with me. It was always worth listening to."

"Roy has told me that together they were good cop, bad cop, him and Moran."

"Yes, Moran was the shouter. We knew they had a good cop, bad cop regime. However, they only shouted when they needed to. What was striking was that their advice was always correct. There and then, I would think, 'What are they on about?' But when I grew up and saw the bigger picture and played at the highest level, I started giving the same advice that Roy and Ronnie had given me."

McManaman has only good things to say about the man who ended up as his manager in 1994.

"Roy Evans is great, a wonderful man. I had a great relationship with him. I thought he was an excellent manager. I think he's been given a hard time and unfair treatment. He got the club into what are *now* the Champions League spots, year in year out, but wasn't given the recognition he deserved.

"I think he was a bit unlucky, too. I mean, our team at the time was great, it just wasn't

good enough to beat Manchester United. Since then, we've learned that Manchester United's team at the time was one of the best in history."

I have heard stories of 'The Spice Boys' from that era. The Liverpool lads were hot property at the time – young, attractive, rich and marketable, attracting interest from high-flying fashion houses like Armani. They also liked a night out, or two. This was at a time when footballers could still go out and move relatively freely about town without being pictured on mobile phones. I have seen photos of the rather loud white suits the LFC team wore before their 1996 FA Cup defeat to Manchester United at Wembley. The suits played a big part in the 'Spice Boys' label sticking at the time when The Spice Girls were emerging as a pop phenomenon.

McManaman was, as one of the biggest names in the team, one of about six or seven players who became known as a Spice Boy. With his wavy hair and star status, he could not escape it. It wasn't a label they appreciated.

"There were six, seven or eight players who fell into that category, and we'd have proven to you that our nickname was ill-deserved. In London, the players went out clubbing, too, and no one batted an eyelid. If we'd won the league, I don't think anybody would

have mentioned it, but it was easy to tag us like that because we hadn't succeeded. We were probably just a couple of players short of winning the league and being a superstar team."

"Did it hurt, being called Spice Boys, or did you just laugh it off?"

"It was a bit of a drag, that's all. The fact the name still comes up now, 20 years later, shows that the press won, quite simply."

As a journalist, I am used to working on the radio and have more or less everybody you ask accept an interview. Now that I have moved into the football sphere, I have been surprised at how difficult it is to get an interview with my generation's footballers.

"Yes, that's how it has become," McManaman admits. "You're only allowed to interview players in the confines of the training ground or with a PR person looking over your shoulder. It's unfortunate. It's not your fault, or other authors of books or certain magazines. It's the press in England who have spoiled everything, to be honest."

"Why?"

"Because you might tell them something on a Friday, then read something completely different on the Saturday. I think every footballer in the country has been through that. So, when the same people – inside the training ground or outside – ask you for a quick word, you naturally turn them down.

"When I played, the press were right on the outside and we passed them every day. They asked all the time if they could speak to me, so we always had confrontations with them. Now, it's more segregated. If somebody writes a whole lot of nonsense, twists and turns your words, you won't trust or talk to that person again. It's as simple as that. Eventually, you run out of people you can trust."

"Did this happen to you a lot?"

"Definitely. All the time. But it was always somebody else's fault, of course, that the articles were unrecognisable; it was the headline writer or editor or somebody else. And, of course, they asked leading questions to get certain answers. It still goes on today. Players and managers just grow tired of it all."

"What was the hardest story for you in the press?"

"One of them was certainly the time when I almost signed for Barcelona. People were having a free-for-all and wrote whatever they wanted. I came out and said what really happened, but nobody was interested in my version. First it was about money, then about this and that. I couldn't control it. It didn't help how many times I said: 'This and that happened.' Unfortunately, people will believe what they read and not necessarily take in what the footballer says or the club. The press are so powerful and so important because people believe what they read in the papers, so they should know their responsibility and tell the truth. Unfortunately, it's all about selling newspapers."

"What actually happened that time between you and Barcelona?"

"Barcelona and Liverpool had agreed a transfer fee of £12million and the club said I could negotiate my personal conditions. When we spoke, we were a million miles away from an agreement, so it didn't happen."

"I read something about you going over and they didn't want to meet you?"

"No, I did go over, but because we already had flight tickets. We flew there and went on to Majorca. There wasn't a meeting – but people like spinning stories the way they want them."

"Did you know that Barcelona wanted to buy you, or did this happen over your head?"

"I had no idea. Liverpool told me after they had agreed the fee."

"How did that feel? Isn't it a strange feeling when people negotiate about you without your knowledge?"

"Exactly! I heard different agents telling me things were afoot. But when Liverpool got an offer of so much money from Barcelona, and accepted it, I started wondering why they wanted me out; if something had happened in the boardroom that I didn't know of. Then I started thinking about myself as a commodity, everybody has a price. This was 1997 and £12million was a lot of money, so Liverpool probably thought, 'Thank you very much, we'll take it.'

"Was this motivation for your wish to leave the club?"

"No, not at all. I didn't go until a couple of years later. So, no, I wasn't bitter they'd tried to sell me, no way. However, a foreign club had wanted me and I hadn't said, 'No, not interested.' Showing will to negotiate with Barcelona, I was signalling I could imagine playing abroad."

So, McManaman realised he wanted to experience football life in Europe and, in 1999, he chose Spanish football and Real Madrid. He was one of the first star names to take advantage of the Bosman ruling and leave English football on a free transfer when his contract expired. Some Liverpool supporters were furious that he could leave the club for nothing, especially considering Barcelona had offered as much as £12million only two years before.

"How did you cope with those who were angry?"

"I was fine. I think Liverpool thought, 'Here's a local lad who's done well. He said he wouldn't play for a club that competes with Liverpool in the league.'

I wanted to go out and play football in Europe, to a different country and a different style of play. Some people appreciated that, but some had difficulties accepting I left the club for free. People said I should have left for a fee. However, I came to the club for free and I left Madrid for free, and that's the way it was.

"Most of the negative reactions came in the press. If Liverpool lost and I played, we lost because I was leaving the club. If we won and I was playing well, it was for totally different reasons. It was hanging over me all the time."

When McManaman sees a talented youngster from Liverpool, regardless of the sport he or she is involved in, he is naturally happy for them if they do well, have success, make money and look after their family. He believes most people in the city are like that.

"We wish each other success."

"You don't think there's jealousy here, too?"

"Sure, without a shadow of a doubt. But that's life. Of course, if somebody does well and makes a lot of money, while others struggle and have hardly anything, people will get envious. But that's for all walks of life, really. It's the same all over the world. There are really nice people as well as idiots everywhere. It's just the way it is."

What made a deep impression on me while working on Liverpool Hearts was when I spoke to John Arne Riise about his court case against his former agent Einar Baardsen, who was subsequently cleared of defrauding Riise. Most of the money from his years at Liverpool was gone and he had to start rebuilding financially in Italy. In the middle of a court case, and with the pressure he was under, he scored one of his finest goals for Norway XI – a perfect long-range strike. When you are a high-profile player and the money is big, financial advisors and agents will pop up out of nowhere. McManaman discovered that.

"There were financial advisors here, there and everywhere, wanting to invest your money, because they'd get a cut doing it. However, you've got to know who to trust and have a small circle of people around you. You see how everybody has an agent now and I'm not sure if it's good or bad. I hope it's good for them, but there are good and bad agents out there.

"I didn't have an agent. I used to speak to Liverpool myself. To me, that was fine. I knew the manager and the people at the club and was fine talking to the club about my contract. I was fine having a chat about it with Roy Evans or Peter Robinson. No problem."

However, when McManaman went to Madrid, he had a couple of solicitors helping him. When he returned to England, to Kevin Keegan's Manchester City, he had solicitors helping him with the contract, but he also talked to Keegan on the phone himself when he got there.

"I see that some may need agents, some who don't like saying 'no' to managers or club chairmen. But I hear thousands of tales of unscrupulous agents and I hope players are well looked after."

"It says a lot about you and your character that at such a high level you thought, 'I'll fix it myself.' It takes intelligence and confidence to do that."

"I think that, the bigger player you become, the bigger the need is for help, because the deals are a lot more complicated. It's not just about how much you make a week, but image rights and that type of thing. When you move abroad you need help with tax issues and all sorts. However, if you're just renegotiating the contract with your first club, it was a no-brainer to me. They offered me my first professional contract when I was about 18. I thought it was fine. I got the next at around 20."

McManaman's mother Irene would go to big games and always kept up to date on whether her son's team had won or not. However, she was not a regular match-goer and then she got very ill from breast cancer. During her son's last season at Anfield, Irene's illness got progressively worse. What was it like having to perform while his mother was so ill?

"My last year at Liverpool was very difficult because my mum was very ill at the time. Also, I only had one bad injury during my 11 years at Liverpool and it was that year. It kept me out of a lot of matches. Knowing she was so ill, and having chosen to leave Liverpool, was very tough."

His mother died aged just 51, only a couple of days after he had played his final game at Anfield. His father was left alone. Steve moved to Spain six weeks later.

"The first couple of months in Madrid were tough because I was alone. My wife was there, of course, but I was away from my dad, who had just lost his life partner.

"It was difficult. I was in a foreign climate and had to work to adapt to it at the same time as I was desperately worried about dad."

"How did you manage to concentrate? Mourning like this takes a lot of energy."

"Yes, but I just had to. You can't let it affect your team-mates, the staff and 80,000 spectators; people who have paid to see the game. You just have to keep it going, be fit enough to train and play. You can say you don't want to play, but you have to get on with things."

His father came over to Spain a few times and felt better for it. The footballer did not have the same opportunity to visit his father because of Real Madrid's hectic schedule.

I tell McManaman how David Fairclough went through the same as him, losing one of his parents much too early, but that, back then, he did not get much support from the team. It was such a macho culture; apparently they did not talk about feelings much. How was a similar situation handled 20 years later?

"I had a lot of support from my team-mates at Liverpool, they knew what was going on. However, they didn't in Madrid. Mum passed away a few weeks before I arrived there and got to know the guys. So, they didn't need to support me. I didn't openly talk about her over there.

"But, since she'd been ill for so many years, everybody at Liverpool knew what the situation was like. I have to say, Gérard Houllier, who was my manager at the time, was absolutely incredible. He always asked me about mum and if I needed time off, that was always fine. He was very supportive through it all."

To All the Readers,
Hope you enjoy the Book
Bes wishes
Steve McManaman

230

Liverpool FC Career: 1990-1999 🦅 *Appearances: 364* 🦅 *Goals: 66*

15

Robbie Fowler
The Altar Boy Who Became God

"Robbie is a great friend of mine. I was lucky to get to bring him up and teach him a few things. He is my son, really."

Ian Rush

 25 May 2005. Ponder that date for a second. It gives most of us Reds good vibrations. The atmosphere that evening and through the night was electric in the heat in Istanbul, where Manchester City's Robbie Fowler celebrated the outcome of a thrilling match at the Atatürk Olimpiyat Stadyumu. The Miracle Final, when mission impossible was accomplished: To catch up with AC Milan's three-goal advantage in six unbelievable minutes of the second half.

The sweet smell of victory spread across the world. It was concentrated in Liverpool and similarly intense in countries like Ireland and Norway. And the jubilations had spread to a house on the island of Tobago, where Jostein and I had just arrived, celebrating the fifth win of the grand trophy, that was now Liverpool Football Club's to keep. We had champagne, and emotions soared high in the weeks and summer months to follow. Liverpool fans all over the globe smiled their way into the summer of 2005. It had an effect. A fruitful one.

The following spring, I was in a delivery room in Trondheim having my firstborn. And I was not alone in feeling what powers a woman's body holds. On Merseyside, there was a baby boom. May 9, 2006, two women in labour in adjoining rooms: In one room Alex, due with her second child; next door, Kerrie, giving birth to her fourth. In and out of the rooms, two expectant fathers. From time to time they would debrief in the corridor, eyeball to eyeball. Who would have theirs first?

It is good to have a team-mate and friend in the corridor on such a special day; the birth of a child is a powerful and strong experience. Imagine then, two team-mates and two of Liverpool FC's biggest stars of all time, having an offspring on the exact same day!

Steven Gerrard and Alex Curran have their little girl Lexie only about an hour before Robbie Fowler and his wife Kerrie welcome Jacob, the first boy in a family of three daughters, into the world. In the corridor, the two newly-fledged fathers celebrate yet another miracle in the aftermath of *that other* miracle.

The Fowler household is at full blast with four children; Madison (12), Jaya (11), Mackenzie (9) and Jacob, the youngest, who turns six in May and is a result of the joy after Istanbul. Robbie had not made the connection between the birth of our children and the miracle final until I had highlighted it along with the rest of the baby boom on Merseyside.

"You know, I hadn't thought of that – but you could be right!" he laughs.

I had tried to get hold of the man for a long time. He had lived and played in Australia, taken coaching certificates in Ireland and – all of a sudden, he was player-manager in the Thai Premier League. Nobody knows where he'll go next. But we know there will be a ball near him. Robbie Fowler – the rebel, God, the natural finisher, the local lad. Suits, fast cars and property king. When he reported in at the very end of my project, it was quite sudden. I spun around quickly, one year's hunt had landed me an exclusive interview. I was a little anxious.

My questions and my project could not have met with a more grounded, attentive and friendly fellow. He had seemed so elevated and inaccessible – but turned out to be the most easy-going, down-to-earth bloke you can imagine. He had just taken his kids to school. The family was back on Merseyside.

His eldest daughter will soon be a teenager, but he still thinks about how he can stretch his playing career a little longer. Ever since he was a boy, playing football was all he wanted to do.

He grew up in Toxteth, a rough neighbourhood in walking distance from Liverpool city centre. The area became well-known during the riots of July 1981. The riot started as the black part of the population protested against the police, and developed into a mass fight between youth and police, where hundreds were wounded and about 500 people arrested. A large number of buildings were so damaged, they had to be torn down, and a lot of cars were trashed. Robbie was only six when the worst riots ravaged his neighbourhood.

He grew up in a catholic home with his mother Marie, older sister Lisa and brothers Anthony and Scott, while his father Robert lived nearby. And the only thing Robbie would think of was football. He played all the time. He was not in an organised team back then, but across the road from them, lay a park where he played every day after school; either with his mates or just with dad, Robert. They discovered early on that Robbie was a natural, but to begin with only his left foot obeyed. So the young football talent would go out in the park five to six times a week with his dad to train his right foot. Untiringly he would shoot balls against the fence.

He wanted nothing more than to become a professional. But as he says…

"You don't just wake up and think you'll be a professional player. Even though I was a gifted player, I had to work hard for my dream."

But motivation was easy, football is a dominant cultural phenomenon in his hometown. Football is wrapped around you.

"There's not much else going on in Liverpool but football. You've got the two football teams dominating the city, and families are divided between them. My family went to the Everton games and I grew up with an interest in football. I wasn't forced into football, I loved playing. Football is a way of life in Liverpool. It's all around you, the papers are full of it, you just can't escape it."

He did not play organised football as early as talents do today. He developed through play and individual training.

"I played football everywhere. I always had a ball with me. If I wasn't playing, I was carrying it around. Kids today have all kinds of computers, iPhones, laptops, iPods, iPads… All I had was a football."

He went to the catholic school of St. Patrick. He played a lot of football with his mates.

In school, the teachers were responsible for suggesting new pupils for trials with Liverpool Schoolboys and eventually Robbie's name was on the list. So he got to try out for U11 Liverpool Schoolboys in Penny Lane, made famous by a certain song.

It wasn't just football and homework that kept little Robbie Fowler occupied in school.

"I don't think anybody knows this, but when I was in junior school, I was an altar boy in the school's church."

At lunchtime, Robbie would be getting the bread and wine ready for Holy Communion, and later he would walk up the aisle with the priest during the service.

I took a deep breath, this was an unknown side to Robbie Fowler's childhood. It made me smile. The biggest profiles and greatest stars of football earn nicknames. There have been a lot of them: The Anfield Iron, Barney Rubble, Crazy Horse, King Kenny, Super Sub, Ginger, Digger, Pinocchio, Mighty Mouse, Captain Fantastic, The Colossus, Quasimodo, The Gentleman, Stan the Man, Razor, to name but a few.

And it was the latter, Razor – or Neil Ruddock – who first came up with the nickname for the boy who had been given a chance by Graeme Souness to play for Liverpool FC's first-team already at 17. A boy who scored goals from any distance and every angle. A guy so unbelievably sharp inside the box, a Toxteth lad who, by one and all the ex-players I have talked to, has been dubbed the most natural finisher Liverpool FC has ever had.

Ruddock's nickname spread quickly among the fans and the press, and since then, Fowler has been called *God*. No less. That really made me smile – with Robbie's little secret from his childhood, I could not help chuckling. "The altar boy turned God." Talk about making the grade!

"All footballers want a nickname. Mine was unbelievable. You can't get any better, in my eyes." He grins.

"You certainly can't get any higher," I throw in, and we both smile while he reassures me he does not go around calling himself God. Then adds:

"When I came into the team, I could do nothing wrong and everything I touched seemed to benefit me or the team… Then Ray (Neil Ruddock) started calling me God. He still does. That's an unbelievable nickname. I've been called a lot of things in my past, but this is without doubt by far the best of them!"

Fowler has certainly been called a number of things both on and off the pitch. You do not score one of the fastest ever hat-tricks, grow up as an Evertonian but choose Liverpool

FC, and operate with great confidence both on the field and in the city with the nickname God, without getting a bit of stick from other teams' supporters. Besides, this particular God was a bit more playful and frisky than *the* Lord God Almighty.

Fowler's most famous stunt was when he 'sniffed' the chalk line in front of the Everton fans after scoring in the 1999 derby at Anfield. He cannot avoid this story because that image of him on all fours is alive and kicking in a lot of people's minds, and is one of the first that pops up when Fowler's name is mentioned.

But first, let us return to where it started: In Penny Lane, trying out for Liverpool Schoolboys. Robbie got picked and started playing for the Under 11s. They trained every Tuesday and Thursday and played matches on Saturdays.

"Being selected for Liverpool Schoolboys, you're deemed among the best of your age group, so there are always talent scouts there – from the top, as well as the lower league clubs."

He was discovered by Liverpool's Jim Aspinall, who came to the Schoolboys' training sessions several times to look at Fowler. The man who drove Steve McManaman to Kenny Dalglish in his car, and made sure the super talent with the wavy hair signed for Liverpool, managed to sign yet another Evertonian, yet another talent that would write his name in Liverpool FC's history books forever.

"Whoever you support, if someone like Liverpool or Everton wants you to sign for them, you listen, whether you like the team or not. When you're given a chance to play and train with them twice a week, you know you'll develop as a player."

"Many of the Evertonians who became Liverpool players say Liverpool FC had a better youth team and talent development than Everton. Do you agree?"

"I don't know, I was always at Liverpool. But I grew up an Everton supporter, no doubt about that. But as much as I was an Evertonian, I stayed at Liverpool FC because I appreciated the club and who they were and what they were about. I went up there and had a great time playing for Malcolm Cook and later Stevie Heighway, who took over. Steve was fantastic and could be very demanding. The Liverpool legend knew how to get the most out of us and did an incredible job with people like Jamie Carragher, Michael Owen and David Thompson. He appreciated good players who worked hard, he talked to us every day and made sure we did the right things. I've always got time for Stevie."

Fowler had fun and developed well at Liverpool's Centre of Excellence. When he was offered a place in the team in his heart, he did not see the point in changing, even as an Everton supporter.

So Robbie Fowler had been accepted into what was then the Liverpool FC Centre of Excellence at the age of 11. Today, kids are recruited to the big clubs' academies as early as six or seven. Back then they would train for an hour at a time – today the academy sessions are much longer.

"I can only talk from my experience and, to be honest, clubs today pick players very, very young. I think that if you want to play football that early, you should play with your friends and have fun, rather than in an organised team. If you're affiliated with one of the big clubs today, you're not even allowed to play for the Schoolboys. The authorities say that would make you play too many football matches. But I'm a little bit biased, I can only say what worked for me."

He is glad he was versatile and had an opportunity to play in different teams when he was young and eager to play:

"The fact I was not just at the academy, or Centre of Excellence, probably made me enjoy the game more. There was never too much pressure, I wasn't manufactured and it didn't become monotonous. Now that they're in one club only from an early age, perhaps they tire and start getting bored with doing the same thing all the time?"

It was a Tuesday night with icy winds and rain, the kind of rain that beats against your body and, combined with the merciless winter winds, makes life insufferable for whoever ventures outdoors.

Robbie had just finished the day's training at Liverpool's Centre of Excellence and was now waiting with his father at the bus stop, freezing, teeth chattering. Robbie's family could never afford a car. Soaking wet, they watched Kenny Dalglish's white Mercedes approach them in the rain. The car slowed down and stopped. Kenny rolled down the window and asked if he could take them home.

"What a manager to do such a thing. And he wasn't just *a* manager, but the manager of probably one of the most successful clubs in the world. He didn't have to stop, but he wanted to. It told me everything; well it confirmed what I already knew, about the kind of man Kenny is. A fantastic player, a fantastic manager and that night he showed me what a magnificent person he is, too."

It was not to be the last time Dalglish gave Fowler a lift as a young lad.

Fowler played altogether 11 seasons over two spells for Liverpool Football Club. His strongest memory from his long service at the club is a friendship that is as strong today as it was then.

"The first time I met Stevie Mac I was with U11 Liverpool Schoolboys, and Stevie, who is three years older than me, played for U14. They trained at the same times as us. I always appreciated good players, and even though he was quite small then, he stood out."

Fowler and McManaman ended up going to the same tournament in Holland and that's where they got to know each other.

"We were fairly similar in size and stature. He was tiny as a kid and ended up playing for Liverpool FC. As he was older, he probably looked down on me, being this little kid."

"And you looked up to him?"

"Oh yeah, of course! He represented hope and possibilities. When I came to Liverpool FC, we became great, great mates. Even though he doesn't play any more, and I still try to play, we speak to each other 5-6 times a week."

McManaman now works as a football pundit, but Fowler feels he still has more to give as a player. He had recently resigned as player-manager for the Thai club Muangthong United, but felt the league level was far higher where he had just come from – Australia, where he had spent two years playing for North Queensland Rovers and Perth Glory. But despite vast distances and time differences the last few years, Macca and Robbie have stayed close friends. McManaman also speaks warmly about his friend.

"He's just a local, working class lad with similar values to myself. We laugh at the same things, joke about the same stuff, have the same mates and good banter. We're a bunch of lads who've been friends since forever. One of us just has to pick up the phone, and they'll all come running. Life is about not forgetting where you're from. Not losing yourself or who you are. That's Robbie, he can do that. He's my best mate."

"McManaman speaks very warmly about you. How would you describe your friendship?"

"Our families are very close and we spend a lot of time together, and Stevie Mac and I have owned horses together, we hang out and he's a great mate. We've played football together, yes, but we have stayed friends and treated each other the same way regardless. We give each other stick, we compliment each other. That's probably why we're such good mates. We can be ourselves, we're not false.

"Can you trust people, being a famous person with a high profile?"

He laughs, breaths out, then pauses:

"Difficult question, really. I'm probably one of most trustworthy people...even if you

239

want to be honest at all times, you can't always be. Because you're a footballer, quite a few hang on your coat-tails. I guess I've always been wary and I think I'm quite a good judge of character."

"Have you ever experienced somebody breaking your trust? Someone who turned out not to be what you thought?"

"No, because I haven't let people get too close. I've got friends outside football but they were friends from before I started playing. And I've got quite a few friends through football. But I haven't given anyone a chance to turn me down. I'm happy with the friends I've got."

Fowler seems an impulsive and fun character – as though he does not care what other people think about him. His career was filled with rumours and speculation in the press about a partying lifestyle, and in the dressing room he quickly learned to adapt and, not least, enjoy all the practical jokes. Besides, he had the ability to take vengeance and gain respect.

"With so many guys together, you've got to handle being on the end of a few practical jokes, and there'll be a lot of banter. You've got to play along. If you seem weak in the dressing room, you'll get a lot of stick, so you've got to give stick. Making the team at such a young age made me learn fast how to hold my own and get back at the others.

On the day Steven Gerrard turned 20, he was with the England squad, training ahead of a match against the Ukraine. The day had started out well, with cake and candles being blown out. His team-mates had called for a speech from the birthday boy, who had blushed and sat down very quickly; Gerrard was a very shy lad. The team had the whole hotel to themselves as always when travelling, so none of the boys locked up their rooms before going into training.

When Gerrard got back, he was in for a shock. There was toothpaste everywhere. Above the mirror, on the bed, across the table. On the wall, a message written in Colgate: *'Happy birthday – you soft-arse.'* Before the national team gathering, Gerrard had bought a lot of clothes that would look good on a newcomer. To his terror, he discovered his bag was gone. He found it in the bathroom, empty; its contents soaked in an overflowing bath.

He spent ages cleaning the room and hanging his clothes to dry, some were completely ruined. He yelled at himself in rage and disappointment but could not report it and had to "play along". As a newcomer in the team, you had better not show weakness. But who had done this?

When Gerrard came in for lunch, knackered, it was impossible to spot the perpetrators in the meal room. All that mess had to be the work of more than one person. All the players just looked up from their food, nodded at him, and carried on eating. Some were probably suppressing a laugh when Stevie came in, way too late, and still in his sweaty training kit.

Gerrard has since revealed in his autobiography that he still suspects Fowler of masterminding the whole thing with Steve McManaman as his accomplice.

When the news leaked to the press, they reported that Fowler was the prime suspect, but he swore on the lives of his daughters (he had none then), and said the only thing he had done was cutting the laces on Gerrard's trainers.

Gerrard also wrote how he thinks Robbie's conscience will one day get the better of him and he will confess to the deed.

Many years have gone and I thought maybe this would be a good day for a remission of sins now that I have got Robbie Fowler in private.

"Was it you?"

"I can't remember.."

"Come on – did you set it up?"

"I possibly did, yeah… It was me, but it would have probably been Stevie Mac too, he's the sensible one, but… I'll put my hand up for that one, yes. But I do believe Stevie Mac was in on it, too."

"Okay, we'll drag him into the dirt with you." We laugh. "How do you think it all up? I'd have gone mad by all this?"

"I've had my share of stick, too. People have messed my hotel room up, torn my clothes to shreds, ripped the handles off my bags. So when you go to pick it up… It's like slap-stick comedy. You're not happy at the time, but looking back, it gives you a chuckle. Then it's funny. And I think it's healthy. If things are too straight-laced, you can get fed up at times.

"I made sure to have a laugh at the right times. Through the week I was serious in training and games, but everyone played practical jokes on each other. I think that's a good thing. It gets us back to normal in the enormous pressure around matches. But even if you don't really enjoy it, there's nothing wrong with it."

It is important not to forget the element of playfulness in high level football, as Fowler points out.

"I think it's reflected in the way you play. Sometimes it's very manufactured and robotic. During my time, we all enjoyed a laugh and a joke and I think it came across in the way we played. We were all good mates, we liked each other, understood one another and it showed on the pitch, too."

"Do you think there's the same banter today?"

"Not as much as it used to be, I don't think. Not like at the start of my career."

The friendship that sprung up between Macca and Robbie is 'God's' strongest Liverpool memory – and baked into the friendship was all the help Fowler got from his friend to enable him to become a better footballer.

"He debuted before me and I looked up to him a lot. In many ways we were quite similar. Both local lads who got into Liverpool's first-team. He took me under his wing, told me what I needed to know and had to accept. He always looked after me. I was like a younger brother to him. I think back on the time I did that stunt against Everton, sniffing chalk, that is – and Steve knew I'd get into trouble, while I didn't realise. I just wanted to get back at them. He was the first one there, trying to get me out of the situation and away from trouble. It's a brotherly thing."

Being worshipped as God in a city with two rival teams could also mean hell. He was the Everton supporter who turned into a massive profile for Liverpool and there is nothing better for an Evertonian than firing at the biggest Liverpool stars. What was it like being worshipped by some, and being a target of abuse for the other half of the city?

There were constant rumours about everything around Fowler and a number of them were printed in the papers as the truth. What annoyed Fowler the most was the speculation he was doing drugs, more specifically cocaine. That hurt him. He was convinced it was smear tactics from Everton fans and decided it was payback time.

"Other clubs' supporters were very, very nasty to me. Some of the songs were really base. But what can you do? I couldn't get in there and defend myself. So to me, revenge was scoring a goal and get back at them. The classic example was when I got down on all fours on the byline in front of the Everton fans. It cost me a few quid."

It was 1999 and he got fined £60,000 – and handed a six-match ban.

"Do you regret the sniffing incident?"

"No! I had planned it as an act of revenge. The only thing I regret is getting fined."

"So this was you saying: 'Stop saying I'm on drugs'?"

"Yes, I'd had so much coming my way from the Evertonians for years and they were as bad as the worst in other clubs. I know people still get abused by fans from other teams.

Gerrard gets his share now. I got some of the same or more, even. The abuse from the Everton fans was pretty nasty and malicious."

"Yes, they do tend to get personal: About one's family, ugly lies."

"Yes, it was very provocative and ugly, but you've just got to accept it."

"Do you really?"

"I think when I played, you just had to, because there was nothing you could say."

With Ian Rush as his tutor, Fowler also learned to shut off the noise of the crowd and concentrate on the game and try to think ahead all possible moves on the pitch. Sometimes it was impossible to shut the fans out – but most of the time he was focused on playing well and scoring goals, so he forgot his surroundings.

"I could have been anywhere, back at my local park, it is quite one-dimensional." But he would be bombarded with verbal abuse from the opposition's fans.

"It didn't really get to me, because I couldn't be bothered with what people were thinking about me. I went out and tried to do my best for Liverpool FC. I always wanted to score goals, I wanted to win matches.

"I always told myself that if I'd been just your average player, they wouldn't have said anything – and that spurred me on. They abused you to try and lessen your performance, and they did that because you're one of the better players. Deep down it's a kind of recognition, although in a very bad form."

One consequence of Robbie Fowler's choice of profession is that he still does not read newspapers.

"They've printed so many stories saying I've done this or that. I just don't read them. If there's one lying right in front of me, I might flip through it, but I don't go out to buy one. I think the only thing completely accurate in the papers is the date."

But he believes papers today are more accurate than they used to be. In contrast with his time at Liverpool FC, where they had no opportunity to talk back to the papers, players now have an opportunity to respond to allegations from the media through social media.

"Social networks like Facebook and Twitter are brilliant – especially Twitter, if players don't recognise what's said about them. It's perfect for people in the public eye."

We can see it today – only minutes after a game. Liverpool players like Luis Suarez, Lucas and Glen Johnson are commenting on the match on Twitter – half a day before the papers reach people's breakfast tables. But Fowler emphasises that players still need to talk to the press.

"But now what they tell the press will probably not be as twisted as it has been before, because now they can correct it on Twitter. So it's a good thing."

Robbie is an active Tweeter himself.

Speaking of social media like Twitter or various blogs, you can read about all those who refer to Liverpool Football Club as their religion. Football is heavy with symbolism and has many parallels to the church, as a Norwegian minister pointed out in "Liverpoolhjerter" (Liverpool Hearts): The black-clad referee as the black-clad priest. All the symbolism of colours, rituals; the chanting in the stands as psalms in a church and the football ground as a place people go to find room for the same needs that others seek in church: Vent their frustration, share joy, worship faith and love and enjoy a strong fellowship between its followers. Besides, a football team often carries the dreams and the answers to people's prayers of hope and happiness.

For some, football as religion is a metaphor; for others, football gives an extra dimension to their personal faith; while to others again, football is *the* religion.

But being worshipped like a god, does that limit what you can say and do, even after your career at a big club like Liverpool FC has ended? Sometimes Fowler has spoken his mind on Twitter and had strong reactions because he, God, cannot say something like that. How is that?

"That's people's opinions. We don't all agree."

"Is it sometimes hard not being able to say what you mean like the rest of us can, because you're a role model?"

"You don't get into football to become a role model. You're still allowed an opinion, it shouldn't be taken away from you just because you're a footballer!"

"Does it limit you in any way, having such a high profile and the nickname God? Does it make you think twice before you say or do certain things?"

"Not really. I think you should always be careful about what you say and do anyway, but at the end of the day, it's just a nickname. If you put too much into it, you'll start getting too big for your boots. I'll never do that."

My project getting to understand the individual player and person in football is coming to an end. It has surprised me how the role of fatherhood has been an important factor to each and every Liverpool FC hero I have met. Behind most success stories, there has been a very supportive father or, in some cases – like for Phil Thompson, Bruce Grobbelaar and Tommy Smith – a very supportive mother. In addition, it is striking to see that everybody who made it in the team and became big stars had some kind of father figure at the club.

Ian Rush even called Robbie Fowler his son.

"Rush was unbelievable to me. I came into the team, did well and scored goals, so he could have hated me, I could have been a threat to his territory. But he took me under his wing and taught me when and where to run, and what to do in different situations. I still have a close relationship with Rushie and we always have a good chat."

"As I've worked with this book, I've discovered that everybody has a father figure in football," I tell him.

"But that's the Liverpool way, the way the club works. Both Rush and Stevie Mac were incredible to me. Look at the players now; Jay Spearing will be fantastic because he learns from Steven Gerrard and Spearing looks up to his idol Gerrard and learns as much as he can from him. Martin Kelly and Jon Flanagan play alongside Jamie Carragher, who is another unbelievable player. His knowledge of football and understanding of the game is brilliant and the lads learn from him."

"Yes, you can tell both Gerrard and Carragher really care about them and are desperate for new, local players to emerge."

"Yes, they want the local youngsters to dominate the team but also to do well for the team, so they can go on to win fame and glory. But at the same time they want these kids to develop because they want to keep to the Liverpool way of doing things. They've learned that from the older players."

We football fans know one thing: a team's performance is as much in a player's head as in his feet. All the Liverpool legends in this book describe Robbie Fowler as the natural goalscorer. I would love to get inside the head of such a natural finisher and find out what goes on in there.

"The answer to that is: I've no idea! Maybe it's logic, where to move and place yourself, where to run. Maybe it's shrewdness and instinct. I think knowledge is a good explanation. You know how players have played in the past, what type of game they play, what type of balls they serve into the box, when they pass a ball and when they don't. There are many things that make you a natural player."

"So you're good at reading the game, too?"

"Yes and I believe that's inherent. That's probably where the 'natural' comes in."

In addition to reading the game well and being a natural finisher, Robbie has rarely been nervous ahead of games. He has had butterflies, yes, but never gone onto the pitch fearing he'll mess up.

"Because I love playing football, I've never gone into a match thinking 'oh no, what if I do this or that…' I always had a positive attitude. I just like playing so much. It's helped me."

"No games have been ruined by nerves for you?"

"It's impossible to be confident all the time – say you haven't scored for 5-10 matches. But I was never nervous about new games because eventually, because you're a good player in a good team, you'll get back to where you should be."

The fact he was not marred by nerves helped him score a lot of goals: 183 in 369 matches. Let us rewind to 2007 when Robbie had made a comeback for Liverpool FC and the club was playing in the second leg of the Champions League semi-final against Chelsea. With the tie heading for a penalty shoot-out, Fowler came on in the closing minutes of extra-time to be the Reds' fifth penalty-taker. All the players stood on the centre spot holding each other.

Steven Gerrard held Robbie and said: "I can't believe you're not ******* yourself!"

"Steven's hand was close to my heart and afterwards he said that it had a normal beat while we stood there, while his was galloping. I just wasn't that nervous."

As it was, Liverpool settled the tie with their fourth penalty, meaning Fowler wasn't required to step up to the spot.

People would pay millions for nerves of steel like Fowler's. A little tension can enhance your performance. But if you are too nervous, your performance goes down, no matter what you are doing. Fowler was apparently born with well-controlled nerves.

"When I was young, only 21, I played for England against Spain in the Euro '96 quarter-finals. Not many people know this, but I was supposed to take the fifth penalty in the resulting shoot-out. In the end I didn't have to, because our goalie David Seaman made a save. But at such an age, I'd been picked to take the final and maybe decisive penalty in a big tournament. It tells you something about my confidence and lack of nerves."

Robert Bernard Fowler played under Graeme Souness, Roy Evans, Gérard Houllier and Rafael Benítez at Liverpool.

"The managers pick the team and have to think of what's best for the club as a whole. As a player, you can be quite self-centred and egotistical and look after yourself. The manager needs to be the least selfish person at the club. He's not only looking after eleven players, but the whole squad of 20-30 men."

So let us go back with Robbie to the different regimes he played under in the red jersey.

"I've got a lot of time for Graeme Souness, he was the one who gave me my chance. I was very young then, but I didn't get to play much under him, because I broke my leg. When I came back, he was gone, but I enjoyed working under him, a real Liverpool legend."

When Souness was sacked, the Bootle Boot Room boy was put in charge.

"Roy Evans was fantastic. The only time I ever fell out with him was when he left me out of the first game of the season against Sheffield Wednesday after Stan Collymore had signed for us. Having scored some 30 goals the previous season, I was dropped. And I was left out of a few games the next season, too. Evans played football the right way. We all loved playing under him, to be honest. He had a reputation for being a nice fellow, but if you got on the wrong side of him… he'd let you know. He was a great manager for me."

The managerial seat was too crowded for two when the club brought in a Frenchman to give the club a lift on the European stage.

"Even though I had a bad time with Houllier, I appreciated him as a good manager. A lot was said in the heat of the moment. Houllier had his team and unfortunately I wasn't in that team as much as I wanted."

"That must have been so frustrating?"

"Yes! Of course, I wanted to play. I moaned, not because I was selfish, but because I wanted to play. I still speak to him when I see him."

Then came the man, the Spaniard, that brought God back to the club, after his round-trip to Leeds and Kevin Keegan's Manchester City.

"Rafa is Rafa. He's been fantastic for the club. I'll always be grateful to him for bringing me back. He actually lives near me, so we speak now and again. He brought me back when Liverpool struggled to score goals. And even if some people say I wasn't so great in my second time around for the club, I think I did quite well. I think I scored twelve in 24 starts. I know I didn't let the team down and I know Rafa wasn't disappointed with my comeback."

It delighted a true Liverpool heart to get a chance to go back to

Anfield. It was 2006. Robbie Fowler loves playing golf and was getting in a few swings. When he got to the second hole his phone rang and he got the question of whether he would consider a return to Liverpool FC.

"It's hard to put those feelings into words. I had an incredible first spell at Liverpool. Then my time at the club was over and I thought I might never reach those heights again. I was away for 5-6 years. Then that call came asking me if I would be interested in coming back. I think it's the first time I quit a round of golf after only two holes!"

He got his clubs and went straight home, heart hammering and face grinning. That same day he had a talk with the club and the next day he signed.

"It all went so quickly and it was unbelievable. I went to Anfield and signed the contract in Rick Parry's office. When I got back into my car, I was screaming! I couldn't believe I was back. To be honest: I never thought I'd have a chance to come back – but it just goes to show anything can happen in football."

248

Liverpool FC Career: 1992-2001 & 2005-2007 🦅 *Appearances: 369* 🦅 *Goals: 183*

16

Everlasting footprints – football has changed but the family remains the same

"I was only in the game for the love of football – and I wanted to bring back happiness to the people of Liverpool."

Bill Shankly

January 2012. I was with my kids, husband Jostein and mother Synnøve at the Bar & Grill in Liverpool with Roy Evans, his wife Mary and their daughter Stacey. The latter had just gained the confidence of our daughter Elvira, who was tired after last night's new year's celebrations with friends at Anfield. Now the two girls held hands tripping across the restaurant floor, and talk flowed easily at the table. Not surprisingly, Roy Evans' girls were as nice as he is.

I looked over at my mum who has helped us so much with the house and kids this past year. Most Liverpool FC heroes I had met over the last year had shared stories of how their dad or mum or both had been there for them when they were kids; talking about their parents who gave them space and trust to be able to live their dreams is what moved me the most.

I still picture Tommy Smith's mother, the widow who dressed up, ordered her only child to don his finest jeans and school blazer, and went to Shankly's office with her hair neatly set. I see Phil Thompson's mum survey her son's chances for a professional contract out of love to her son. I think about how June could barely contain the happy news – that Thommo would have a contract offer on his birthday – and how she bubbled over on their way home. And I imagine Doris May Rush patiently patching clothes for her tenth child.

I think of Philly Carragher who travels everywhere with his grandson James to see his father play and always has something positive to tell his adult son who is guaranteed to call, or look him up, as soon as possible after a match.

Dave McManaman is on the sideline. Deep in concentration, he follows every move his kid makes, be it on grass or gravel. He stores all his observations so he can share them with his son after the game. And not least: I imagine Tom Fairclough coming home from work to see a new window smashed in the house, without ever telling his son off.

I had been surprised by John Barnes' strength, and his thoughts about racism, as well as his ability to rise above what went on for many years. Barnes has reminded us that mental strength could be many things. The power of mind really can make you perform the most incredible feats even during immense pressure. 'Digger' also told us how important it is for us parents to equip our children with confidence as armour against evil; which comes in useful in many situations in life.

Something Roy Evans said about coaching springs to mind: "You've got to be ultra critical on the odd occasion. Perhaps only a couple of times a year. If you yell and shout at your players all the time, it loses effect. It's just the same with child rearing."

I had never in my life expected to be inspired as a mother by writing a book about football. But meeting all these magnificent representatives for Liverpool Football Club has made me reflect on the importance of parenthood and family loyalty. It is no secret that being a parent is an important task. But the stories in this book have taught me that you really can do anything if you have got dedicated parents who support you and back you all the way.

Money will not necessarily help your kid succeed. A lot of stars on the English football scene have come from poor working class neighbourhoods. Behind them usually a mother or a father who provides the support, attention and, not least, the self-confidence they need.

The father figures in football are important. The Liverpool Way, as Fowler says. Because talent is not the only thing that needs to be fed in football. You must make sure you build relationships within the club. There are a lot of father-son relationships in the history of Liverpool FC, but they have probably never before been so clearly and systematically defined. Keegan's father figures were Smith and Shankly, Rush had Kenny, Neal had Paisley, McManaman had Evans and Moran. Evans had Fagan, Callaghan had Shankly and Fowler had Rush. And we could go on listing the father figures of the game. It shows us that you depend on people to take care of you, take you under their wings, if you are to be successful and go all the way to the top.

A conspicuous number of the ex-players I have met have lost one of their parents way too early in life: Alan Kennedy, David Fairclough, Tommy Smith, Phil Neal, Steve McManaman – and Bruce Grobbelaar too, in a way. Losing a parent like this is a momentous experience and has a strong effect on a young person. Perhaps it adds to your independence. It makes you step up, take more responsibility; and amid all your vulnerability and humility, you become more thick-skinned and better equipped for tough competition.

There has been a change in culture from the '70s' hard, macho, fend-for-yourself mentality to today, when players support each other through difficult times in a different and more articulate way. Globalisation of football with new technology and communication forms on the web, with all the social media, makes information – also on personal matters – quickly available. At the same time, it gives supporters all over the world an opportunity to express their sympathy to those who need it: The big, red family will rally.

There is no doubt that family ties are strong in a club like Liverpool FC. If you have succeeded at the club, you will forever hold a special position in this huge, inclusive family. And the big sons take care of each other and meet across the generations through work for the Former Players' Association, charity work and social gatherings. The heroes of Liverpool Football Club have each other, and they know the family is there for them when they need it. David Fairclough has felt that more than anyone these last years. But also Kenny Dalglish is happy for the support and friendship of his old team-mates, backing him when he feels the pressure of being manager in one of the world's biggest football clubs. Especially in times of trouble, it is good to be able to sit down with old team-mates, knowledgeable guys.

The family remains the same after all these years, but football has changed radically since Ian Callaghan had his debut and took over from the legendary Billy Liddell. Money and marketing forces are gigantic nowadays. Players are constantly bought and sold; the game is quicker and teams rotate more frequently within bigger squads, where numerous languages can be heard. Scientific methods have long since made their entry into football. Physiology, analytic tools and dietetics have gained more focus.

The top players in the Premier League have become superstars, and their personal life has become transparent and public property. Rumours spread quickly through social media. In Cally and Smith's time, you could knock on their door and ask for an autograph and have a chat. Today, top flight football can be quite lonely. But as modern forms of communication can spread rumours about players within seconds, they are also useful tools for the players to arrest untruths about themselves, and a new and practical way to communicate with fans. And the fans are just as loyal, and have an equally strong feeling of ownership and love of the club as fans before, even though supporters today are spread all over the globe.

My journey is at its end. On the way I have discovered different connections from what I had expected. I feel incredibly privileged to have been allowed to ask questions and dig around to see new angles to footballing life, and how top flight football has developed. And with that development, the new and different challenges football professionals face today.

I am lucky to have met so many personalities, each standing out and will remain Liverpool FC heroes forever. I will never forget them or their wise words, and the stories from their lives. Liverpool Football Club are privileged to have such loyal and fantastic representatives that help us remember the magic of the last 50 years of the club's history.

By reaching the top with Liverpool FC, the Liverpool heroes have left permanent footprints It must be a great feeling knowing you have achieved something that has brought so much joy and meant so much to millions of people all over the world. It is an overwhelming thought.

They have all got a hero status that nobody can take away from them. And we need heroes. They lift us and surprise us by achieving something we did not think was possible. They tie our lives together in shared experiences and a common history.

And they are basically just like you and me.

Acknowledgements

First and foremost I would like to express my sincere gratitude to all the genuine Liverpool FC heroes for their time, invaluable thoughts and stories; as well as photos for this book: Ian Callaghan, Tommy Smith, Phil Thompson, Kevin Keegan, Phil Neal, Roy Evans, Alan Kennedy, David Fairclough, Bruce Grobbelaar, Ian Rush, John Barnes, Steve McManaman, Robbie Fowler and Jamie Carragher. It has been a true joy meeting every single one of you, and Liverpool FC are very lucky to have such sterling ambassadors.

I am grateful to so many, but it may be easy to forget everyone when you have worked so long with a project and met with a host of good helpers along the way. I am bound to you all for your contributions. There are a lot of you: Friends, family, colleagues and members of the Facebook group 'Liverpoolhjerter' (Liverpool Hearts) as well as my Twitter followers (@Liverpool_heart). Furthermore, all my readers out there who have given me inspiration with their enthusiasm and anticipation before this book and after "Liverpoolhjerter".

Thanks to Elisabeth and Ingvart Strand Mølster, Sola Jonsen, Mali Finborud Nøren, Siv Limstrand, Mary and Stacey Evans, Philly Carragher, Ganka (Gery) Turmanova, Sue Neal, Thomas Larsen Bergheim, Elisabeth Kjølholdt, Haakon Forren, Bodil Tafjord, Johan Ivar Ansnes, Ingeborg Refsnes, Kaya Herstad, Chris Carney, Kristian Ravnevand, Ole Magnus Røen, André Øien, Eric Doig, Pål Christian Møller, Tom Bolstad, Johan Mathis Gaup, Håkon Hake-Steffensen, LFCHistory.net, Michael Woodburn, Scott George, Tom Fairclough, The Liverpool IRREGULARS, Spice Boys, Kristin og Ida Estil Jacobsen, Pål Tore Holten, David Hillyard, Magne Ek, Mediehuset Altaposten, Surnadal Sparebank, Det faglitterære fond, Fredrik Skagen, and all the great Liverbird clubs I have collaborated with on my book tour. NRK, Line Gevelt Andersen, fact checkers Torbjørn Flatin, Jonny Stokkeland, Chris Wood (who has also done valuable research as well as English language vetting).

I would also like to thank Liverpool FC Supporters' Club Scandinavian Branch and their secretary Tore Hansen. The club has been a fabulous partner in my projects and Tore has been an invaluable sparring partner along the way.

It has been a delight working with the skilful and all Red photographer, Tony Wolliscroft. Thank you Tony, for taking time inbetween your tours with great bands around the world, to capture the beautiful portraits for this book! Kamilla and Tage Herstad, and their children Tia Louise and William Shankly: Liverpool wouldn't be the same without you.

Special recognition to my publishers, Sport Media, and the knowledgeable and competent crew: Simon Hughes, John Hynes, William Hughes, Chris McLoughlin, Roy Gilfoyle, Rick Cooke, Colin Sumpter, Lee Ashun, Adam Oldfield, Gary Gilliland, Claire Brown, Karen Cadman, my editors – Ken Rogers for his assistance and not least Steve Hanrahan and Paul Dove, who have pulled their weight making this book the best possible.

I also want to thank Liverpool Football Club; Linda Pizzuti, John W. Henry, Ian Ayre, Damien Comolli, LFC Press Office, Debbie Bristow and Marie-Louise Culbert and my consultants Otto Ulseth, Lars Steinar Ansnes and Ole Magne Ansnes. Kathrine Hake-Steffensen for super translation to English as well as a vigilant proof-reading eye on the Norwegian version. Designer Bernt Dag Ravnevand for yet another wonderful collaboration. Gro Eide also deserves thanks for excellent promo work and ingenious ideas.

Finally I would like to thank my family who have supported and helped me on the way. My children's wonderful grandmothers: My mother Synnøve Beldo Lund and my mother-in-law Gudrun Ansnes, and to my beautiful children Elvira and Elias who are an endless supply of inspiration and joy. Last, but not least: I would like to thank my husband Jostein Ansnes, who has supported and guided me all the way, and also kept Family Ltd afloat. Thank you for helping me with the pieces of this big puzzle and see me through this incredible journey into Liverpool FC.

To my dad, Steinar Lund. I know you would have loved joining me on this journey into football.

Liverpool FC Heroes is written by Ragnhild Lund Ansnes
Translated into English by: Kathrine Hake-Steffensen
Design: Bernt Dag Ravnevand
Cover: Lee Ashun
Consultants: Otto Ulseth, Jostein Ansnes, Lars Steinar Ansnes, Ole Magne Ansnes and Chris Wood
Executive Editor: Ken Rogers
Senior Editor: Steve Hanrahan
Senior Production Editor: Paul Dove

Published by: Trinity Mirror Sport Media
PO Box 48, Old Hall Street, Liverpool L69 3EB.

Printed and bound in Slovenia by arrangement with KINT Ljubljana

The author of this book has been supported financially by Det faglitterære fond.

Published 2012
First edition

ISBN: 9781906802950

Photographs: Ragnhild Lund Ansnes, Trinity Mirror, PA Photos, Getty Images,
Liverpool FC & Athletic Grounds and the players' private photographs.
From book release Alta: CPM/Johan Mathis Gaup. From Alan Kennedy chapter: Gro Eide.
Portrait photographs: Tony Wolliscroft

Facebook: Liverpool FC Heroes
www.liverpoolheroes.com